Josie Dew has cycled som... continents and 47 countries ...
The survivor of several wonky knees and a handful of worn-out bottom brackets, she is still firmly fixed in the saddle. She has written seven books about her travels: *The Wind in My Wheels* (shortlisted for the 1992 British Books Travel Writer of the Year Award), *Travels in a Strange State: Cycling Across the USA*, *A Ride in the Neon Sun*, *The Sun in My Eyes*, *Slow Coast Home*, *Saddled at Sea* (one of the *Daily Mirror*'s 'summer season top travel reads') and, most recently, *Long Cloud Ride*.

For more information on Josie, her books and her travels, visit www.josiedew.co.uk

Praise for Josie Dew

'Josie's native resilience, not to mention her unquenchable optimism, prove indispensable and her entertaining chronicle of a singular adventure is both amusing and poignant'
Good Book Guide

'It is her well-developed sense of the ridiculous which makes her adventures so entertaining'
Today

'Dew excels at recreating and evoking the quaint and sometimes bizarre idiosyncratic behaviour and events she encounters'
Adventure Travel

'Josie is an acute observer of foreign lands . . . a highly

Also by Josie Dew

THE WIND IN MY WHEELS
A RIDE IN THE NEON SUN
THE SUN IN MY EYES
SLOW COAST HOME
SADDLED AT SEA
LONG CLOUD RIDE

TRAVELS IN A STRANGE STATE

Cycling Across the U.S.A.

JOSIE DEW

Drawings by
Melanie Dew

Maps by
Peter Wilson

sphere

SPHERE

First published in Great Britain in 1994 by Little, Brown and Company
Published in 1995 by Warner Books
Reprinted 1995, 1996, 1997, 1998, 1999, 2001
Reprinted by Time Warner Paperbacks in 2003
This edition published by Time Warner Paperbacks in 2004
Reprinted by Sphere in 2008, 2009, 2012

A CIP catalogue record for this book
is available from the British Library.

ISBN 978-0-7515-3529-7

Printed and bound in Great Britain by
Clays Ltd, St Ives plc

Papers used by Sphere are from well-managed forests
and other responsible sources.

MIX
Paper from
responsible sources
FSC   FSC® C104740
www.fsc.org

Sphere
An imprint of
Little, Brown Book Group
100 Victoria Embankment
London EC4Y 0DY

An Hachette UK Company
www.hachette.co.uk

www.littlebrown.co.uk

FOR IDRIS
ALWAYS STRONG
MAY BE GONE
BUT NEVER
FORGOTTEN

Contents

Contents

Acknowledgements

I owe a whole lot of thanks to the following, without whose help I would probably still have gone on this trip but quite possibly never returned:

To my parents for being on supportive stand-by and for sending out emergency supplies of bits of bicycle to wherever I may be at a moment's whim; to my mad map-man Peter'osed Wilson for all his deeply touching and heart-stirring actions and for surfacing from Bosnia alive; to Melanie (Meme) Dew for once again turning her well-seasoned hand to the drawings despite being surrounded/curtailed/hampered by Freddie and Alex; to Ward with love wherever you are for my Guyana Back-of-Beyond Hash House Harriers Fun-Run T-shirt and for not suing me; to Mrs Serena Hazlenut Churchill (a.k.a. Block'ed) for express-ing no interest whatsoever in The Sequel and for eating my honey; to Makl Thomson (a.k.a. Red'ed) for being my Canadian Overseas Correspondent, building me my trusty mount and for doing his 'Bit To Save The Split'; to Jimmy Holmes my Jam-Man – 'Totemo Oishii Desu'; to my editor Hilary Foakes for spurring me forth for more, and for initi-ating me to the joyful hazards of rock climbing on yonder distant (Kentish) cliff face; to Val Porter for so expertly trans-lating my efforts into English and for enlightening me to the fact that Cod is a six-foot monster rather than a one-foot fil-let; to Vic and Karen and Joe and Sam Gibson for boosting my Liverpudlian sales by purchasing a book for every family member whether they liked it or not; to Karen's Mum and Dad, Paul and Hazel for expressing such enthusiasm and

interest; to Vic's Mum, Joan, for so wisely agreeing with me
that Ward got what he deserved; to Nick Crane, John
Pilkington, Hallam and Carole Murray and the Mighty Quin
for the Hand and Shears at the Bricklayers Arms; to Sally
Newman and Lucinda Boyle and Jessie Brill at The Traveller's
Bookshop for indispensable books and tips and maps and
chat; to Harriet and Andrew Currie and to Astrid and
Nicola at Nomad bookshop for putting me in the window
and for providing worldly words of advice; to Tim Hughes,
Trevor Roberts, Sue Hall and Lisa Warburton and gang at
the indispensable Cyclists' Touring Club; to Chas Roberts
at Roberts Cycles for an indispensable bike; to David
Stewart-Clark and Les Young at Stuart Bikes and to Grant
Young at Condor Cycles for indispensable bike bits; to
James ex-Surecraft-Shaw at DS Cycles for rummaging
around for a set of Modolo brake hooks; to Jeremy Yeo at
Weald Bicycles for being more than just my local friendly
bike shop; to the 'never-leave-home-without-it' Rohan who
kitted me out in quality gear to be reckoned with; to the
North Face for quality equipment that is hard to beat; to
Chris Bell (Mr Eggring Man) for precision-made nigh-on
indestructible circular chainrings; to John North for nigh-
on indestructible Karrimor panniers; to Wayne Doran for
nigh-on indestructible Tika panniers; to the wizardly inven-
tors and manufacturers of the life-saving sonic-zapping Dog
Dazer; to Simon Doughty at NTi for seating my rear so
comfortably on a titanium railed Georgena Terry saddle
(P.S. the socks are lovely); to Carolla at Codex Trading
Company Ltd for SeeU limb-flashing devices which startle
motorists; to Winifred Dalby and Debbie Smith at
Intermediate Technology – a charity well-worth cycling or
doing anything for; to Jo Leslie for lots; to Oliver Cooper for
lots of things; to Patrick Field and his *Breathing Spaces* for
lots of other things; to Helen Caldwell and Mark Renwick
for the Independent Traveller's World and for ignoring my
nonsensical assertions that their brother's a fireman when
he most definitely isn't; to Emile Joachim at R.G. Lewis
Photographic Specialists for such specialist advice; to Mr

Sherwood and Mr Churcher at Sendean for performing specialist surgery on my camera and bringing it back to life at a moment's notice; to Graham Mackintosh (Mr Baja Mann) for teaching me a culinary thing or two about downing a rattlesnake; to Kermit and Ursula Bartlett for letting me eat my way through their Californian house and home and Dairy Shelf and Nut Drawer, and what's more, inviting me back to do it again; to Cherry Schaeffer and Sophie (the Shih Tzu sticky-bun-devouring hound) for so good-naturedly putting up with a couple of Over the Water nutcases. PS. Sorry about the handlebars; to Chris and Carol and the boys for the death-defying lop-sided knife and the home-grown broccoli; to the other Chris up yonder, who is always with me; to Moira McDonald for recognizing my striped bottom and to Kevin Whitelaw for taking me to the skies above the Golden Gate and for enlightening me as to where on my anatomy my 'zygo-maticus major' lies; to David Peoples and Rob Robert-son at IBIS cycles for so efficiently getting me back into fuctioning order again; to the Thousand Oaks Racket Club for my two-mile swims; to Berdie and Mike Mikalson, John and Vala Mosier, Tom and Marge Jackson, Steve and Barbara Reinhard, Peg and Dick Mergenhagen, Bob and Gunda Lewis, Terri and Gordon Ness, Elizabeth and Dennis Bonney, Jim and Judy Stockhausen, all for taking a lone rider under their wing and for being the sort of people whom you wish didn't live half way across the world; and to all the many other charitable State-side souls whose names I shall never know but who came my way, helped me, directed me, fed me, sheltered me – wherever you are, one big and heart-felt thank you.

During my travels in America I was raising money for Intermediate Technology (IT) which is a British charity that works with rural communities in the Third World. It enables poor people to develop and use productive technologies and methods which give them more control over their lives

and which contribute to the long-term development of their
countries.

Intermediate Technology
Myson House, Railway Terrace
Rugby CV21 3HT

TRAVELS IN A
STRANGE STATE

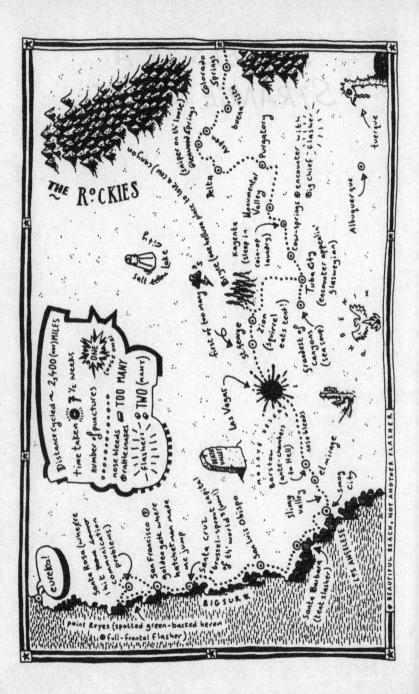

1

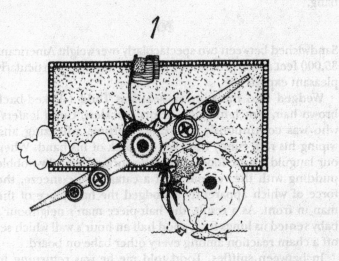

Roll on America

'It's better to know nothing than know what ain't so.'
(American saying)

 Two days before I was to leave for America, my father handed me an article which he had thoughtfully cut out of the London *Evening Standard*:

Murder Toll in U.S. Hits 24,000

More than 24,000 Americans were murdered last year, a total that was the highest in U.S. history...

...A year which saw the rest of the world become safer for America saw this nation become less safe for its own citizens...

... the record carnage will continue to skyrocket in the days, months and years ahead...

My father was always one for getting my travels off with a bang.

∞

Sandwiched between two spectacularly overweight Americans 35,000 feet above ground for 12 hours was not a particularly pleasant experience.

Wedged into the window seat was Todd (slicked-back brown hair, crotch-hugging 'pants', sockless, Gucci loafers) who was continuously sneezing, sniffing, wheezing and wiping his red, runny nose on the back of his hand. When our languid plastic food arrived he sprayed my jelly-wobble pudding with the remnants of a catastrophic sneeze, the force of which apparently dislodged the hair piece of the man in front. As a result, the hair-piece man's neighbour's baby vented its lungs for a good half an hour's wail which set off a chain reaction among every other babe on board.

In between sniffles, Todd told me he was returning to Oakland after a four-day business trip in London. He was 'into Real Estate', golf and food.

Ben, on my left, was even more of a 'larger-than-life' character than Todd. 'They call me Big Ben,' he chortled as I offered him my jelly-wobble pudding. I had been put off this delectable dessert not only by Todd's formidable fountain sneeze but also by Big Ben's choice of attire.

Hugging his ample midriff was a lime green Crimplene shirt ten sizes too small – the bottom buttons had burst open to reveal an unappetizing suet-white expanse of blubber. An obscenely short pair of shimmery nylon shorts struggled to conceal his nether regions. I wondered why on earth he was dressed like that, leaving London on a cold, grey January morning.

I was off to San Francisco but only a few hours earlier I had very nearly made it no further than Customs. Passing my luggage through the X-ray machine had caused quite a stir. I was ushered to one side as quizzical hands delved into my handlebar bag and extricated my Dog Dazer.

'What's this?' demanded the woman official accusingly.

'It's a Dog Dazer,' I said helpfully.

She gave me a Gestapo-type look. I thought I had better elaborate.

'It's a device I use for teaching dogs a lesson. When I'm cycling and a dog gives chase, I push that button to emit a high-pitched noise which affects their hearing and hopefully stops them in their tracks.'

She eyed me suspiciously.

'What's all this for?'

'That's the gaffa tape I put round it so that I can attach a bungee cord, which I can then attach to my handlebar bag for easy access.'

I visualized a bubble rise from her head which said: Suspect bomb?

A security man was summoned who then disappeared with my Dog Dazer for further investigation while I was left to be scrutinized by the X-ray machine woman.

'It's harmless, but I've never seen anything like it,' the security man finally announced and I scurried to catch my flight.

But we didn't get very far very fast. Two people had failed to turn up for the flight despite their luggage being on board and so a fidgety hour was spent as baggage handlers sifted through a few hundred bags in order to remove them.

Todd offered me some peanuts and said, 'I sure hope they bring the drink soon – keeps them old nerves at bay.'

He asked me where I was going and what I was doing. I told him I was going to California to cycle down the coast to Mexico. He said I had to be crazy.

A little later he said that there were some guys in Los Angeles who had set up a nudist bowling alley.

'Anything goes there,' he said. 'Say, you be careful.'

I was met at the airport by Elizabeth Bonney, an elegant ex-opera singer and former Bed-and-Breakfast owner who came from New Zealand; a sort of Kiri te Kanawa character. She was a friend of my father's; he had first met her when he went to San Francisco a few years ago on a business trip. When he discovered that all the hotels were full because of a bankers' conference he went in search of a Bed-and-Breakfast and found Elizabeth Bonney's. But when he rang the bell there was no reply. It was getting dark and late and his waiting taxi didn't. While he dithered on the steps, pondering his next move, the door suddenly burst open and Elizabeth Bonney stood there, wrapped in nothing more than a bath towel. My father went in and that was that. They have kept in touch ever since.

The day I arrived, tragedy had struck the Bonney household: Racing Car, the goldfish, had died. It had belongēd to seven-year-old Mark Bonney and as I stepped through the front door he welcomed me with: 'Hi! Racing Car's in the garbage.'

The house was a gigantic one tucked away in a corner off Nineteenth Avenue. The Bonneys had just moved in but were just about to move out so that the builders could move in and tear the place apart. I thought this was a shame. I liked the house as it was and could quite easily have lived there very happily. There was a bright, white kitchen, sweeping staircases and a grand piano beside which Elizabeth would sing pitch-perfectly. When I looked out of the windows at the front of the house, I glimpsed my first sightings of the Pacific. That night I lay awake listening to the mournful sound of fog horns out to sea.

2

Shoot the Breeze

I thought I was safe, but I was wrong. In a country where English was the mother tongue, I had presumed I would have no problem in making myself understood. Apart from the fact that 97 languages are spoken in Los Angeles alone, I almost managed to make myself more coherent in Polish when in Poland than I did in English in America.

Pulling into an Exxon 'gas' station, I went and asked the attendant if I could fill up on water.

'Fill up on *whaaat*?' he said.

I said, 'Water, please.'

'Wart-her? I ain't never heard of that make,' he said. 'All we got is in them pumps.'

'I'm not talking about a make of petrol.' The mention of that word produced further looks of incomprehension.

'Look, kid,' he said, spitting out a well-chewed globule of fluorescent green gum, 'you want gas, you help yourself. Right?'

'No,' I said, 'I don't want gas, I'm on a bicycle. I want some water to drink. Your toilets are locked so I was wondering where there's a tap so I can fill up my bottles.'

'Are you crazy or what?' He stuck another piece of fluorescent gum in his mouth and continued ruminating like a cow. I was getting myself into deeper water: I didn't know that in America taps are not taps – they are faucets. I thought I would give it one more try.

'I'm very thirsty,' I said, 'and I'm looking for some of that clear liquid that comes out of pipes for free.'

'You ain't looking for waah-der, are you? Hell kid, why didn-cha-say?'

That afternoon I stopped at Safeways in Santa Rosa and hit more communication problems.

'Paper or plastic?' asked the supermarket check-out girl with a cheesy, have-a-nice-day grin.

Peering into my wallet I said, 'Ummm . . . I think I've got the exact change.'

The check-out girl burst into laughter, as did the man behind me in the queue (or, as I was later to be corrected, 'in line').

The 'paper' she was referring to was not monetary notes or cheques but a sturdy brown paper bag, and the 'plastic' was not a credit card but the supermarket-brand carrier.

Whether you want paper or plastic, you don't pack your own. Someone always does it for you and woe betide those who interfere by trying to give a helping hand to the shopping-packer to pack your own shopping. They don't like it at all. In fact they positively hate it and, despite the fixed grin, they can even get a trifle shirty. I tried to help once because I felt a bit useless just standing there, watching the packer do all the work and putting all the squashable things in the bottom and all the heavy items on top, when I could have been saving my bananas from being squidged as well as speeding up procedures. But it was the first and last time I tried that one, as I sensed vehement vibes passing from packer to shopper.

*

I rode out of Santa Rosa wondering where I would camp that night. Suddenly, a white car swerved erratically into the hard shoulder, nearly knocking me into the ditch. An elderly lady with a radiant smile jumped out and trotted down the shoulder towards me, apparently oblivious to the near miss.

'Hey, where you from?' she asked excitedly, adding before I could answer, 'Say, we're bikers you know too. Got British-made Curly Hetchins. I'm Grace, and' (pointing to the erratic driver) 'that's my husband Ernie.'

'Hi there!' he called.

'You fancy a shower or something to eat?' Grace said. 'We know what it's like to be on the road. Isn't that right, Ernie?'

'Sure we do, Gracie,' affirmed the voice from within.

I had scarcely managed to utter a word before Grace added, 'C'mon, drop by or stay the night – we live just down the road in Sebastopol. Right, Ernie?'

'Right, Gracie. Just down the road. Not far.'

Grace jotted down their address.

'We'll put the tea on,' she said. 'Any problem – call us.'

With that, she and Ernie disappeared up the road as erratically as they had arrived.

When I appeared half an hour later, Grace greeted me like a long-lost offspring and gave me such a vigorous hug that I was momentarily winded. Ernie wasn't there.

'He's gone out on his bike looking for you. He was real worried you'd not find us.'

I must have missed Ernie on the road when I stopped off at a nursery to buy Grace a bunch of flowers. The flower girl had been built like a tank and her neck hung in ribbons of fat, a concertina of cellulite. Her T-shirt said: Semi-Vegetarian. When she learnt that I was cycling alone in California she said, 'Hey, that's neat, but you must be kinda crazy.'

As I was about to leave with my flowers, a huge turquoise parrot landed on the till, squawking, 'Dan Quayle – get serious!'

Ernie returned from his fruitless search and found Grace giving me a guided tour of their small bungalow. Forty years earlier her father had started to build it in a haphazard manner, adding bits on willy-nilly when money and time allowed. It was all slanting angles, sloping walls and doors that didn't quite fit – a home with character. The heating came through a vent in the middle of the living-room floor and Grace would stand over it, letting the warm air blow up her skirt. She only stepped off it when Ernie said he could smell her smouldering.

Ernie and Grace were Quakers. As we sat down to a supper of noodle soup, toast, cheese and orange segments, they clasped hold of my hands and bowed their heads for a moment of thoughtful silence until I was hit by a sudden sneezing attack which dispersed any religious air with a bang.

Grace told me about the earthquake in October, 1989.

'It was felt all over California,' she said. 'I was out biking at the time – on my way to the grocery store – when I thought, gee, I must be going all dizzy, because I couldn't cycle straight. It took me a while to realize it was the ground that was shuddering and going all funny and not me. Then I fell off my bike and hurt my arm. But I was one of the lucky ones.'

'Was the biggest 'quake since 1906,' said Ernie. 'Why, it killed 62 people, it did. And, guess what? More folks were more upset about it interrupting the World Series game between the Giants and the Oakland A's than they were about it knocking out part of the Bay Bridge in rush hour.'

I asked if he had a tried and tested method of surviving an earthquake.

'Well,' said Ernie, 'stand beneath a doorframe or clamber for cover under a heavy table or desk. And then, I suggest you pray.'

They told me that the University of California at Berkeley Seismographical Research Centre provided a Dial-a-Quake phone number for a 24-hour report on rumblings not only in the area but around the globe.

'They say you can find out if that was a 'quake or just a big truck trundling past!' chuckled Ernie.

As it turned out, I experienced an 'earthquake' which I found rather fun. At the time the earth moved, I was in a San

Francisco museum visiting an earthquake exhibition. Along with a squad of sniggering school kids, I stood on a small platform waiting in eager anticipation of being stimulated by a simulator. Then controls were activated; things rumbled and shuddered and buildings fell down around us. People laughed. It seems that's the sort of thing Americans like doing.

That evening Ernie and Grace left me alone in the house, apologizing profusely that they had to go to a Quaker meeting. Grace's 97-year-old mother had died recently and I was given her room. They flicked on the TV before leaving and told me to lock the doors and make myself at home. So I did.

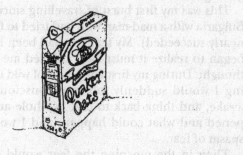

I spent the evening reading through old issues of *National Geographic*, intrigued by how death comes quickly for victims of trap-jaw ants, and the like, as the TV flickered in the background. I was distracted from a 'Dance of the Electronic Bee' article when a programme came on about the Royal Family with a smarmy narrator saying, 'The beautiful Diana shows us the perfect example of fulfilled motherhood and loving independence. Don't we just all love her!'

That was too much. I went to bed.

I had come to California with the intention of cycling south to Mexico. Instead I found myself heading north towards Alaska, mainly because most people I met told me that if I entered Mexico I would die. It was a rough and unruly country, they said, full of rapes, robberies and murders and no place for a girl to be travelling alone. I suspect this was the usual humbug that people feel inclined to pass on about foreign places – stories they have heard and headlines they have heeded – for it is usually fear of the unfamiliar that is frightening. But then, if I did an about turn and told people I was heading for Alaska, they told me gruesome stories of grizzly bear attacks and murderous drunkards. And when I said I'd just stay in California then, they said the state was crawling with crazies and psychos.

So I found myself cycling in figures of eight – one moment determinedly thinking: I'm going to Mexico, I'll see for myself what it's like – make up my own mind; and the next getting cold feet and heading north to bear country.

This was my first burst of travelling since a close shave in Bulgaria with a mad-man who had tried to finish me off (and nearly succeeded). My feathers had been ruffled and I now began to realize it must have affected me more than I had thought. During my first few nights of wild Californian camping I would suddenly jolt into consciousness, wide-eyed awake, and think back to that hell-hole and what had happened and what could happen, and I would shiver with a spasm of fear.

Then in the morning the fear would dissolve with the darkness and I would yawn, stretch, breakfast, roll up my tent and hit the road with gusto.

I swung back round towards San Francisco. I had made up my mind to head south.

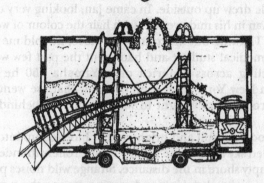

3

Land of the Chemically Sensitive

The sun was sliding slowly into the Pacific, turning the sky all colours under and over the sun as I arrived at the youth hostel in Point Reyes National Park. Bob, the warden, was lighting the wood-burning stove inside. The place was like a cosy log cabin, apart from the icy dormitories.

After I paid Bob $8, he showed me the immaculate kitchen and told me the rules. There was a sink for washing dishes, a sink for rinsing dishes and a sink for sterilizing dishes. There was a panoply of dustbins: one for recycled plastics, one for recycled tins, one for recycled glass, one for recycled paper, one for compost and one for real rubbish.

'And make sure you don't get your garbage mixed up. We like things right. In the morning we give you a chore to do, so come to me at the desk and say, "Bob, give me a job".'

The hostel was practically empty. I had briefly caught sight of a skinny, forlorn girl disappearing into the toilets, never to be seen again. At about 9pm there was a distant roar and a motorcycle drew up outside. In came Jan, looking very cold, a Dutchman in his mid-twenties with hair the colour of wood-shavings. Thawing out in front of the stove, he told me that he was a medical student and had spent the past few weeks motorcycling across America on a Yamaha 850 he had bought in New York. After a bit of a chit-chat, we went out into the cold January night to walk up the hill behind the hostel.

The moon was full and bright and as I looked up into the star-studded sky I heard the mighty Pacific rollers thundering on the empty shore in the distance. Strange wild noises punctuated the night, shrieking and rasping among the swaying shadows of the trees.

I wondered if there were mountain lions lurking in wait. Bob had told me that many still roamed the park but assured me they rarely attacked humans. Generations of hunters have dubbed these wild cats pumas, painters, panthers, cougars, catamounts and more but, unlike lions and tigers, the mountain lion cannot roar. Instead it purrs and occasionally howls – a howl that is said to sound like a woman's scream.

Bob did let slip that there had recently been two fatal attacks by mountain lions: one victim a five-year-old boy in Montana, the other an 18-year-old man killed while jogging along an abandoned Colorado logging road.

Jan wanted to go on a midnight hike down to the thunderous ocean but I didn't fancy it. I was filled with a sudden shudder of exhilarated fear. I wondered what I was doing out in the dark, sinister, shadowed Californian hillside with a Dutch motorcyclist in a land rumoured to be teeming with wild cats and crazed psychopathic killers.

A howl like a woman's scream sliced through the night, stabbing icy pins into my back. I turned and fled towards the distant light of the hostel, hearing Jan's heavy-booted footsteps close behind. I ran and ran, scared that something horrible was about to happen, my breath smoking from me.

I burst through the door into the reassuring light of the hostel's common room and when Jan arrived, panting and chill-cheeked, we burst into a relieved chorus of breathless laughter. California was doing strange things to me.

In the morning I noticed a woman who had arrived overnight. She had hair as coarse as a toilet brush and cut in pudding-basin style. Her spectacles were as big as dinner plates. Stretched across her hefty chest was a yellow T-shirt emblazoned with the words: IF GOD IS YOUR CO-PILOT, SWITCH SEATS.

As I washed the floor of the showers (my assigned task) and extracted the unappealing tangle of hairs from the plug-hole, she told me that her husband had recently been killed by a truck which had swerved into him as he stood on the sidewalk (pavement to you and me). The driver of the truck had once been a friend of theirs and worked in the same company as her husband, but 'they'd fallen out ever since my husband reported him for drink driving. He was drunk when he killed Jeff.'

I walked fifteen miles that day through mountain lion territory and down along the long, empty stretch of Limantour Beach. It was cool but clear and the booming Pacific surf crashed upon the barren, hard-packed sandy shore.

I sat in a dune at the end of Limantour Spit, eating banana-and-honey sandwiches, close to a clan of snoozing harbour seals sunning themselves on the sandbank. Bob had given me a rundown on some of the wildlife that I might come across and had handed me a photocopied description which he had written. Feeling as if I had flashed back to a school biology field trip, I read: 'Harbour seals are distinguished from other species of seals and sealions by their dark and light spotted coats and their lack of external earmuffs.' I took it he meant earflaps.

For this trip I had come prepared and brought a pair of mini-binoculars which I now trained (like a true ornithologist) on a pair of preening brown pelicans or 'pelis' as Bob called them. I had never gone bird spotting before but,

armed with 'bins' and a bird book on loan from the hostel,
I found the whole procedure surprisingly entertaining. I
even began to feel a slight (and I reiterate, 'slight') understanding for that most curious of species, the anoraked
train-spotter. Rather worryingly, I was overcome by a similar
thrill of spotting and jotting down in a spiral-bound note-
book. All I lacked was a thermos of tea and a
bacofoil-wrapped meat paste sandwich and . . . well, I suppose, a train or two.

I did a lot of stomach-wriggling that afternoon, inching
my way towards unsuspecting feathered specimens busily
preening themselves on wind-blown tussocks. I ticked off
ring-necked duck, ocean warblers, belted kingfishers,
smoked-back bacon – I mean green-backed heron, crossbills,
hooded mergansers, passerines, (motor) scoters and turkey
vultures. The peregrine falcon, alas, remained elusive which
is more than can be said for the peregrinating pants-dropper.
Training binoculars on some unidentifiable low-swooping
feathered flight, I was alarmed to pick up a full-frontal flasher
in my sights standing erect on yonder distant dune top. He
stared manically in my direction. Waiting for nobody I
dropped my apparatus, picked up my books and scarpered.
Bloody pervs . . .

There were some new arrivals that night in the hostel. Mary-
Lu had flown over from New York to meet her Billy Idol
look-a-like son, an actor 'from Frisco'. They had come to
Point Reyes National Park to 'get away from the fast life,
man', and Billy's overbearing voice could be heard through-

out the hostel telling people how he was on the point of 'making it big'.

Most curious of all was my lower bunk mate, Lorraine, an elderly woman with a squint and a thicket of matted purple-grey hair. Although the night was icy, she went around throwing open every window and propping open every door in order to get a 'spiritually-cleansing draught', as she put it. I am all for a bit of fresh air but I felt that having a body-numbing gale howling through the dorm was taking things to extremes. Lorraine wouldn't hear otherwise.

'I'm chemically sensitive,' she told me. 'Allergic to all these horrors we've made for ourselves. I've sold my home in Los Angeles and I'm living out of my car to escape from earthly pollution. I'm just living to let go – to let God take me. It's the hardest thing I've done.'

Outside The Epicenter Store in Olema a notice caught my eye:

Women's Anger Workshop

Situation: Nice girls DO GET ANGRY, but were never shown how to effectively express this unladylike and unattractive emotion.

Call Nancy Pratt (a licensed counsellor for help) NOW, and learn how to release those emotions.

A dented red Mustang swung into the parking lot and a woman bulging out of her rose-pink lurex pants stepped out. She dragged a disenchanted mutt into the grocery store and soon reappeared with a Diet Coke and a colossal ice cream. Taking her first mouthful, she tripped up on the dog's lead and dropped her cone in the gutter.

'Ah shit!' she screamed. 'You good-for-nothing lousy dawg. Look what you made me go and do, goddam it. You want your neck wrung or what? Jeez!'

She threw the dog into the back of the Mustang, the bumper of which had a sticker saying: UPPITY WOMEN UNITE. Then she gunned off down the road. A recent graduate from Nancy Pratt's angry workshop?

At Stinson Beach I turned off onto a dirt track and rode up over Mount Tamalpais. Here, back in the 1970s, the mountain bike had been conceived by the likes of Charlie Kelly, Gary Fisher and Joe Breeze who raced down the mountainside on old souped-up cruisers. Today it has become such a hot-spot for two-wheeled speed merchants that rangers use radar guns and fine offenders $200 for breaking the bicycle speed limit of 15mph.

At the top I met a Park Ranger, a Yogi Bear cartoon character in his wide-brimmed hat and breeches. On learning that I was bound for Mexico, he said, 'Hey, kid – you head down there you'll get fleeced.'

The trail led me bouncing across the barren wilds with the misty, thick-wooded valleys on one side and rolling ochre hills plunging down to the swirling blue Pacific on the other. I thought what a wondrous city San Francisco would be to live in. Within minutes you could ride out across the Golden Gate and be up here in the sea-skirted ruggedness of the Marin mountains.

Cycling through Sausalito past the house-boats (more house than boat) I met Boe, an effusive black chef on a chopper with a pearly smile that stretched from ear to ear. He said he would show me the bike route to the bridge and so we rode along together.

When Boe wasn't working in his cafe (where we stopped for a drink), he danced and wrote books about dances related to astronomy.

'You know, we've all become so far removed from our animal instincts,' he said, 'and cosmic dancing helps to realign our lives. I kinda believe it brings out a form of subconcious savageness in us.' He flashed me another of his dazzling, maniacal grins.

*

I crossed the bridge slowly, savouring a world famous land-mark 8,981 feet long and 220 feet above water. The setting sun turned the Golden Gate's girders to fire and I kept stopping to peer over the side, far down into the turbulent tides below – tides infamous for sweeping away any prisoner who attempted to make a swim for it in the days of Alcatraz.

Halfway across I dismounted again and looked over the railings, imagining what it would feel like to commit suicide by jumping. Not much fun, I decided. A dope-smoking man carrying a hatchet appeared at my side.

'Hey babe,' he said, 'think about it first. Long and hard.'

He had once met a guy who had come out here to kill himself and climbed up onto the railings.

'You know what?' said the hatchet man, 'He told me that just as he let go he had this shit-awful feeling that he'd done the wrong thing. He wanted to live, not die.'

'How do you know that,' I said incredulously, 'if he's dead?'

'Cos he survived. Pretty cool, huh? The lucky bugger survived the fall and was picked up by a sail boat. Apart from being real fucked up, he's a new man.'

🕸

I wore nothing more than a surgeon's green gown as I lay flat on my back on a bed as narrow and hard as a plank of ply-wood. I was in a chiropractic centre not far from Nob Hill and was about to have my back snap-cracked back into position. A few days earlier, while I was straining to open a non-opening sliding window, something in my shoulder had pinged. As a result I couldn't move my neck more than 45 degrees either way, which made cycling highly precarious and decidedly painful.

Before prostrating myself, I had been shown a video explaining the 'practise of chiropractic and applied kinesi-ology' which, from the way it was presented, resembled more a cross between *Star Trek* and the *Magic Roundabout* than a medical enlightenment. It was a science fiction of spaceship-like environments, Zebedee bouncy things and cosmic characters. It didn't give me much faith for what was to come, but then nor did the doctor who was positioned to instigate some bone-crushing 'treatment': his name was Doctor Payne.

Held against a viewing machine were two X-rays of my spine, which looked pretty impressive to me. Doctor Payne thought otherwise.

'You've got the spine of a 60-year-old,' he said encouragingly. 'I'd say you need at least a year's treatment to get you back into shape.'

'I haven't got time for more than one,' I told him, 'so do what you can.'

This was a mistake. I should have left there and then. It felt as if Doctor Payne had compressed a year's treatment not only into half an hour but into every bone in my body. I was contorted into every conceivable position possible, whereupon Doctor Payne would command me to relax (as if, with left leg entwined painfully round neck, such a thing were possible). Taking a vice-like hold of my head in his hands, he twisted it through 180 degrees and then gave it a violent snap-crack tug which felt as though it had been yanked off its hinges and into his hands. *This* was remedial treatment?

An hour later, clutching a bag of bones which sufficed as my body, I staggered out of that Payneful practice – and that's just what I thought it was: practice. I was the guinea-pig upon whom he practised his not so delicate techniques. I felt like emergency-ward material for the nearest hospital. A spritely octogenarian helped me on to the bus, bless her, and I collapsed back at the Bonneys.

The next day I was better. Just like that. I changed my mind. Doctor Payne's performance had paid off and I sallied forth for the Pacific Coastal Highway.

4

Lob Me a Bud

In Half Moon Bay I was camped next to a 40-foot RV (an abbreviation no one now expands into 'recreational vehicle') that resembled a space-age torpedo. Its occupant ambled over and said, 'Hey! Know what? You're sleeping in the Pumpkin Capital of the world!'

My watch said 6.10am. I had just crawled out of my tent in a soporific state and this struck me as an unusual way to bid good morning.

'Yes siree,' he continued, with far too much rapture for that hour, 'and I'll tell you summin' else, it's Martin Luther King day and I ain't going nowhere on them roads.' With that, he waddled off to the toilet block, contentedly muttering to himself.

The next morning, at 5.52am, I had another unusual awakening. I was bedded down in the Santa Cruz AYH-Hostel ('NO REFUNDS') sleeping above a Dutch girl in a two-bunk room, when a piercing Robotic voice from the street below jolted me from my slumber.

'Stand back . . . I warn you . . . Stand back . . . You are too close . . . I repeat . . . too close . . .'

Then, amidst a sudden cacophony of shrill-wailing sirens, came the Dalek-scream rant: 'I have been tampered with . . . I have been tampered with . . . I have been tampered with . . .'

It was a Santa Cruz interpretation of a car alarm.

'Santa Cruz is for cruisin',' said the hip dude clad in a 'KISS MY ASS' T-shirt. I left him slumped in front of the TV watching Jack Nicholson doing things to Faye Dunaway and walked out into the brilliant January sunshine.

I walked for miles down endless blocks (some still badly damaged from the 1989 earthquake) full of motels – the Daze Inn, the Dream Inn, the Comfort Inn, the Vagabond Inn – until I hit the Santa Cruz cops, all shirt-sleeves and shades and armed to the hilt with hip-holstered pistols. The streets around the sea-front had been sealed off as a suspect bomb had been found in a parked RV. I gave the area a wide berth before clambering up onto the Boardwalk, 'the place', I read, 'to see and to be seen' if you had anyone to look at or anything to show in summer.

It was winter, albeit a sunny and warm one, and the Boardwalk was boarded up. No one was around. The place was dead. I felt happy. As I strolled with a springing gait along the beachfront, I hummed the Drifters' 'Under the board-walk . . . I'll be having fun . . . under the boardwalk . . . boar-oard walk . . .' I kept pausing to gaze up at the garish pinks and greens and purples and oranges of the 1924 Giant Dipper roller-coaster, the 1911 merry-go-round, the casinos and the chip houses, and tried to visualize it in summer – a frantic, frenzied whirring of screams and colour.

I had the beach virtually to myself. I found a windless spot and sprawled out on the sand, soaking up the body-glowing but melanistic sunny rays of a typical Californian winter. It felt good. I flicked on my short-wave radio. Tuning into NPR (National Public Radio), I was told that by the year 2000 the majority of commuters would have microwaves in their cars. From what I had seen of America so far, I could well believe it.

THUD!

A pair of bare brown feet landed in the sand beside me. They had jumped down from the Boardwalk and were attached to a brawny little Mexican.

'Hi there!' he said. 'You want to make friend?'

'I wasn't planning on it,' I said.

'Hey, where you from?'

'England.'

'Aaah – Inglaterra. Life is beautiful . . . non?'

'It's pretty good,' I said.

'You like Santa Cruz? Is the Brussels Sprout Capital of the world. I once live in New York but then I transplant. Now Santa Cruz my home. Hey! You wanna make screw with me?'

'No thanks.'

'Non? OK, no problem. I buy you chips.'

I walked down the pier past rows of parked cars: souped-up Chevies gleaming in the sun and old Cadillacs from the sixties – glorious fish-tailed monsters.

As I leaned over the side looking down into the sea a big, brown pelican landed in ungainly fashion on the railings beside me. Then its mate swooped into view, descending from the sky as gracefully as a sack of potatoes, frantically braking with its wings, feet splayed out in crash-landing mode and, I am convinced, eyes tightly shut. It made it, but only just.

Barking away with reverberating gusto, a herd of huge sealions basked just above the water level on the wooden struts of the pier. There were one or two slightly more energetic ones whose shiny, glistening heads bobbed momentarily out to sea before disappearing and then emerged with hoarse vociferations beneath the pier. Mexican fishermen were everywhere.

I rode onwards, southwards, past fields of brussels sprouts, artichokes and 'PICK-YOUR-OWN' kiwi fruit. Then I was back on the furious fastness of Highway 1 through Marina, Sand City and Seaside – fun-and-sun sounding places, but I saw no boats, no sea, no sand. There was only block after block of concrete, flashing neon and traffic lights, gas stations, motels, drive-ins and fast food. And trash. The gutter was awash with giant milkshake beakers, beer cans, broken glass, fast-food throw-aways. It was the first litter-strewn road I had seen.

And then it suddenly stopped.

I had entered Monterey, all spick'n'span and scenic. Houses worth big bucks clung to the hillside overlooking the yacht-studded bay. Steinbeck would find it hard to recognize his Cannery Row these days: all but one of the fish canneries have been replaced and overwhelmed with gaudy souvenir shops, galleries and seafood restaurants.

But 17-Mile Drive proved a spectacular 17-Mile Cycle around the peninsula from Pacific Grove to Carmel. The coastal road meandered past such sights as Cypress Point (a point packed with cypresses), Lone Cypress (a wave-lashed rock with an old, gnarled, lone cypress) and Seal Rock – yes, you guessed it, a wave-lashed rock covered with seals.

From the sweet-scented shade of the cypress woods, I emerged at the famous Pebble Beach Golf Course where, for a mere $225, the rich and the famous do their thing in 18 holes.

'Know what?' said an elegantly dressed, elderly woman outside Carmel's Safeway. 'Doris Day runs a guest house just down the road where animals are not only welcome but expected.'

'Oh . . . really?' I said.

'Where's your friend, dear?' the woman enquired.

'I haven't got one.'

'Now you're not telling me you're travelling all alone?'

'I certainly am.'

'Good heavens,' she continued in her unplaceable accent, 'You must be either brave or stupid or both.'

'No, just stupid,' I said.

'But it's so dangerous out there for a young girl like you. And on a bicycle of all things. Why not hire a car or take the bus – you'd be so much safer. Why, whatever does your mother think? Look, why not come home with me?'

'Well, thank you,' I said, 'but I'm just looking forward to riding along the coast to the campsite at Big Sur while the weather's nice.'

Rummaging in her Safeway shopping bag, she said, 'Here, love, at least take these,' and she handed me a box of Triscuits, which tasted like Shredded Wheat.

'I'm from Kingston-upon-Thames originally,' she said. 'Do you know it?'

I told her my brother was studying at Kingston Poly.

'Well, fancy that!' she said. 'I've been here since '52 but, you know what, my favourite place is Freshwater on the Isle of Wight.'

Big Sur sure was beautiful. Highway 1 turned into a 90-mile strip of sparsely inhabited coastline, a twisting and turning ride flanked on one side by the craggy Santa Lucia Mountains and on the other by melodramatic rocky drops down into the blue but belligerent Pacific. Big Sur and beyond is not only renowned for its beauty but also for its thick, swirling sea mists that suddenly engulf you in greyness. But I struck lucky. It was hot and clear. Stripped down to T-shirt and shorts and with salt-streaked cheeks, I had to keep reminding myself that this was January, not June.

As I panted up the side of one hefty hillock a massive RV, the size of a bus, pulled alongside. Incongruously, it was called Wilderness and towed a BMW as its run-around car. Up at the helm were two affluent Americans. The passenger window was lowered and a woman's head popped out from her air-conditioned world.

'Sure looks a great way to lose a hundred pounds,' she observed jauntily.

Later, another motorized monstrosity ('Lazy Daze') lurched alongside.

'Jeez!' called the helmsman. 'Looks like one loaded bike. Hell kid – you got guts or what?'

An ice-cold can of Budweiser was lobbed my way.

'May take some of the pain out of it,' he chuckled, before accelerating off in a flurry of fumes.

While I was drinking a bottle of strawberry-and-kiwi juice outside a store near Plaskett Creek, a roofless jeep screeched to a halt and out leapt a Cindy Lauper look-alike dressed in a glitzy, snug-hugging lycra bodysuit. Wearing a Walkman, she boogied her way towards me as she gyrated to the groovy beat – man. She looked well spaced out.

'Wow! Hi there – how're ya doin'?' she said, before ejecting her chewing gum into a flower pot.

Before I had a chance to reply that I was doing real good, she said, 'You've gotta be that crazy biker, right? A real cute guy at the gas station up the road said he'd seen you. First serious biker he'd seen all year, he said. Yeah, guess he's right – you look real loaded. I guess you gotta be nuts to do that. Right? Neat road, though. Hey, wanna come to a party?'

Stacey, it turned out, was driving from San Francisco to Los Angeles, a mere 500 miles just for an all-night rave before driving all the way back again the next morning.

Awestruck, I said, 'That's like driving to Scotland and back.' It was incomprehensible to me, to travel so far for so short a time.

'Hell,' said Stacey, 'it ain't far. It's just down the road.'

I had forgotten that America is a big country where things come big: bodies, cars, distances – a country where people think nothing of driving 50 miles to pick up a pizza.

Stopping in Cambria, I met a mustachioed man in a cowboy hat as he swayed out of Cammozzis Saloon.

'Know what?' he said. '*Arachniphobia* was filmed here.'

Never mind spiders, I thought; they should have made it on butterflies. The coastal road was littered with their corpses while the live ones fluttered and coloured the breezy skies. The magnificent Monarch (*Danus plerippus*) is reputedly one of nature's greatest mysteries. During its annual migration from Canada to Mexico, the Monarch's flight can exceed 2,000 miles (sometimes covering as much as 80 miles in a day) while it overcomes all types of natural batterings from winds, mountain ranges and storms. Judging from the number of flailing and flattened bodies, they were apparently not so successful at surviving collisions with fast-speeding windscreens. I later read that harming a Monarch is a $1,000 offence. Seemingly someone, somewhere could make a lot of money.

Super Bowl Sunday was the day to be cycling – the day when 120 million Americans (half the population) settled down to the serious business of ball-game watching. The road was mine. In Minneapolis, Minnesota, the Buffalo Bills were fighting it out against the Washington Red Skins.

The importance of Super Bowl to the American psyche is incalculable. Not only are vast sums staked on its outcome (it is said that the Mafia derives most of its annual income from the event) but also there is claimed to be a correlation between the result and the performance of the US stock-market.

Rolling through Nipomo, I turned up at Bill Deneen's Home Hostel. On the door was pinned a note:

Smoking

Smokers cannot stay here.
Kick your addiction and
you are welcome.
If you smoke while you
are here pay an extra
$10.00 and leave.

Wearing dark glasses and with long, shaggy white hair topped by a large, black top hat, Bill looked like a mixture of something from *Alice in Wonderland* and what the dog had brought in. He was into organic grow-your-owns, self-sufficiency, recycling (the average American throws away 600lb of packing a year, he said) and saving water. On the issue of toilet flushing, he said: 'Yellow is mellow; brown goes down.'

Bill was not into cars either: horses and carts were his scene and he took me for a brisk trot around the four-cars-per-family neighbourhood in his prize shining black buggy. The local dogs didn't take too kindly to this unCalifornian conveyance and gave chase in the manner recognized by cyclists worldwide, snapping and snarling and baring their teeth. My Dog Dazer taught this lot a lesson. A quick blast on the button was all that was needed to send these nasty hounds skidding to a violent halt as if they had just head-butted a brick wall. Stunned, they slunk away ignominiously, their tails between their legs.

Bill was mightily impressed, so much so that he let me off cleaning duties back at the hostel. Instead, he ordered me to play my rusty Mozart party piece on the piano.

At a junction south of Santa Maria, I asked a man in a pink Mustang where the nearest grocery store was. He clutched the top of his steering wheel with outstretched arms and stared freakishly ahead. He said nothing. He looked shell-shocked. I didn't think I had asked a particularly taxing question but, then, you never know with some people. I rephrased my query.

'Is there somewhere I could get some food around here please?'

Silence.

I shuffled uncomfortably. Slowly, he turned to face me with demonic, penetrating eyes and said in low, slow monotone, 'Don't fuck with me.'

I thought of that quote by J. Turkey Junior: 'I know you believe you understand what you think I said, but I'm not sure you realize that what you heard is not what I meant.' I was about to retreat when a leopard-skin boot hit the gas and the car gunned off with an impressive squeal of burning rubber.

I just caught sight of a large sticker on his bumper:

The Armed Forces:

Not just a job,
A total waste of fucking time.

And I thought: Ah, there's more to that than meets the eye.

I stood astride my crossbar and slugged a mouthful of water in contemplative mood. It was hot. There was nothing around except a dusty, parched expanse of nothingness.

Then a rattling brown Oldsmobile pulled up. A woman who looked like Dolly Parton rolled down the window.

'Drives me nuts,' she said inexplicably. 'How about you?'

'Pardon?' I said.

'That line of pylons marching off into the distance. Drives me nuts. Ain't that what you're looking at?'

Was Dolly off her rocker?

'Umm . . . no, not exactly,' I said. 'I was just wondering where I might find some food.'

She told me but it wasn't much use. ' 'Bout a 50-minute drive,' she said, before adding, 'Say, be careful. There's a lot of crazy people out there.'

'I know,' I said, 'I think I've just met some.'

Mrs Frances Colt Rose wasn't crazy – generous, garrulous and perhaps a touch unusual, but certainly not crazy. I had met her outside the delicatessen in Santa Ynez. A woman of sixty-something, dressed in the khaki uniform of a US park ranger, seemed like a pretty safe bet to ask about camping at Lake Cachuma.

'Well, hon,' she said, 'you're most welcome to come and stay in my home. Isn't this just a darling of a town? I've lived here 30 years – I'm well known in this neighbourhood so I assure you you'll be real safe with me.'

Frances' long, blue-and-white clapboard bungalow was one of those homes where everything gleams and nothing is out of place. Doing things like removing a magazine from the perfectly fanned coffee-table display or drying your hands on a perfectly folded towel felt as if you were causing chaos to flawless order.

I was introduced to Butterball and Precious, her two fat and fluffy cats, who instantly took to a sweaty cyclist by purring in reverberating unison, dribbling and entwining themselves in continuous figures-of-eight around my ankles.

'Aren't they just darlings?' said Frances lovingly.

I agreed that, yes, they were very darling indeed. All four of us adjourned to the living room and Frances announced that it was my room for as long as I wanted. She apologized for not being able to offer me a bedroom but since her children had left home she rented out the three spare rooms to lodgers. One was a shy Hispanic girl who, when I briefly bumped into her in the hall, said something like, '*Trabajo mucho pero gano poco*,' to which I replied, 'Yes, it's a lovely sunny day, isn't it?' because I didn't have a clue what she said.

Another lodger was a man who kept himself to himself and who made rather a lot of unsavoury sounds in the bathroom. Then there was middle-aged Mary from Beverly Hills, bedecked in jewellery, masked in make-up, dressed to impress and looking every bit like a Hollywood Queen – or Dragon. Frances said she seemed to have a new boyfriend each day.

In such an immaculate house I felt like a ragamuffin – as if everything I touched, I tainted. Rather than dirty Frances' floor with my dusty old panniers, sleeping bag and body, I pitched my tent under the washing line in the back garden. Frances thought me a trifle odd and got the wrong idea.

'Privacy is something I greatly respect,' she said.

I didn't need much persuasion to take up her offer to use the shower and washing machine and to eat her food. Over a bowl of gazpacho soup, she told me that her first husband had been killed in the Second World War and, because of that, 'I feel real patriotic. America's just a great country,' she said with fervour.

That evening Brian, the next door neighbour, dropped in.

'Josie,' Frances announced, 'I'd like you to meet a fellow countryman.'

Brian had originally hailed from Portsmouth but had been based in California for the past 30 years. During the war he had been evacuated to Midhurst in Sussex. When I told him I lived just down the road from there, Frances found this a fascinating coincidence and exclaimed, 'Why . . . is that so?' Pause. 'Whale I never.'

The following day I met Brian's Hungarian wife, Ilona, who invited me round for freshly squeezed orange juice and home-baked Hungarian cakes. Although Brian had adopted an Americanized twang, I could still detect the archetypal reserved Englishman in him. Ilona was another matter – a

hyperactive, flamboyant character who talked as if there was
no tomorrow. She was clad in a colourful clash of leggings,
short skirt, frilly top and woolly hat (for a hot day). Her
biggest wish was to head off alone to see the world with no
commitments and no time schedules; and she confided in
me that she had bought a back-pack (kept hidden from
Brian) so that she could go off on secret missions into the
mountains while Brian was at work.

'That's why the house is such a mess,' she said.

She was in the middle of telling me how she had fled
Hungary during the 1956 uprising when she suddenly said,
'You know, Brian is always complaining how I can never make
rice pudding like his mother did. And you know what I tell
him? I say that's because I'm not your mother.'

Frances had gone out to work when I returned from
Ilona's. On the table was the backdoor key and a note It
said:

> Hi Josie Dear,
> Call me at work if any questions
> need to be answered.
>
> > > Frances.
>
> PS. Share my darling house but
> know I love it a great deal!

While I was packing up my bike the next morning, Ilona
came round to see me off and handed me a box of fig rolls,
a bag of warm-baked cup-cakes, some orange juice, bananas
and stamps 'so you write us'.

Frances asked if my bike had a name. I have always been
slightly suspicious of people who give names to their
machines, much as I am of those who call their cars things
like Herbie, Gus, Steamer or Nigel. But I admitted to Frances
that I had recently christened my mount 'Starcraft' after a
hideously gargantuan mobile home-cum-camper that had
passed me.

'Well, you and Starcraft take it easy now,' she said, before
subjecting me to a bone-crunching bear hug.

Loaded up and weighed down, I trundled off over the San Rafael Mountains to Santa Barbara.

When I pulled into the State Beach Campground at Carpinteria, the ranger asked, 'Do you have anything valuable with you?'

A little tentatively, I said, 'Umm . . . well . . .yes, sort of. A passport, a few dollars, a camera and a bicycle. Why?'

'Well, I don't want to alarm you,' said the ranger, 'but there's a tent slasher on the loose. There's some crazy guy going round at night slashing people's tents while they're in them, holding them at knife point and robbing them of everything: money, valuables, sleeping bag, clothes and food. He hasn't injured anybody yet but I just thought I'd better tell you.'

'Oh . . . er . . . I see,' I stuttered. 'Thank you. I appreciate it.'

'You're welcome. Oh, and I should say he usually strikes when the freight train passes – the noise camouflages any commotion he causes. I'm afraid there's nothing we can do. The campground's an open one and the cops aren't interested. You have yourself a nice day now.'

As a precaution, the ranger agreed to lock my bike in the cleaning cupboard. I asked if he would be so good as to lock me in there too, but he said it was against park rules.

It was on occasions like these when I wished I was travelling with the Fort Knox security of a mammoth RV, surrounded by alarms, locks and peace of mind instead of a few square feet of flimsy nylon and easily accessible zips.

Being so early in the season (and no doubt for other reasons), the tent section was empty apart from one solitary nylon dome. I approached the young couple sitting beside it on a pile of firewood.

'Have you heard about the tent slasher?' I asked.

'Yep,' they said, 'and we're debating whether we should pack up and leave, even though we've just arrived.'

Rob and Zoradi were from Bristol (the first British I had met) and had spent the past few weeks driving from Florida to Los Angeles. As we chatted on in a faintly perturbed fashion about the lunatic on the loose, a station wagon pulled up and out jumped Tom Muir, a decidedly attractive yacht builder from Seattle.

We all stood around deliberating on the likelihood of our surviving the night intact. A nervously jocular air prevailed as we opted to stick it out and stay put and build ourselves a barricade. We discussed possible survival techniques and equipment. I said that if the tent-slasher was more canine than human, just leave everything up to me and I would handle him single-handedly with my trusty Dog Dazer – as long as he wasn't deaf. Failing that, I said, I possessed an impressive assortment of weaponry: a whistle (upon which, should the need arise, I could deliver the internationally recognized distress signal of six quick blasts followed a minute later by another six blasts), a sturdy bicycle pump (which, speaking from experience, is useful for hitting undesirable types over the head or in the genitalia) and some dental floss (trip wires or strangulation).

No one, I admit, looked any more confident.

'Never mind my tent,' said Tom, 'I'm sleeping in the truck.'

He said he would have invited me to sleep with him (an offer which momentarily gave me heart palpitations) but, alas, his surfboards were dearer to him than I was. (His wife had finally granted him permission to disappear for a week's solo surfing holiday.) He removed his boards from the roof and stored them inside just in case the nocturnal stalker should possess an affinity for surfing.

I think I would have preferred to be with Rob and Zoradi in their tent. Rob had been in the Marines and was one of those brawny action-man characters who stalk around with sizeable sheath knives attached to their belts. His was a mean-looking dagger, certainly not something I'd like to find myself the wrong end of, and what's more, Rob knew how to use it. I said that the only thing I could do with a knife was to chop an onion or carve the Sunday roast.

I pitched my tent practically on top of Rob and Zoradi's – I didn't want to risk the chance of my 'held at knife-point' blood-curdling scream going unheard. We sat around a blazing log fire deep into the night as a stack of six-packs slowly diminished. Tom believed that inebriation was the best way to tackle whatever we might have to tackle.

'Maybe,' I said, 'we should hijack one of those tank-like RVs to sleep in safe and sound.'

'Not worth the risk,' Tom said. 'We'd be shot. Everybody in California has a gun.'

'Florida's full of guns too,' Rob remarked. 'And RVs. Second-hand ones. It seems that every well-off couple buys one of these monsters when they've hit retirement and then they embark on their mandatory transcontinental adventure to Florida. There the husband dies of old age, obesity or gun-shot wounds, leaving the wife who can't drive these beasts to sell it and take the bus home.'

That was Rob's myth, anyway.

Whenever I spotted a sinister shadow lurking in the blackness of the trees I would gallantly leap into action by steering Rob towards whatever it was to investigate, knife at the ready. Meanwhile Tom, Zoradi and I would shout encouragement as we monitored his progress from the safety of the fire.

At one point the dark, sinister form of an old bearded man appeared, dragging what sounded like a sack of chains. The whites of his eyes gleamed as the light of the fire caught them and then he slunk away, vanishing into the woods, more like an apparition than a solid body form. The sight of him made us immediately stop talking and stare. The same thought came to us all: Is that him? No one moved. No one got up to stop him. The fire crackled on.

Finally the dreaded moment arrived. Bedtime. For a modicum of protection, I climbed into my sleeping bag with my cycling helmet on as I didn't fancy half my head being slashed along with the tent.

The night was not a good one as far as sleep was concerned. Every time a 100 or so car freight train noisily reverberated past I sat bolt upright, waiting for a steely blade to slice through my home and for the words, 'Put ya hands in the air and gimme all ya money . . . and clothes . . . and food . . . and sleeping bag . . . and sheet sleeping bag . . . and helmet . . .'

The most serious dilemma was that I thought my bladder would truly burst. By about 4am I was more than desperate; I had reached emergency level but I was too scared to venture out alone in the dark to the distant toilet block. I have had some nasty experiences in campground toilets and I didn't want to add to that collection, even if it meant bursting my internal version of the Thames Flood Barrier. In the end it was mind over matter, or more importantly, mind over bladder, and I survived until the first tawny streaks of sky appeared in the east.

5

Getting Nowhere Fast

I sat in the Soup Connection, a self-service restaurant in a suburb of Los Angeles. A notice informed me that I could replenish my plate as many times as my stomach allowed with soups and salads, pizzas and pancakes and pies, cookies and muffins and more. But no doggy bags allowed. The place was a cyclist's paradise – no, a glutton's paradise, which amounts to the same thing really. For $4 it was possible to sit in my seat and eat for a week, which goes some way to explaining why you don't see many thin people in America. Astonishingly, there are over three million people in the US weighing over 500–600lbs; in English, that is a phenomenal 35–42 stone.

There were certainly no thin people in the Soup Connection. Even calling them fat would have been a compliment. No, these people were big and I mean *real* BIG. How big? Well, they were as expansive as ten normal-sized people rolled into one. No kidding. They were monsters.

I couldn't stop staring at the couple on the next table who were speed-shovelling their way through a mountain of food as if there was no tomorrow which, in their case, there probably wouldn't be. Their sights were focused on their food. They didn't speak, they scarcely breathed, they scarcely chewed. They just shovelled and swallowed, shovelled and swallowed, and only looked up to throw back their fully-mouthed heads for large, slurping swigs of Diet Coke.

I could go some way to understanding their prodigious appetites if they had fasted for a year but, no, these people hadn't eaten for two minutes – the time it took for them to belch and wobble over to the canteen to replenish their plates. Frankly, it was grotesque. Most of the Soup Connection's clientele had appetites greater than an army of elephants; mine, I hasten to add, included. I did myself proud as an 'all-you-can-eat, stuff-your-gob' beginner. Occasionally I caught sight of my Soup Connection companions, Kermit and Ursula Bartlett, over the top of my mammoth leaning tower of pizza. They looked at their watches and announced, 'You're doing well. You've been eating continuously for over an hour.'

This was a considerable improvement over my first visit, when I couldn't even make it to seconds, let alone sevenths. It was due not so much to lack of a big appetite as to a big mouth; I talked more than I ate. Again I had been with Kermit and Ursula (I cooked for them in London before they 'transplanted' to California) and was so pleased to see them that conversation outweighed consumption.

Kermit, a lovely lovable man, was a native Californian who had grown up in the Los Angeles area in the 1930s when it 'used to be a great place to live' – unspoilt by smog and freeways and murderous street gangs. His mother had been of the houseproud sort who clean the house before the cleaning lady comes. Kermit called me the daughter he had never had.

Ursula, his gregarious German wife, was tiny, even tinier than five-foot-nothing me – though this fact she resolutely disputed.

They had lived in Germany, London and Philadelphia but now their home was California, in a sort of countrified suburb of Los Angeles. The city of Moorpark had barely existed only ten to fifteen years ago. Now it was like countless similar communities which were mushrooming out of the beautiful hills and mountains of Southern California so fast that you could actually stand and watch them grow. Cheapish and cheerful housing, they called it. Certainly they were not the ugly, run-of-the-mill concrete blocks that have so blighted many a British town. The style was pseudo-Mediterranean stucco villa with sunny pantiled roofs.

I had planned to stay a day or two in Moorpark, say hello to Ursula and Kermit, sleep in a bed, have a bath, wash my clothes, read my post and move on before they asked me to, but I was still there weeks later. It was an easy place to get used to. The sun shone, my washing got washed, I slept in a bed, I wallowed in the bath, I swam in the pool, played tennis and frequented the Soup Connection.

What is more, Ursula was happy for me to stay as long as possible. All that was asked of me in return for an easy life was to do things with food. Ursula hated cooking even more than she hated the look and taste of porridge. 'Prison food', she called it and would watch in horror as I gleefully worked my way through gargantuan amounts.

Ursula would have loved a house without a kitchen. She literally recoiled at the thought of having to prepare something to eat. In that way, she called me the perfect house guest and I became her built-in cooker.

There was something unusual about Moorpark but it was several days before it suddenly dawned on me why I felt faintly uneasy. No one ever went anywhere under their own steam. The only people I occasionally passed on the flower-lined pavements (perfectly manicured by hard-worked, underpaid Mexican labourers) were either shell-suited dog walkers or Walkman-topped joggers. Unless you fell into either of those categories (or a mixture of both), there was apparently no reason to head out on foot.

There was none of that sense of community which is found in any European town or city. You couldn't trot down to a corner shop to pick up a paper or a pint of milk or swap a bit of gossip with the locals – the nearest shops were a car ride away in the Mall along a dangerously traffic-laden highway. You couldn't nip round the corner to post a letter because there were no post boxes – the Mall was all or nothing. Nor did people pass the time of day on street corners or cross the road to greet friends, any more than people in Britain chat on the M1/M25 intersection. It's not that this lack of streetlife cohesion is necessarily wrong; it's just different and strangely sad.

California is America's most populous state and it is a place which was born of and for the car. Everybody drives everywhere. I found it incomprehensible, as did many motorists. A man once said to me in a Seven Eleven, 'We drive somewhere and then drive back and then wonder why the hell we went.' It's no wonder the world is being slowly poisoned to death.

Los Angeles is more or less held together by an intricate network of five-laned, car-crammed highways. Public transport is virtually non-existent, certainly in Moorpark. I had been there only four days when I said to Ursula, somewhat naïvely, that I fancied taking the train into Los Angeles.

Ursula laughed. 'What train?' she said.

I had seen that Moorpark had a railway but I hadn't realized that it was only for freight.

'Well, I'll take the bus then,' I said.

Again, this was wishful thinking. The only way to get downtown was by car or, if you liked dicing with death, bicycle. Apparently three-year-old Chris Harrison relished an element of danger. I read in the paper that he was stopped by police who found him dressed in pyjamas and riding his tricycle along the freeway at 2am.

I found such a dependency on cars decidedly depressing. Woody Allen once said about Los Angeles that 'the only cultural advantage is that you can make a right turn on a red light'. That sort of sums it up, really.

But the place intrigued me. I found it incredibly exciting, depressing, superficial, materialistic, money-orientated, car-infested and smoggy. Down at the Thousand Oaks Tennis Club the ladies' changing-room talk was of affairs (both monetary and sexual), face-lifts and flesh-puckered tucks. It seemed that all along the coast of Southern California people lived to be lithe-limbed. Many were self-conscious and self-obsessed with surgically-adjusted bodies trying to establish their place in the cosmos.

Even European Ursula had become incredibly Americanized. She thought I was truly mad when I washed up in the sink instead of using the dishwasher, or chopped and sliced with a knife instead of using the Moulinex, or used the (quicker) hand tin-opener instead of the electric one, or hung out the washing on my improvised line of bungee cords instead of using the dryer, or opened the window if I felt hot instead of closing it and turning on the air-conditioner, or used a toothbrush attached to my hand instead of a motor, or cycled instead of driving, or sifted through the garbage reusing useful 'rubbish', or walked out of the door to walk the dog (a black standard poodle who ate bananas) instead of climbing into the car and driving ten miles in order to walk the dog, or suggested parking the car in a space at the rear of the near-full Mall parking lot even if it meant a longer walk rather than driving around in exhausting circles searching for a space nearest to the shops to save on valuable leg power (but not time), or said that I preferred to sleep in the wilds on the ground with a rock in my back rather than in a sumptuously swish hotel . . .

But despite having nothing in common apart from size, we got on a treat.

One morning I was working my way through the never-ending wadge of the Los Angeles *Sunday Times* when, reaching the travel section, I spotted a flight to Hawaii for $109. The following Sunday I was on it with the Pacific far below, and heading for the 'Fiftieth State of Heaven'. Beside me was black Monique from Martinique, a Hare Krishna. On boarding the plane I had found her in my designated window seat, happily chanting away to herself in a state of meaningful meditation. In her palms she gently rolled together a string of harlequin-coloured wooden beads. She emitted an air of benevolent calm and sweet sandalwood. After about two hours she suddenly removed a book from her bag, wrote a message on the inside front cover, and handed it to me.

'For you,' she said. 'Thank you for letting me have your seat.'

The book, by 'His Divine Grace' A.C. Bhaktivedanta Swami Prabhupada, was *Beyond Birth and Death* in which 'India's most renowned Vedic authority presents startling evidence of the soul's incredible journey after death'. Quivering on a wing high up in the clouds when all faith is put in a giant and glorified airborne tin can, I found Monique's offering distinctly ominous.

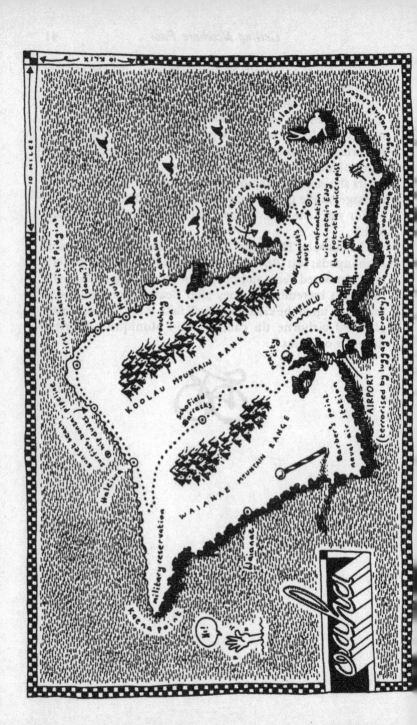

6

Life's a Beach

'They paved paradise and put up a parking lot.'
(Joni Mitchell)

It was a 2,400-mile flight to reach what Mark Twain had called 'the loveliest fleet of islands that lies anchored in any ocean'. Of all Hawaii's 162 islands, only seven are inhabited and I was heading for the most heavily inhabited of the lot – Oahu.

Before arriving, my concept of Hawaii was of a distant tropical island roamed by grass-skirted, hip-swaying hula girls and *Hawaii Five-O* film crews. And I had gleaned from the *National Geographic* that the state fish was a tiny creature with a pig-like snout called a *Humuhumunukunuku-pua'au* (pronounced: hoo-moo-hoo-moo-noo-koo-noo-koo-ah-poo-ah-ah). Only the latter of these facts was correct, and a fish would not get me very far. Nor would my lack of wheels. I had left my mount in Moorpark because the airline and travel agency had told me (incorrectly) that bicycles were not accepted on inter-island flights. Assuming a handful of small, compact islands, I had decided I would hire a bike on each one for a quick scoot round for a few days.

It was February. As I stepped off the plane in Honolulu ('Protected Harbour') the first thing to hit me was the tropical heat. The second was an unmanned, out-of-control airport baggage trolley that took me unawares from behind, at speed, leaving me with a dented shin and a bruised ankle.

I felt lost. I had never gone anywhere without my bike before and I was already missing Starcraft. Whereas I would usually just fling my bags on my bike and sally forth with ease, I was now burdened with cumbersome baggage and had to start looking for a vehicle to get me out.

I lumbered on to *TheBus* and stood wedged among a multi-hued stew of passengers as we inched our way laboriously in the teeming bumper-to-bumper traffic of downtown Honolulu. I was heading for one of the most densely populated areas on earth: Waikiki ('Spouting Water'), where around 110,000 people rub shoulders with each other on the boulevards and beaches in an area covering only seven-tenths of a square mile. About half of these people are tourists; another 30,000 are commuters who cater to the tourists; and the remaining 25,000 actually call Waikiki home.

TheBus moved on in jerking spasms while my nose was pressed ever closer into the tropical armpits of the tightly packed passengers. Phew! Was it hot! The smell of sweaty flesh was intoxicating.

Crammed against the glass partition was Bob Allnutt from Maryland, looking a touch hot and flustered. I homed in straight away on the tell-tale sign of a cyclist – a handlebar bag hanging from his shoulder. Bob said he was a freelance travel photographer and had come to Hawaii for a ten-day cycle ride around the island of Maui. He admitted he was a little worried because he did not know where his bike was. From his bag he extracted *Six Islands On Two Wheels*, a guide book which had given him the idea. Bob said he had been told that there would be no problem about putting bikes on the inter-island flights.

Looking as though he would expire at any moment was Carl, a dentist with a ballooning belly, who was sweating heavily on a seat beside me.

'Teeth are the only thing in the world that fascinate me,' he said. 'Teeth and my girlfriend, that is. But I see a lot more teeth than I do of her 'cos she lives over your ways in Yorkshire. Guess I must be doing something wrong 'cos I can't for the life of me get her to move from Harrogate to Hawaii.'

Peering over his shoulder into a street scene of gridlock chaos, I said, 'Maybe you'd be better off if you moved to the moors.'

Two teenagers in shades, baseball boots and baggy shorts were sitting down behind Carl.

'Wow man! Check that chick,' cooed one as a bikini-clad Michelle Pfeiffer look-alike crossed the road.

A man called Benny prodded my shoulder and said, 'Here for long?' His rotund form was tightly encapsulated in a T-shirt saying:

EAT
RUN
STAY
FIT

'I'm not sure,' I said. 'Maybe a couple of weeks. I'm planning on cycling around all the islands.'

'Jeez, you be careful now. This ain't the place it used to be. Hell no – this ain't no paradise for sure. Full of crazy weirdos, if you ask me. Why, just the other week a pretty young thing was pulled off her bike on the Big Island – raped then murdered. Never caught the killers. Don't want to put you off but . . . well, take it easy. There are better places than this.'

*

I checked into Waikiki's Interclub Hostel and took the last bed. The first people I came across in my dusty dorm of eight were two girls from Sweden jet-setting around the world for a year. Their identical T-shirts said: ANNA AND TINA WORLD TOUR 1992.

I dropped my bags on to my bunk with relief and then trotted off past burger stalls, shops selling plastic hula dolls, the Outrigger Hotel and down to the world-famous Waikiki Beach just in time to face a falling sun fire-balling its way into the ocean.

❀

My first priority was to find some wheels. After a fruitless day traipsing around every bicycle hire shop in the vicinity, I discovered that hiring a small, standard shift, non-airconditioned car from the likes of Hertz, Avis and Budget was only about $5 a day more expensive than hiring a rusty, badly maintained, single-speed bone-shaker. I ended up buying a brand new Raleigh Eclipse mountain bike which the shop agreed to buy back off me for 70 per cent of the original price – a pleasing bit of wheeler-dealing.

I sat on a bench on the beach in the shade of a gently rustling palm tree. Behind me Kalakua Avenue bustled with throngs of tourists and traffic and obsequiously smiling Japanese businessmen. In front of me lay the sun-seekers and the surf-kings of Waikiki beach. I had never seen such an incredible hotchpotch of faces. Nowhere else in the world can you find such a mixed, polyglot, integrated lot.

Every major race is represented in Hawaii. More than 50 ethnic groups have added their genes, their traditions, customs, ways of life, food, views and prospects to the brew. So much blood has mingled over so many years of intermarriage that it is often impossible to place people in a specific racial category.

The original Hawaiians are dwindling away fast and now form barely ten per cent of the population. Their history stretches way back to between AD 500 and AD 900 when Polynesians (originally South East Asians) from the Marquesas and Tahiti arrived on Hawaii in huge canoes, some with double hulls, after being guided by wind, sea current and stars across thousands of miles of open, unknown ocean in search of new land. With them they brought their families, household possessions, pigs, barkless dogs, chickens and rats (overlooked stowaways), coconuts, taro, sugar-cane, bread-fruit, sweet-potatoes, bananas and mulberry plantings. For generations, the islanders lived in their grass houses, making canoes and tapa cloth and eating taro, fish and tropical fruit and vegetables, undisturbed by the outside world.

Then towards the end of the eighteenth century Captain Cook arrived with his ships and posse of sailors. The Hawaiians called these strange, pale newcomers *haoles* or 'those without breath' on account of their death-like complexion. One native who returned to shore after going on board described seeing men with wrinkled skins, sparkling eyes, white foreheads and angular heads (three-cornered hats) who spoke a strange language and breathed fire from their mouths.

During the next hundred years the white man's diseases of typhoid, cholera, measles, mumps, 'flu, tuberculosis, small-pox and VD ravaged the Hawaiians, reducing the native population by over 80 per cent. Then with the influx of races – Chinese, Japanese, Samoan, Korean, British, American, Filipino, Norwegian, Russian, Polish, German, Spanish, Portuguese, Afro-American, Puerto Rican and American Indian (to name just a few) – the Hawaiians liter-ally bred themselves out of existence.

An old man as white-headed as a mountain and with a leathery, lined face sat down on the bench beside me. He smiled, then deliberately rolled himself a cigarette and read a dog-eared Chinese newspaper. The man wore baggy blue calf-length trousers and shoddy flip-flops. He looked as if he had just stepped out of a paddy field.

Soon, copper-coloured clouds glowed in the west and the sun slid slowly over the edge of the ocean as I sauntered back to the hostel.

It didn't take long to realize that Hawaii wasn't a paradise for all. Riding through high-rise Honolulu, I passed a park covered with makeshift tents and the cardboard homes of the homeless. Yet in one sense it *was* their paradise. As one tarpaulin-homed man told me: 'Where else in the world can I sleep out year round in temperatures of 70 and 80 degrees?'

A few days later I read in the *Star Bulletin* about their outcry when the police evicted them. Mainland US cities, not so dependent on tourism, are more tolerant of citizens who have fallen through the social net, but in Hawaii the tourist industry has a dread that low-lifers, loafers and down-and-outs will ensconce themselves on Oahu's beaches.

The most beautiful beaches are on the leeward stretch of coast around Waianae ('Mullet Waters'). Several people warned me not to venture there alone because of the intense territoriality of the locals – Oahu's last stand for the ethnic Hawaiians. Here *haoles* were said to be given a hard time, tormented or even physically attacked. Safety was not something I would find there, they said, adding that everywhere else was risky, if not downright dangerous.

There was a pervasive sense of bitterness. Rich outsiders were infringing upon the locals' territory, dispossessing them of land which for generations had been passed on to them by their own people. It was easy to understand the growing sense of bitterness and deep dislike that was now spreading rapidly from Hawaiian to *haole*.

Even if you tried to camp by the laws and regulations, Hawaii was a headache. On arrival I had presumed I could pitch my tent safely in any little secluded spot I fancied. I was wrong. Official camping on Oahu was made as inconveniently complicated as possible and it revolved around bureaucracy, form-filling and sour-faced officials.

To camp in a state park campground, I needed a permit. To obtain a permit, I had to locate first the Department of Forestry and then the Division of State Parks in downtown Honolulu. After being wrongly directed by a scooter-riding policeman and much searching, I eventually found it. By then I was ten minutes late: the offices had closed at 4.15pm.

I returned the next morning and was served by a surly woman who said that I had to write a letter stating my name, address, 'phone number, the number of people in my party, the type of permit required, the duration of my stay and at which state park I was requesting to camp – all *at least* one week in advance.

I said I wanted a permit for tomorrow night, Wednesday. 'Impossible,' she said. 'Like I say, you have to apply at least a week in advance.'

Flexibility was forbidden. If I had a permit for one park but was unable to make it there for the particular night I had reserved because of, say, mechanical or bodily malfunctions, and if I then headed for a more convenient park for which I failed to have a permit, my entrance would be prohibited.

'So what am I expected to do if I don't have another twenty hilly miles in me and am not allowed to camp off the beaten track?' I asked the sour-faced woman. 'Sleep on the hard shoulder?'

'I guess so,' she said helpfully, visibly brightening at the prospect.

I gave up. Instead I tried my luck at the City and County of Honolulu Department of Parks and Recreation in King Street.

'Hello,' I said to the Japanese-looking man, 'I'd like a permit to camp at Kualoa Park tomorrow night, Wednesday, and one for Haleiwa Beach Park on Thursday.'

'You cannot camp on these days,' said the man. He never once looked me in the eye – his gaze constantly focused somewhere near my covered tummy button.

'Why not?' I asked.

'Because on these two days of the week the parks are closed.'

I thought there must be a conspiracy against me. After all, I was in America, the world's superpower, and not some African backwater. But it was becoming obvious that it was far less complicated to get married (in Las Vegas you can be wed within 15 minutes of proposing) than to go camping.

When I asked my Japanese man why the parks closed on the nights that I wanted to sleep there, he told my navel that it was due to the homeless problem in Hawaii. Closing at random for two nights a week prevented squatters from setting up a permanent base in the parks.

I gave up for good and cycled back towards Waikiki, stopping to buy Jack London's *South Sea Tales* in a bookshop. As I was browsing, a cheerful girl approached me with a clipboard in hand.

'Excuse me,' she said, 'I'm Marcy and I'm doing a survey on public hygiene for the university. Would you mind filling out a form?'

Not at all. The form had questions like:

Do you always / sometimes / never wash your hands after going to the toilet?

Do you always / sometimes / never use soap?

Do you wash your hands out of habit or necessity?

Who would you say spends more time washing their hands. Men or Women?

How many seconds on average do you think a
person takes to wash their hands?
3 : 5 : 10 : 15 : 25

I put down my book and stood in the aisle pretending to
wash my hands: turning on the imaginary tap, getting a good
suds with the soap and drying off nicely on the hand-towel. A
worried nearby browser edged away from me. I circled '15'
on the form. When I next washed my hands for real, I timed
myself. I took a surprisingly swift six seconds. Well, you live
and learn.

I rode out of Waikiki beneath the domineering shadow of
Diamond Head volcano in a sudden, road-sweeping shower.
Palm trees waved their spiky fronds in wild gesticulation as
the squally, warm, wet wind blew with a vengeance off the
frothy ocean, flicking spray from angry waves.

I passed a postman in a white pudding-basin helmet,
shorts, long white socks and rain-splashed shoes. He flashed
me a smile and dived into his van for cover, shouting the
friendly Hawaiian greeting of '*Aloha*!' followed by a hasty
'Shit!' as he banged his head on the roof.

By the time I had reached Hanauma Bay State Underwater
Park, the sun had reappeared. The heat increased, the road
steamed, the wind smelt salty, fresh and raw.

Hanauma Bay is known for its prize snorkelling but I didn't
have a snorkel. Nor did I fancy leaving my money on the
beach while I went for a dip in clear waters thick with fierce-
coloured fish. Instead, I walked along a sea-cliff on the left of
the bay to 'Toilet Bowl', where I sat in the sun and watched
two young local lads splashing and guffawing in this bowl-
shaped phenomenon, the water rising and falling as the
waves filled and emptied the pool through its bizarre natural lava plumbing. The boys, brown skin glistening, floated
up and down looking for all the world as though they were
bobbing about in the pan of an enormous flushing toilet.

Heading back to Highway 72, I skirted round
Kohelepelepe ('Fringed Vagina'), a dormant volcano more
commonly known as Koko Crater. Legends abound in Hawaii

and the legend around Koko is that the great fire goddess
Pele had a sister called Kapo. Instead of a magic carpet, Kapo
had a magical flying vagina that she could send 'anywhere,
any place, any time'. When Kamapua'a, the pig-god,
launched a rape attack on Pele, Kapo came to the rescue by
dispatching her vagina to act as a decoy, luring Kamapua'a to
Koko Head where it formed the crater before flying away.
Thus the elusive magical vagina had disappeared before
Kamapua'a, leaping in hot pursuit, had gained any sexual
gratification. Such are the titillating tales of Hawaii.

The warm trade winds bowled me along the coast and past
Sandy Beach, renowned for its body-surfing and famous for
breaking more necks and backs than anywhere else in the
world. Rather than add to this painful statistic, I went
paddling instead.

I was on my way to Kailua Bay, the home of Laura Schmidt – a friend I had met in Honolulu. As I rode past Bellows Air Force Base ('inactive', so my map said), a beaten-up jeep passed and then did a U-turn, crawling past on the opposite side of the road before doing another U-turn and again passing suspiciously slowly. Finally it ground to a halt and a small, squat man with curly black hair and a grimy face leaned out of the doorless side and shouted something at me as I approached. Smelling a rat, I swerved out into the empty opposite lane to give this suspect character a wide berth, my eyes focused dead ahead. Heartbeats quickened. The jeep passed again, slowed and stopped. Again the man called to me. This time I stopped. I didn't fancy being followed by a 'crazy' who might knock me off my bike at any moment. I decided to see what he wanted.

'Hey! Wanna do some boat modelling?' he said.

The first thought to flash into my mind was fashioning Airfix model boats.

'You look real sporty,' he said. 'D'ya fancy being photographed in some real neat swimwear? It's a whole lotta fun and the money's good. Captain Eddy's the name – real pleased to meet you.'

Modelling! The idea was preposterous, and most definitely suspect. Whoever heard of a five-foot-nothing short-ass with pulsating calf muscles being asked to model?

'I'm not interested, thanks,' I said.

'Hey, come on, babe,' he said, with a leering and shifty-eyed look. 'You don't trust me, huh? Think I look a mess? That's 'cos I've been giving the boat a fresh coat of paint. Take a look at this.'

He produced a tattered wallet from his pocket and flipped it open to show me a police identification card of himself.

'See, a part-time cop. I work for the force Downtown. There's sure no need to be worried – I'm safe all right and I'll make sure you are too,' he said with a sly smile.

'Piss off,' I said, 'I'm meeting my body-building friend up the road and I don't think he'd like it – or you.'

What I needed now was to turbo-boost my way up the road in order to make a hasty and impressive 'don't mess with me' exit. Instead my foot fumbled for my toe-clip and I lurched off up the hill with about as much urgency as a snail in labour. In short, I was still easy prey.

The jeep drew level and Captain Eddy flicked me his business card.

'Think about it,' he said, 'there ain't no rush. I kinda like you and I guess I'm gonna see you again soon – yeah, real soon.'

He threw back his head with a repulsive laugh before swinging the jeep round and accelerating off in the direction from which he had come.

When I arrived at Laura and Jack Schmidt's house, I told them about my encounter with Captain Eddy. They looked worried and told me about a recent spate of attacks that had taken place up on the Pali Highway. Women drivers who had stopped or broken down had been raped or sexually assaulted by a man posing as a policeman. I thought: Was that him?

Laura and Jack lived in a long, wooden bungalow with their two pretty young daughters, Jessica and Jennifer. Jack, a pilot for Hawaiian Airlines, flew on the inter-island routes and so he was home every night. It was a good life, he said. He had moved to Oahu from rainy Seattle some 16 years before but he was becoming more and more disillusioned with Hawaii.

'It's no longer the paradise it once was,' he said. 'Violence is everywhere. These days there are too many attacks and rapes and murders and disappearing tourists. There's a hell of a lot of racial hatred out there – it's just not the sort of environment I want to bring up my daughters in. I've been thinking about moving to the Cook Islands – they seem like a neat place to live.'

I took a step outside into the garden and was severely reprimanded by a savage black dog. Laura was most apologetic.

'We haven't had him long,' she said, 'we got him as a guard dog ever since we got burgled. Before that happened, I'd always felt so safe here. At night Jack and I would always leave the porch door open next to our room to get the through breeze. Now we never do. We close all the windows and lock all the doors.'

She told me about the burglary. 'It was late in the evening. Jack was on the 'phone in his office at the other end of the house while I had stretched out on the couch and dozed off for a while. Then suddenly I woke up and had this awful feeling that someone else was in the house. And then I saw him – a dark shadow creeping out of the bedroom. I screamed and screamed and he ran out of the porch door and disappeared into the night. Jack came running and found me in a terrible state. It took me a long time to get over it. It was just so scary. Now we've gotten ourselves the dog, kinda makes us feel a little more secure.'

I read a story to Jennifer before she went to bed. When I arrived she had been dressed in an angelic fairy outfit and was dancing and singing while she half-watched a full-volume video called *Yeller* about a big, bounding dog doing heroic things while the ear-rattling, sing-song music burst forth.

'TV's my favourite thing in the whole wide world,' she said. And I thought: What a shame.

Later that night, over a pasta supper, Laura told me about their cat, which had disappeared. A few days later it was found dead on the beach and with much sadness they gave it a state burial, flowers and all. Not long after this, a neighbour rang up to announce happily that she had found their cat. Laura said, 'But you can't have – he's dead.'

It turned out that they had buried the wrong one.

The next morning Jack tried to dissuade me from continuing my ride around the island.

'It's just not safe,' he said. 'We'd love you to stay, make

this your base for a few days – maybe go on some short day rides or else you could take it easy on the beach. There's a lot of bad people on this island and I wouldn't want you to meet any.'

Then he got me to speak to an Australian friend from work.

'Look,' said the voice on the other end of the line, 'it's not *if* something will happen to you, but *when*.'

With such words of encouragement rebounding in my head I packed up, hugged goodbye, promised to ring and rode north out of Kailua. Before leaving town I stopped off at the Food Pantry supermarket and had my first encounter with a preposterous Martian-voiced talking till.

'. . . 59 cents . . . 2 dollars 65 . . . 17 cents . . . 1 dollar forty . . . that is 5 dollars 32 . . . and 18 cents change . . . thank you for shopping at the Food Pantry . . . have a nice day . . . oh, and watch out for those Captain Eddies . . . remember this is Hawaii . . . a paradise crawling with crazies . . .'

I rode on up the coast with the clear outline of the spinal Koolau range of fierce, purple-green mountains forming a bulwark on my left while the incessant pounding of the Pacific collided with the reef on the other side. Smashed and crumpled wrecks of cars lay incongruously harsh and ugly against the stark and verdant beauty – wrecks sprawled with graffiti and left to rust in their graves in otherwise beautiful mountain streams, lush jungle-like woods or crescent, white-sand beaches. I was surprised by the neglect, the broken glass at the roadside (hundreds of smashed beer bottles – it was said the locals liked their drink), crisp packets, sweet packets, cigarette packets and cans – an endless supply of littery eye-sores. There were dead dogs, too.

In Kahuku I stopped for a rest in the shade and heard two local boys chatting nearby in pidgin. Pidgin is an extraordinary language to hear: a few words leap out at you, words you half recognize but which throw little light on what is being said. The language evolved during the plantation days of the last century when Hawaiians and *haoles* had to communicate with migrant Chinese, Japanese and Portuguese. A simple common language was needed so that workers could quickly understand each other, and the colourful, companionable vernacular of pidgin was born.

The boys' chattering sounded to me something like: 'Hey! howzit brah? Hele on. Da lolo buggah – one wid da cockaroach – man was he swell head. Li'chs an' Lil'dat da'kine wahine in da'kine trouble, as her big Hawaiian blalah, get plenty hu hu an' den da tita was hele on. Some say ono dis kaukau! OK. Les go.'

I didn't pick up a lot of pidgin but I knew that I certainly wouldn't take it as a compliment if I was called a 'lolo buggah pakiki head'.

I hit Sunset Beach, the surfers' strip, and leaned my bike against a toilet block. After emerging from the well-soiled *Wahine* side, I sat on an overlooking tussock and watched the beach scene. Bodies of bronzed muscle prevailed, with surfboards either underarm or underfoot. Out towards the reef, more talented muscle performed a wave-crested ballet, expertly balanced and skimming among breaking rollers of mountainous sea. Here, when conditions are right, the surf can build up into a mighty azure wall of some 40 feet of solid liquid power. Riding the waves in such spots as the Bonzai Pipeline, the Pinballs or the Rubber Duckies is the stuff of surfer's dreams.

Captain James Cook was the first white man to report seeing surfers in Hawaii. The kings of the islands rode the waves on *olos* – large planks of sugar-pine and coachwood. The sport was surrounded in mystery and ritual, and when the Calvinist missionaries arrived they considered surfing to be a form of paganism, and they banned it.

The surfers of Sunset were no longer royalty but mainly Californians who came here to fulfil their dreams. Now their lives revolved around surfboard designs (single fins, pintails, trusters, swallow tails), surfers, surfing and surfing talk. Little else mattered. The sea meant everything.

A big body with a triangular torso came and sat down beside me, glistening, fresh from the sea. He looked like something out of the Chippendales.

'Hey babe,' he drawled, 'how're ya doin'?'

I always found this sort of 'right-on' greeting a bit hard to answer in suitable surfing mode. Should I shock them and respond in a typically pompous English style like, 'Very well thank you. How are you?', or with a more swinging, 'I'm doin' real good'?

But none of these sounded or felt quite right. I listened to how the hip-dudes responded to each other and I decided that if I wanted to be one of them (which I didn't) I would have to adopt a sort of laid-back West Coast drawl like, 'Hey radical – that's cool, man.' But that wasn't me. Instead I just replied to Mr Think-a-lot-of-himself Chippendale, 'Fine thanks, but I'm a bit hot.'

'You biking far?' he asked.

'Well, I'm planning on riding round all the islands and then . . . I'm not sure . . . maybe down to Mexico.'

'Get serious! That's fucking manic, man – that's serious biking!' Then he said, 'Hey, I'll tell you what, babe – you should hole up here for a while. It's a real happening place. Cool crowd.'

One of his hip mates, crammed into the sort of overly brief, tight trunks that threaten emasculation, sauntered over and lobbed Mr Chippendale an ice-cold six-pack of Rolling Rock. He said, 'Swell, man,' and I thought: Do these people *really* talk like this?

I booked in down the road at the Vacation Hostel, a crashpad for surfers, where I took the last bunk in a room with three boys. It was dark, dirty and cramped. There was sand everywhere: in my bed, on the floor, in the basin. The toilet was blocked but not with sand. On the gritty wet floor were a couple of used condoms.

Emerging from the bathroom, I walked back into the murkiness of my room and was faced with the bare backside of some surfing maestro changing from lycra trunks into baggy day-glo shorts.

'Whoops – sorry!' I said.

'Hey, no sweat man,' he said breezily, 'We're all one big happy family here.'

Greg was a plumber from the mainland who had come to Hawaii for a holiday, found a part-time job and stayed. He had been on Hawaii for nearly two years. He surfed in the morning, plumbed in the afternoon and partied all night.

'Yeah – life's pretty fucking cool,' he said.

Later I lay on the top bunk in the sultry heat and listened to the rain beating on the corrugated-iron roof all night, bouncing off the banana leaves outside my mosquito-mesh windows. It didn't sound promising. But dawn came quiet, clear and cool. I left the surf-kings to their slumber, their sand, their sea and their Bonzai Pipelines.

Heading back inland towards Honolulu, I passed fields and fields of Dole pineapples and Del Monte tropical fruit. The sun was hot by now and the air smelt sweet and sickly, as if I was cycling with my nose immersed in an immense bowlful of tinned pineapple.

Then I came upon Schofield Barracks, 'Home of the Infantry, Tropic Lightning'. Hawaii is the most militarized state in America and my map of Oahu was covered in beige pockets of military reservations. The soldiers and their families tend to keep exclusively to themselves; they live in their own fenced-off, guarded world; they swim at their own beaches, attend their own schools and churches, shop at their own stores. The local Hawaiians don't like the soldiers. To them they are 'jar-heads'.

As I crested the hilltop that looked down upon the high-rises of Honolulu and the sea-speckled flotilla of boats in Pearl Harbor (which, in 1941, had been called the world's strongest fortress) I wondered what it must have looked like 50 years earlier on that blue, cloudless December morning as the Japanese planes were strafing and bombs were falling, ships sinking and two and a half thousand people dying. It was a day that, President Franklin D. Roosevelt said, 'will live in infamy'.

The Americans had been taken totally unawares. So confident were the Japanese pilots that they wore white cloths around their heads that read *Hissho* – 'Certain Victory'. It was the calamity of this attack on Pearl Harbor that propelled the United States into the Second World War.

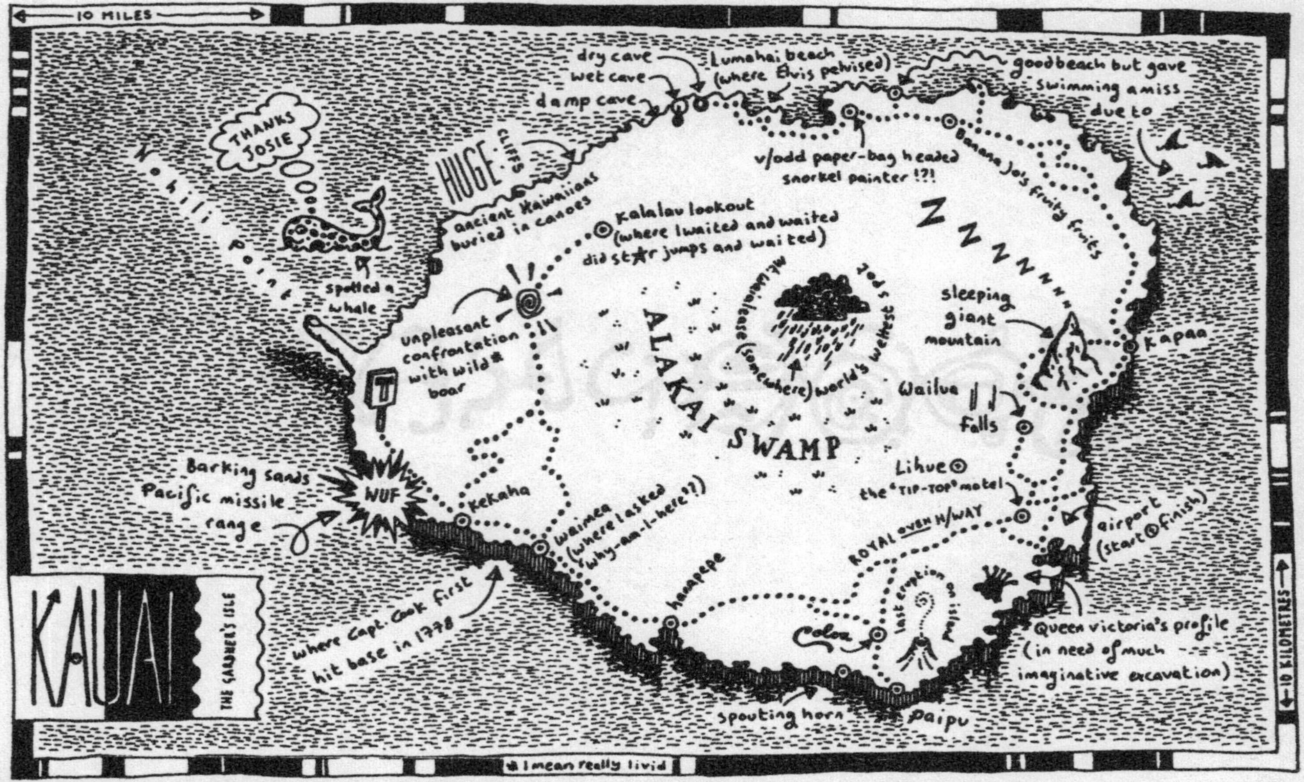
10 MILES
10 KILOMETRES
KAUAI
THE GARDENER'S ISLE
THANKS JOSIE
Nohili Point
spotted a whale
HUGE: CLIFFS
ancient Hawaiians buried in canoes
dry cave
wet cave
damp cave
Lumahai beach (where Elvis pelvised)
good beach but gave swimming a miss due to
v/odd paper-bag headed snorkel painter !?!
Banana Jo's fruity fruits
Kalalau lookout (where I waited and waited did st★r jumps and waited)
unpleasant confrontation with wild* boar
mt. Waialeale (somewhere) world's wettest spot
ALAKAI SWAMP
Z Z Z z z z
sleeping giant mountain
Kapaa
Wailua falls
Lihue
the 'TIP-TOP' motel
airport (start finish)
ROYAL OVEN H/WAY
last eruption on island
Queen Victoria's profile (in need of much imaginative excavation)
Koloa
Paipu
spouting horn
hanapepe
Waimea (where I asked why-am-I-here?!)
Kekaha
Barking sands Pacific missile range
WUF
where Capt. Cook first hit base in 1778
* I mean really livid

7

The Land of
Liquid Sunshine

It was Valentine weekend. Honolulu airport was bustling with sweethearts and jaunty holiday-makers as I bought the last ticket that day for an Aloha Airline flight to Kauai. Luckily the information I had been given in Los Angeles proved to be wrong: taking a bike on the inter-island flights was not only possible but easy – no packaging, no dismantling, no trouble.

Leis were big business. Practically everyone was garlanded with these big flowering necklaces, traditionally given to island visitors on arrival or departure. The heady smell of mokihina, ilima, lehua and plumeria flowers mingled with an abundance of sweat. It was very hot.

The couple in front of me in the queue kept looking at me. Then the husband, Clarence, turned round and said, 'Hi there! Know what? You're the spitting image of our daughter.'

'Oh, am I?'

'Gee,' remarked his wife, June, 'the likeness is uncanny.'

Whether it was because of my uncanny likeness to their off-spring or whether it was because they were just plain friendly, they adopted a rather enthusiastic parental affinity to me, and tried to give me some money to 'keep yourself safe, hon'. Then they wrote down their address (they lived in Maryland) and said that when I came to visit them they would buy me supper on top of a mountain overlooking their home. It sounded an appetizing offer. But where exactly *was* Maryland? Some place way away.

Kauai, the Garden Isle, was a swift 18-minute flight. As we descended towards the airport, the land beyond my porthole looked very green. It also looked very wet.

On Kauai, they call a light shower a 'blessing' and they call rain 'liquid sunshine'. As I cycled up the road from the airport to Lihue, buffeted by mighty winds and fighting through a torrential downpour, there was nothing sunny about this rain. I checked into the Tip Top Motel soaked and exhausted, despite riding barely three miles. I pushed my bike straight from the parking lot into my room and closed the door on the elements. The Tip Top was my first ever motel. It was basic but clean with a rather loud linoleum floor and nails for hooks on which my jacket slowly drip-dried.

That night a Valentine's party raged until the early hours in the 'Portakabin' school next door. Every now and then I peered through the bouncing rain outside my frosted-slat window and watched silhouetted couples cavorting on the classroom dance floor.

In fitful bouts of sleep I dreamed, not of romance, but of skimming across the ocean surface on a grass strimmer like a motorized witch's broomstick. I was heading for a distant desert island – I could see its outline on the horizon – but before I reached it I ran out of petrol and fell, for what seemed forever, into the sea.

The following morning I again took to the skies but in something which I hoped would prove a little more reliable than my flying strimmer. I went for an airborne tour of the island in a helicopter.

I didn't really want to – not because I was afraid of my first ride in a chopper but because I felt that helping to finance noise pollution and swooping intrusively into otherwise inaccessible areas with a clamorous bunch of cooing tourists was not really the way this island, or islanders, wanted to be seen. It seemed a harsh, mendacious and deceptive way to pry into dense and verdant nooks and crannies that belonged to ancient Hawaiians, many of whom were buried in their canoes in the most improbable and unlikely places – like the 4,000-foot cliff faces of the spectacular Na Pali coastline.

But when I read that helicopters (apart from the noise) actually inflict less impact on the ecosystem than hikers, I didn't believe it but at least it gave me a slightly clearer conscience. So I signed up.

Before I and the three other passengers (Americans) climbed into the helicopter, we first had to be weighed to get the balance right. Hank, the pilot, said, 'And make sure you don't swop seats or else we'll turn upside down.' Then Thelma, half of a honeymooning couple from Texas, asked the question that was in most of our minds but which we didn't dare to air.

'Excuse me, Hank,' she said, taking a deep breath (we knew what was coming), 'have you had any real bad accidents?'

'Well, any accident is bad news in a chopper for sure,' said Hank, 'but I'll give you a better answer when we get back down.'

And off we went, rotating into the blue with a clacketing roar.

Carpets of emerald cane fields shimmered in the sun. Seconds later we had hurtled into rain as we swooped towards mist-shrouded Mount Waialeale, the wettest place on earth, which boasts an astounding 40 feet of precipitation a year. For a while we hovered among countless rainbows beside a thousand waterfalls tumbling down the lush jungle flanks of the mountain before buzzing on.

Through the big bubble windscreen we saw the looming, chiselled red bedrock of Waimea Canyon – the 'Grand Canyon of the Pacific', according to Hank's narration through my headphones. When he wasn't rattling on in corny chatter, he switched us on to what was supposed to be a soul-stirring musical interlude as we clattered over the Alakai Swamp. Thelma and her brand new husband Kurt found such elevator Muzak moving: they took a momentary respite from their rather nauseous repetition of 'Wow!' and 'Woo!' and 'Magic!' and 'My Gad!' to exchange a starry eye-locked smile and a lip-smacking kiss. The other passenger, a mousy middle-aged woman, never uttered a squeak.

I pushed back my headphones and gingerly stuck half my head out of the small, sliding side window. My Gad! I thought as the cold, forcing wind slapped into my face – this was magic! Wow! I felt as if I was back on my flying strimmer.

We speed-crested a sharp ridge of red-ruffled mountains so close that I thought we would slap-bang into the side and then I yelled 'Woooooo!' in unison with the hand-clasping honeymooners as the land, virtually touchable one second, ended abruptly and plummeted down a vertical 4,000-foot cliff into the swirling seas. We were skimming past the wrinkled weathered faces of precipitous lava valleys and cliffs like jagged ramparts that spilled down Kauai's magnificent Na Pali coast.

The Barking Sands airfield and Pacific missile range was

just around the headland from these inaccessible corrugated cliffs and for a moment, as I peered wide-eyed down into the boisterous seas, I spotted a couple of torpedoes far more impressive than anything man could make: they were hump-backed whales. It was the winter season for these 40-ton missiles, migrating to frolic, mate and give birth in the pro-creative warm waters of these South Pacific islands.

With my stomach back in place, I paid a visit to the police sta-tion in Lihue where, I had been told, I could buy a permit for camping.

'We're closed,' said the gum-chewing cop as he reclined in his chair, feet on the desk, mirror-shades pushed back on his head. Among an assortment of telephones and papers scat-tered over his desk were a smouldering ashtray, a can of beer and a gun holster. I felt as if I had just stepped into a laid-back film set for *Miami Vice*.

'It's the holiday weekend,' he said perfunctorily. 'You can't get no permit till Toosday.'

As I walked out, I passed a poster on the wall:

DON'T LET ALCOHOL TURN CHRISTMAS EVE
INTO CHRISTMAS MOURNING.

I joined the Kaumuali'i ('Royal Oven') Highway and rode past the Hoary Head mountains in which supposedly Queen Victoria's profile lay. I spotted a rocky outcrop which resem-bled something that could just pass as a nose and chin, but as for Queen Victoria's likeness – well, a bit of imaginative exca-vating was needed.

I had seen the 'Grand Canyon of the Pacific' from the sky; now I was seeing (and feeling) it from the saddle. Up I went, only this time very, very slowly. I left behind the heat, the sugar refinery stacks and Waimea (the coastal town where in 1778 Captain Cook had first touched land) and climbed a canyon road which twisted and turned its way up an inces-santly steep and tortuous route. Blood-red earth lay all around, its fire-coloured dust sticking to my T-shirt and shiny, sweat-wet skin. Then all of a sudden it rained in a heavy, body-pummelling shower that turned sweat to shivers. My arms broke out into goosebumps, or 'chicken skin', as it's known in the local pidgin.

When I looked back way down below – past a carpeted expanse of brilliant green fields of billowing cane, past the small cluster of tin-topped houses and on down to the dazzling white sand and surf – it was all still bathed in a glorious shimmering sunlight.

The rain turned heavier and then I was enveloped in a thick, freezing mist. So much for sight seeing! The vibrant reds and russets and purples and golds of the gorge might just as well have been any grey, bleak, inner-city suburbia for all I could tell. As I toiled upwards hour after hour, tired, hungry and wet, I thought: Why am I doing this? I don't have to be here. This is horrible. I'm not trying to prove anything to anyone. The world's not going to be a more jubilant place just because I've made it to the top. What's the point in cycling 4,000 feet into a freezing cloud of murk when I can't see anything anyway? I can't even take a different route down the other side, because there isn't one. And I've already seen this canyon from the sky.

I did an about turn and shot back down the mountainside. Actually I didn't, though I should have done, had I been sensible. Instead I was gripped by an inexplicable urge to keep going – I mustn't give up, even though I hated every painstaking push on the pedals. It's a funny old world: I wanted desperately not to be doing what I was doing – but then again, I did. Maybe I shall grow out of it one day.

As I muttered to myself in self-pitying waves of dispirited incoherence, something tumbled down the woodside bank and landed in front of me on the mud-red road in an ungainly and humiliating heap.

I got a shock.

It was a big, black and rather pissed-off wild boar, sporting decidedly off-putting four-inch tusks. It picked itself up, snorted and then caught sight of me.

It stared.

Standing motionless astride my mount, I stared back. We had both been startled and we both stared – both scared – neither of us quite sure what to make of each other.

As our gazes interlocked I could see it thinking: Jeez! What the hell've we got here?

I was thinking along similar lines. I had been warned that wild boars can be dangerous. In fact, more people are killed in the South Pacific by feral pigs than by sharks. Certainly this four-legged swine was not something to be argued with. It bucked its head, pawed the ground and looked as if it was revving up for a charge.

I thought: Don't you even *think* about it.

Then I shouted. In fact I believe it was more like a primeval battle cry, a warbling roar that reverberated off the rocks. King Boar, looking faintly bemused, decided that I was worth neither time nor effort and turned tail, trotting off into the dungeon-dark and dripping woods.

Finally I arrived in Kokee State Park and came across a cluster of log cabins on the edge of the forest. One cabin had been rented for the weekend by a waggish bunch of New Age hippies who were in the midst of celebrating a few combined birthdays. Dan, with his long, tangled hair, was unpacking his beaten-up, been-around VW camper van when he spotted me emerging from the mist, looking a little the worse for wear. He handed me an apple-banana (a dwarf, sweet banana that tastes like an apple) and said, 'Fuck, man – where've *you* come from?'

Feeling in no mood to mince my words, I said, 'The bottom.'

'Holy Jesus!' he exclaimed.

There were about 15 of them altogether, gathered around the log-burning stove in various beer-befuddled states and puffing away on *pakalolo* ('crazy tobacco'), a local name for pot which more often was referred to as just plain old Maui Wowie.

They were all mainlanders from the west coast who had uprooted to live among the laid-back *aloha* spirit of Hawaii. Compared to frantic and fast California, Hawaii did seem to exude an incredibly unbuttoned and carefree air. It was not surprising, then, that a couple of the most hackneyed mottos in circulation were 'Hang Loose' and 'Life's a Beach!'.

We sat around for hours eating taco chips and chatting until late. They said that there was plenty of room for me to bed down in the cabin if Woody and Abraham nudged over a bit. I said I would prefer to put up my tent outside in the rain. Woody said I gotta be crazy.

By morning it had stopped raining but it was still very cold and misty and dripping. Despite Dan saying that I wouldn't see a thing because of the mist, I left to climb the last thousand feet up to Kalalau Lookout where, if it was clear, you could peer down over a 4,000-foot drop to the jagged-edged Na Pali coast. It wasn't clear but I waited . . . and waited. I walked around in the swirling cloud and did star-jumps to keep warm.

Then a jeep appeared and a well-built middle-aged couple from Ohio clambered out. I felt like saying: Oh! Hi, oh! But I didn't. Instead, the man said, 'Goddam it!'

'I told you it wouldn't be worth our while, honey,' said the woman, 'but you wouldn't listen. I guess you're now gonna say it's all *my* fault. Huh?'

'Hell, Madge,' he said, 'if you hadn't wanted to see these rocks so bad, I would never have come. Now you're not gonna tell me you think I would rather get up at some god-forsaken hour just to come and see some lousy canyon than play a leisurely round of golf are you? Jeez!'

With that, they turned round and disappeared back into the gloom.

I continued jumping up and down overlooking the Lookout that I could be looking out over if I wasn't looking at cloud. I thought: I know you're in there somewhere. And then a red *'apapane* (a Hawaiian honeycreeper) winged past.

Suddenly a laser of tunnelling sunlight burned through the mist, illuminating the red-cliffed ravine that plummeted far down into the Pacific. Swooping into view a great-frigate with an eight-foot wing span wheeled in the wind – a magnificent flying flash in a knife of strong, hard, brilliant light. And I knew then it had all been worthwhile. Rain, boars, star-jumps and all.

I rode along the Coconut Coast, stopping at Banana Joe's fruit stand where I ate frothy Smoothies and icy Frosties (machine-whipped, tropical delicacies) until I had expanded two-fold, and bought an avocado the size of a small football (everything in Hawaii grows so *big*). At Kilauea Lighthouse, the northernmost tip of the main Hawaiian islands, a short walk took me to the edge of the Kilauea National Wildlife Refuge where, attached to the fence surrounding it, a sign said:

AREA BEYOND THIS SIGN CLOSED.

BIRDS ONLY BEYOND THIS SIGN.

And I wondered what type of plumed wonder you had to be to understand *that*.

Banana Joe had told me that, if I was lucky, I might spot some red-footed boobies down here. I scanned skyways and seaways but no booby came my way. Instead I came across a possible booby-trap: a man (of sorts) sitting atop a cliff in front of an easel, painting a sweeping panorama of Hanalei's tantalizing coastline and valley. On his head he wore a brown paper bag and a snorkel.

Intent on scrutinizing his artwork through his swimming mask, he didn't flinch a muscle when I pulled up beside him. He remained so motionless that for a moment I mistook him for a cardboard cut-out, like one of those glaringly hideous billboards that Americans so often erect in areas of out-standing natural beauty. But this was a cardboard cut-out of a highly sophisticated nature – one that could mix paints and scratch and sneeze.

I stopped and stared and then said hello. Slowly, he put down his paint-brush, wiped his hands, and spoke. He told me he was from Los Angeles (well, they do say that California is the land of fruit and nuts) and that he had once been a member of the Ku Klux Klan. This was all very well but what I really wanted to know was why he was wearing a snorkel when sitting in the sun fully clothed while painting a picture on top of a hill.

Without a hint of facetiousness, he said, 'Whenever I paint the sea, I always wear my mask because it conjures up an oceanic atmosphere and gives me more perception for the water – more a feeling to express myself. Like a kind of sixth sense, I guess.'

And he was so serious, so earnest, that I actually believed him.

Coasting into Hanalei ('Lei-Making Town') I heard, 'Hey – England!' It was New Age Dan and Bonnie (from the Kokee State Park log cabin) who, emerging from Big Save Supermarket, had spotted me but forgotten my name. They told me to come and stay.

Their house was halfway up the hillside and made from the wood of an old sugar mill. I put up my tent in the jungle-garden among huge-leafed plants and banana, papaya, passionfruit, orange and lime trees. Giant fern fans pro-vided perfect shade; cascading bushes of bougainvillaea and violet bell-shaped blossomed jacaranda mingled with the hypnotic scents of plumeria and ginger flowers. Beside the house tumbled a sparkling mountain river, continuously filling the air with its cheery sounds.

An old cast-iron bathtub sat on some rocks by the river, surrounded by gently swaying hibiscus and birds of paradise. I shooed away log-sized frogs and cleared out a carpet of star-jasmine flowers before pouring bucketfuls of cool mountain water into the tub. Then I lay in the water in the sun, gazing up into vivid green sun-dappled trees that dangled with Tarzan creepers as thick as legs. Electric-coloured birds flitted to and fro and I thought: No five-star hotel could beat this tubbed wonder.

Down at the bottom of the valley, beneath dark lava cliffs and lush tropical jungle, lay a perfect crescent of white sand – the stuff of which movies are made. Lumahai Beach ('Twist of Fingers') had indeed seen a star or two in its time, like Mitzi Gaynor, who did some hairy things in *South Pacific*. All along this coast, Hollywood legends have frolicked and been filmed in the sun and the surf: *Fantasy Island*, *Raiders of the Lost Ark*, *The Thorn Birds*. Elvis the King had hip-swayed through *Blue Pacific*, and King Kong had set up base amidst much destruction.

Dan, Bonnie and I left early one morning along a sometimes muddy, rocky, slippery but always precipitous path that roller-coasted its way up and down Na Pali ('The Cliffs'). I was bitten alive by life-sucking mosquitos but I didn't mind (too much) as the scenery made up for it. I had flown over it, cycled up it and now I was walking into its heart. With tortuous walls of jagged cliff, Na Pali felt like a fortress, impregnable and safe. Late in the last century Koolau, a leper, escaped into one of these remote valleys when pursued by a small army complete with cannon. But they never found him. Koolau had been saved by the formidable but friendly Na Pali.

It was the middle of the night and I was peacefully slumbering in my tent on Anini Beach when I was rudely awoken by a man shouting at my door. Now what? I thought.

'Oi! Park Ranger – permit. Hey! You in there. Park Ranger – permit!'

I unzipped, and was blinded by the powerful beam of a torch.

'I can't see,' I said, aggravated and sleepy. 'Can you switch off your torch a moment?'

Unfortunately I had hit upon another one of those Anglo-American communication problems. The man behind the beam would have interpreted my request as, 'Can you switch off your burning piece of wood a moment?' In America, torches are flashlights. The torch remained on.

'Oi! Permit?' he shouted again.

'I haven't got one,' I said. And then he said something about arrest and I remembered what Dan had told me about how strict park rangers were on camping and about the German who, a few months ago, had been camping on Secret Beach and had been held at gunpoint, put under arrest and had his tent destroyed. But that was when there had been a murderer on the loose.

I wangled my way out of it by explaining that I had been to the police to get a permit but being Valentine's weekend they had shut up shop and, seeing as Lihue was the only place on the island to obtain a permit, I wasn't going to cycle a daily 60-mile round trip just because of some cockeyed camping procedure when I could be doing far more worthwhile things like wolfing down endless mango, pineapple and coconut Smoothies at Banana Joe's. It did the trick. He fined me $5 and left.

A ghost crab woke me next morning by trying to dig a hole somewhere near my head. I spent the next hour mainly under water as I swam along the reef among the vermilion, emerald, turquoise and silver-coloured fish – red-lipped parrots, blue-spotted cows, moorish idols, threadfin butterflies – all sparkling like jewels in the sunlit seas.

Sitting on the beach in the shade of a gently rattling palm tree, I ate a locally grown bunch of bananas for breakfast and listened to the news on the radio. It didn't sound promising. On Oahu a man had been killed by a shark. His surfboard had been bitten in two. I stopped chewing midbanana and thought that perhaps I had better stick to paddling in future.

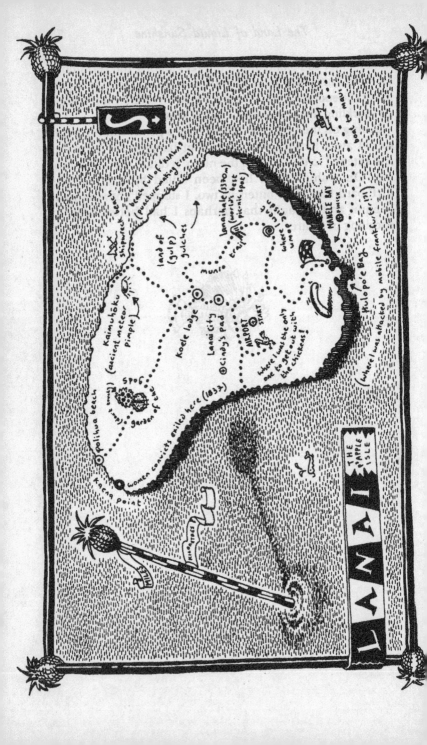

8

Hang Loose Lanai

The Twin Otter landed on pear-shaped Lanai, the Pineapple Island. I was with four other passengers but, apart from a crateful of chickens, I was the only one to disembark. No more than a handful of tourists visit Lanai, which is one of the many reasons it feels such a special place.

The tiny airport was situated literally in the midst of a pineapple plantation. I wheeled my bike across the tarmac and it was like entering an Italian village in siesta time. Nothing stirred. The sun beat down. All was quiet.

Then Tarsus appeared. He seemed just as surprised to see me as I was to see him. Tarsus was the baggage-handler, mechanic and airport control, all in one, but I think he was probably asleep when we landed. Rubbing his eyes and yawning, he stretched out on a bench in the shade and watched me pack up my bike. Tarsus was most definitely of the 'hang loose' type.

After a while he summoned enough energy to prop himself up on an elbow, slide on his fluorescent-framed Oakley shades and tell me he had grown up on Lanai but moved to Oahu in his late teens. Recently he had moved back to Lanai because, although he was not much more than 30, he found 'the pace of life there too fast'. A few evenings a week he worked in the bar of the newly built Manele Bay Hotel.

Before I left, Tarsus gave me a burger and four cartons of Aloha Airline orange juice. 'Take it easy,' he said.

Still nothing stirred as I rode the road to the little town, ambitiously named Lanai City, where nearly all of the island's 2,500 residents live. Bumping down the rickety, unpaved back streets, weaving among scuttling chickens and the odd free-range goat and pig, I passed clusters of small, brightly coloured, tin-topped clapboard houses with luxuriant jungle-gardens in their front yards. Papaya trees prevailed, laden with orangy-yellow fruit, while tropical flowers and colourful bushes spilled over every wall and fence. Wondrously, there was no traffic. There were no nauseous clouds of fumes or head-crunching wails of temperamental car alarms. Instead the air was crisp and clear; the only sounds were of crowing cocks, barking dogs and birdsong, and the happy voices of children playing and laughing.

As I passed down Jacaranda Avenue, an oldish Filipino wearing a worn, broad-rimmed hat trotted across the road and said, 'Hi there! I'm Victor.'

'Hello, Victor,' I replied.

'Welcome to Lanai,' said Victor, warmly shaking my hand. This was no tourist-catching ploy but just a fine example of the open friendliness and candid good humour of the people.

I rode into a square bordered by tall Norfolk pines. A few school children with summery smiles were playing tag on the grass and a handful of octogenarians sat on the benches, smoking and chatting. Not a lot else was happening. Across the road were two old wooden grocery stores, all dark and disorganized inside with tins and boxes stacked higgledy-piggledy on the floor.

There was no sanitized state-of-the-art shopping mall

here – just stores with character where the customers seemed more interested in gossiping than shopping. No one hurried.

❀

More permit problems. Lanai had only one small spot where it was possible to camp. Everywhere else was illegal. I found the administration building but was refused a permit by a Hawaiian woman with a fixed grin.

'You must call us one month in advance to reserve a place,' she smiled.

I said that I had tried ringing from Kauai but the line was always engaged. I'd tried again at Lanai airport with a similar result.

'Ah, that is because we have no telephone at the moment,' she explained.

'Well, how am I supposed to ring you if you have nothing on which to be rung?'

The woman shrugged her shoulders and just laughed. I asked how many spaces the campsite had.

'Six.'

'And they're all full?'

'Three are taken,' she said, 'but the other three are closed off. We are cutting the spaces down.'

When I enquired why, she looked at her fingernails and emitted a titter. I didn't feel I was getting very far very fast.

'Can you open a closed-off space just for one night?' I asked.

'No, not possible.'

'I'll just have to go and find a small bit of beach to sleep on, then,' I said, being the difficult child that I am.

'No, not possible. The beaches are patrolled and you will be evicted,' she said, with considerable pleasure.

'Is this because Lanai is privately owned?'

'Sure it is.'

In 1922, the entrepreneur James D. Dole had bought the island off an old missionary family for $1.1 million which, at 18 miles long by 13 miles wide, worked out at a mere $12 per acre. He converted it from ranchland to a giant pineapple plantation by planting 16,000 acres of pineapples. This made it the largest single pineapple plantation in the world.

Today, high-powered David Murdoch owns the conglomerate Castle and Cook (which had taken over control from Dole in the 1950s) so that now Lanai is known as The Private Isle. The pineapples which have been the island's mainstay for 70 years are rapidly being faded out in the face of competition from other countries like the Philippines and Central America, where the fruit can be grown far more economically.

Recently, Murdoch poured millions of dollars into building two luxurious hotels on the island – the Lodge at Koele, and Manele Bay – and gave preference to the displaced pineapple workers in hiring staff. But cheapskate campers were not encouraged by Murdoch.

Knowing only too well what the answer would be, I said, 'So if I can't camp in the campsite and I can't camp anywhere else on the island, where do I sleep?'

'Well, we have two new hotels where I'm sure you would be most comfortable,' said the woman with glee. As the prices started at $275 for a standard room (and were well over $1,000 for a suite and a butler) I should hope that I *would* be comfortable.

Cindy Heckman, the housing manager for Castle and Cook, had overheard my unproductive conversation with her grinning colleague. Big, jocular and immediately likeable, Cindy took me by the arm and led me outside.

'Listen,' she said, 'I'm from Oklahoma and I know what

you're up against – brick-wall bureaucracy. You're most welcome to come and stay with me.'

I camped beneath the pine trees in Cindy's garden for three nights. She told me to come and go and use her white clapboard bungalow as I pleased while she was out at work. I wasn't lent any keys because Cindy never locked her door or, for that matter, removed the keys from her station-wagon. An old Chinese man down in the square, who saw me habitually locking up my bike said, 'No need for that; nobody take nothing round here.'

I asked Cindy what it was like living on quiet, trustworthy Lanai after Oklahoma City.

'Great,' she said, 'but I have to take the boat to Maui at least once a month for sanity's sake.'

One morning I set off early to ride the Munro Trail, a mountainous ridge studded with tall, spindly Norfolk pines which gave it the bristle-haired look of an angry, arch-backed cat.

The dirt track climbed steadily – through mud, through rainforest, through guava groves and past disorderly bushes of thimbleberries. There were strawberries, too. For an hour, I did more foraging and eating than cycling. Then, with a mouthful of freshly plucked fruit, I suddenly spotted an axis deer clinging precariously to a red and rocky precipice. These were what the well-off hunters staying at Koele Lodge came to shoot. Later I spotted one of those deer-stalkers creeping through nearby undergrowth. Togged out in camouflage gear, his face smeared in war-paint and with rifle at the ready, I think he thought he was Rambo.

To my left, there were 'gulches' 2,000 feet deep – great red wounds cut into Lanai's windward side, plunging down towards the sea. Here, in days of old, Lanai's warriors fought battles with Kalaniopuu, the conquering warrior king, and his savage fighters from the Big Island. Spread out way down below on the south side was a wide basin of land densely spiked with mottled green pineapple plantations.

I had the place to myself. Apart from Rambo, I had seen no one. A few hours and a lot of wild guavas later, I puffed to a halt on top of 3,370-foot Lanaihale. And what a view! I sat in a sunny rocky nook, munching my packed lunch and looking out over the deep blue Pacific. It was so clear I could see five other islands looming out of the sea like shimmering mirages. The sunny conical peaks of their major volcanoes – Haleakala on Maui, and Mauna Loa and Mauna Kea on the Big Island – soared into the skies like celestial islands floating above a halo of cloud, disembodied in space, ethereal but real.

Sitting alone on top of that mountain on a small island in the middle of the Pacific, I suddenly felt ridiculously happy. An electric spark glowed through my blood as I sat there smiling absurdly and utterly content.

A little further down, on the other side of the track I stumbled across a rock engraved with the words:

When fog bathes the peaks along the Munro Trail,
When tall pines become mere silhouettes within the restless clouds,
When the mist occasionally parts to permit a glimpse of the sun's reflection in the sea far below –
That is when Lana'i becomes frozen in time.
At these times, you can hear the earth . . . feel the air . . . smell the wind's bounty and see history.
It is here . . . on Lana'i . . . that you can touch the very soul of man.

David H. Murdoch

And I thought: Murdoch, you romantic swashbuckler, you. But I knew where he was coming from.

Then, with the wind up my tail, I turned into a real wild child. I jumped on my mount and careered at breakneck speeds through bright, airy woods, dropping and spinning down the other side of the mountain. I bounced over roots, skidded on dusty-dirt corners, slalomed round rocks and rocketed over gullies. The hot wind rushed through my hair, sweat cooling in streaks as the rough red track leaped up to meet me. The mountain was mine. I was the Munro Trail Speed King, a manic flying machine.

And then . . . BOOMPH! I was brought rapidly down to earth. My front wheel sank into sand and I shot from my saddle, torpedoing through the air to land flat on my back on a fiery-red dune. Suddenly the wind had gone. The speed had stopped. All was silent and I lay still – very still. I opened my eyes and stared at the sky. With torn shorts and ruddy, mud-splattered face, I thought: What am I doing? Is this normal behaviour for a 26-year-old? I thought back to home – to my friends, a lot of them married, with children, with 'sensible jobs'. Should I, I wondered, be behaving with a little more sophistication, a little more panache? In short: should I be acting my age and not my shoe size?

But why? Hawaii had caught me, picked me up and spun me round. I loved the place. I was happy. And I thought: What a feeling – what a day!

Lanai certainly doesn't go out of its way to cater for tourists, and I hope it never does. There are no signs pointing you to the sights; you have to ask a local or feel your way. Once you get there, there are no gaudy tourist stalls selling gimmicky rubbish, or ugly paved parking lots for buses and cars, or ice-cream and burger booths, or TOILETS signs. In fact there are no tourists. The place is yours and, like the Garden of the Gods, it is the same now as it was when it was inhabited by the man-eating spirits and fiendish, fear-inspiring ghouls of legend. Not for nothing was Lanai called the 'Forbidden Island'. It was not until early in the fifteenth century, after Maui's King Kaalaneo had banished his troublesome son to Lanai to rid it of its spirits, that people began to settle on the island.

A woman in the Dis 'n' Dat store sketched me rough directions to the Garden of the Gods. The red volcanic-dirt road took me through a criss-cross of green and gold pineapple fields before entering a tunnel of bleached pine trees where the wind moaned in long, eerie sighs. Then it was back out into the hot sun and a hard, parched, desert-like landscape dotted with giant yucca plants.

The Garden of the Gods was a weird, unearthly plateau spread with weathered lava rocks and boulders and tortured, raw-baked areas of ancient lava flows that changed colour continually as the sun moved across the sky turning the rocks from purple, red and orange to subtle shades of sulphur yellow.

Lying in the shade of a palm tree on Hulopo'e beach, I tuned into the local news on my mini radio. Another surfer had been attacked by a shark but, apart from losing his foot, he was fine. On Oahu an ambulance driver, racing along to aid a heart-attack victim, had suffered a heart attack himself and crashed. The heart-attack man died because the ambulance never arrived because the ambulance driver was dead.

Then there was a programme featuring Check-it-out Linda, who was investigating a case where a woman called Cindy-Lu sent off for six pairs of cheap pantyhose from a mail-order catalogue and was charged twice as much as advertised. Four months and many 'phone calls and letters later, her goods finally arrived but when she tried them on 'they only came up to my . . . well – let's just say a certain point. They were kids' size.'

Check-it-out Linda checked out the case. As a result Cindy-Lu received so many free pairs of pantyhose that she set up a stall in her back yard and sold 'DISCOUNT PANTYHOSE' to the public, much as one might a surplus of homegrown carrots.

I had left the misty-cool hills of Lanai City behind to roll down to Hulopo'e beach – the beach where the fixed-grin administration building woman had told me I couldn't camp. Experience proved otherwise. No permit was ever requested, nor was the 'campsite' full. There was only one couple camping: Annette and Warren, restaurant owners from Breckenridge, Colorado, who were the first cycle-tourers I had met since arriving in America two months before. They had come to Hawaii for a few weeks' holiday but decided to live here. Just like that – and just like everyone else I seemed to meet, mainly mainlanders, who had come initially for a holiday and, falling in love with what they found, stayed put.

One morning a kayaker appeared and put up his big dome tent beside me. Ron ran kayaking courses on Maui. He was also a professional masseur and before long he had me flat out on top of a beach-side picnic table 'working me over', as he put it. I have to admit it was blissful. Below me was the hot white sand, while above bright red parrots skipped among rustling palm fronds and a mere pace or two away the whooosh, whooosh of the Pacific swept upon the beach. At one point, as things were being done to my coccyx like they had never been done before, I suddenly saw a 50-foot hump-back whale breaching – catapulting itself out of the sea like a 40-ton torpedo. By the time Ron had pummelled my shoulder blades into oblivion, a posse of porpoises and dolphins were larking in the bay. This was a massage parlour with a difference.

When I had first arrived on Hulopo'e beach, Annette and Warren had warned me about the surrounding thorny Kiawe trees. The sand around the campsite was littered with their wickedly sharp needles which not only made for hazardous walking (their inch-long thorns shot through your sole like nails) but could also cause multiple punctures. Carrying my bike to my tent in order to keep the tyres hole-free, my ploy back-fired when I stepped on a thorn, yelped, and promptly dropped my bike on the equivalent of a bed of nails. For two months I had managed to remain puncture-free and then suddenly, in the space of a second, I had acquired 14. Ron told me to blame the missionaries who were said to have introduced the Kiawe trees as a way of making the naked natives wear shoes.

It became evident why the authorities were doing all that they could to stamp out camping. Just up the hill behind our tents was the Manele Bay Hotel. The management did not appreciate a handful of beachbums sleeping for free within sight of hotel customers who were paying $500 for their rooms.

The Manele Bay had been built in the style of an airy, sumptuous Mediterranean villa – stucco, bright tiles and layered grandiose gardens with rockeries and stepping stones and waterfalls. At night the pathways were lit by burning torches.

Every day I walked up the hotel's gravel path from the beach to have a snoop around, fill up on ice, use the ritzy toilets to brush my teeth and wash my smalls (when no one was looking) and to read in the library. I was just the sort of person the Manele Bay didn't want. The place smelled of money, from the architecture to the furnishings to the customers.

Once, as I was leafing my way through *Hawaiian Antiquities and Folklore* in the library, an expensively dressed man with a bulbous belly and a jewel-studded Rolex said, 'You interested in legends?'

'I'm getting to be,' I said. 'Hawaii's got some good ones.' And I told him I was just reading about the Garden of the Gods. 'Have you been there?' I asked.

'Hell no. Churches don't interest me.'

'It's not a church,' I said, 'it's a bunch of rocks.'

'Even more of a reason not to go there, wherever it is.

Traipsing round nature's not my idea of fun. I've come here for a holiday and I'm not moving from that pool.' Then he said, 'Neat hotel. Been here long?'

'Well actually,' I said, 'I'm not staying here. I'm camping on the beach.'

'Oh – really. You're one of those guys, huh?' And he moved away.

One of the many attractions about Hawaii is that it doesn't have any snakes. But it does have its fair share of creepy things that make your skin crawl, one of which I was to meet that evening on my way back from the hotel.

Crawling into my tent, I suddenly saw something that looked like a long, mobile frankfurter which scooted beneath my sleeping bag. I shot back out of the tent in hasty reverse and, quivering, assessed the situation. There was something in there that I most definitely didn't like. How had it got in? The door had been firmly zipped shut. Gingerly, with bike light in hand, I went on a reconnaissance, stepping ever so cautiously around my tent. I found a small hole.

I reassessed the situation. Whatever was in there had teeth.

Arming myself with Kiawe branches, I ventured forth to do battle. What I found was not pleasant. The Mobile Frankfurter was in fact a giant poisonous centipede – a snake with legs which moved like a bullet.

After a lot of shrieking and leaping on my part, and a lot of slivery darting on the centipede's, I succeeded in catapulting it into oblivion. At least I thought I had – until it came back. Every time I flicked it away, it returned like a vengeful homing pigeon gone berserk. Finally I managed to devise a trap whereby it fell into my porridge pan (empty at the time), and with outstretched arms, I scurried worriedly across to the other end of the beach, where I released it. Sleep was not something I had a lot of that night. I kept imagining that I could hear the sound of its teeth sawing through my tent. In the morning I had a nasty turn when I found it curled up in the leaves of my freshly plucked pineapple.

I left Lanai after that.

9

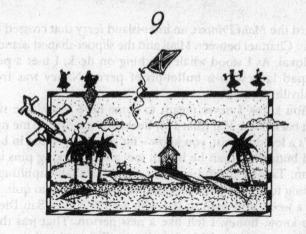

Jawaiian
Delicacies

Hawaii is home to the wili-wili tree (used for canoes) and also to the Phallic Rock which as legend has it, could make you pregnant. Early Hawaiian women made offerings to it in the hope of fertility, and photographs of this rock tend to make rather fetching postcards for tittering tourists (such as myself) to send home with some whimsical schoolgirl sentiment scrawled on the back. I thought that my mother might be slightly offended when this picture of a petrified, six-foot, ready-for-action apparatus dropped through the letter-box but, no: surprisingly it won prime position on the kitchen pinboard, where it has remained ever since. It seems to make for a lively conversation piece when her friends drop by for morning coffee.

To reach the ancient Phallic Rock I had first to jump on

board the *Maui Princess*, an inter-island ferry that crossed the Auau Channel between Maui and the slipper-shaped island of Molokai. As I stood whale-watching on deck, I met a pear-shaped lady with a bullet-proof perm. Nancy was from Nashville, Tennessee.

'You know, I never meant to come here at all,' she said, 'but back home Hal (that's my husband) was driving me nuts. He's a lepidopterist, you know – far more interested in bugs and butterflies than he is with me, always sticking pins into them. Talking to him is about as intellectually uplifting as talking to QE2 – that's the goldfish. So I decided to quit, just for a week, and went to stay with a girlfriend in San Diego. You know, honey, I felt like a new person. That was three weeks ago now and I had such a swell time that I thought, well, why go home? I sent Hal a postcard and told him not to forget to change QE2's water and that there's a pile of pizzas in the deep-freeze. Ain't Hawaii real cute? I'll tell you what I've discovered: there's more to life than your husband!' And with that she waddled off towards the bow.

The ferry docked at the wharf in Kaunakakai and I left Nancy with her new-found freedom waving excitedly as she climbed into the minibus for a day tour of Molokai. I rode off past the big 'ALOHA' sign and embarked upon my pilgrimage to Phallic Rock.

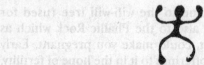

A few hours later, I found it in a pine forest surrounded by a small gaggle of sniggering schoolboys who, whenever the teacher turned her back, added to the copious graffiti already carved upon it. Wisecracks and raucous banter surrounded me. One cocky youth said, 'When I grow up I wanna be phallic like this rock!' which resulted in howls of laughter. The shame-faced teacher led them away after that and peace prevailed.

A short walk through the forest took me to Kalaupapa Overlook. Nearby, the world's highest sea cliffs, some 4,000 feet high, arched their backs against the pounding surf on Molokai's north shore. Far down below me the green plateau of Kalaupapa Peninsula, separated from the rest of the island by a vertical 2,000-foot wall of lava rock, jutted out into the tumultuous seas. Because of its remote and isolated location, the eastern windswept base of Kalaupapa (Kalawao) was selected in 1866 as the place to confine the disfigured victims of leprosy.

Through crude diagnostic testing, anyone who was suspected as suffering from any skin disorder (even sunburn) was ruthlessly rounded up by heartless hunters who roamed the islands in search of their prey. The pitiful captives would be ripped away from their families and villages, placed in a cage and sailed into the treacherous waters off Kalaupapa where their cage was opened and they were cast over the side of the ship. No one was spared; young and old alike were hurled into the sea. The weak and the sick drowned. Those who made it to the shore known as Makanalua (the 'Living Grave') were greeted by a band of maimed bodies – bodies who, having been deprived of families, friends, love, their country and apparently even God, had become wild savages. The newcomers would be bludgeoned and beaten and raped by horrifically deformed and filthy creatures – innocent outcasts whose only crime was contracting leprosy.

The settlement at Kalawao endured a painful history of hardship, anarchy and misery and the outside world all but turned its back on the lepers until the arrival in 1873 of Joseph de Veuster, a Belgian Catholic priest, known as Father Damien. During an intended two-week stay on Hawaii, he learned of the plight of Molokai's forgotten exiles and chose to spend the rest of his life on the island. He saw the lepers not as bedevilled or rabid beasts but as Children of God. He lived among them, establishing order and devoting his life to serving their spiritual and physical needs until in 1889, after 16 years of dedicated work, he contracted the disease himself and died at the age of 49, the 'Martyr of Molokai'.

I had planned to camp atop these cliffs in the cool mountain air of Pala'au State Park, but I changed my mind. The fetid, wooded campsite was derelict, dark and eerie, and strewn with wind-blown litter. There was no water and the soiled toilet shed was covered in scrawls of sordid graffiti. The whole place had an unpleasant, threatening air and I had the feeling I was being watched, even though there was no one around. The wind moaning through the trees sounded sinister and mean. An empty beer can, blowing noisily across some stones, made me turn my head with a start. I hurried to my bike and returned to the road. It was the right move. Later that evening a local in Kaunakakai told me that a girl had recently been found murdered up there. And this on Molokai, the supposed 'Friendly Isle'.

I rode on, stopping to eat a tuna sandwich beside the seaside grove of royal coconut palms – tall and graceful trees that Mark Twain described as 'feather dusters hit by lightning'. Wooden notices warned you not to go walking among these palms because of falling coconuts. Every now and then when the wind whips up there are those who, ignoring such warnings, fall victim to an aerial bombardment of plummeting hefty 'five pounders' and are hit on the head and die.

Much of Hawaii was in the throes of a 'Say No To Drugs' campaign, including the small and nondescript dusty settlement of Kualapu'u. Here I was escorted out of town by a bevy of toddlers on trikes with 'No Hope In Dope' flags fluttering from their rears.

Round the corner I came across a lake claimed to be the largest rubber-lined reservoir in the world. I stood for a moment among the lakeside coffee plantations, trying hard to muster suitable enthusiasm for this watery wonder and debating whether my contemplation of it would give life new meaning. I decided it wouldn't and so, unmoved, moved on.

Finding water on Molokai was not always easy. Before climbing up over Puu Nana, I stopped at a farm building to ask if I could fill my bottles. A man in dusty overalls apologized and said that they didn't have any as they weren't connected to the water system. The nearest place was the small airport down the road. The farmer told me how opposed he was to the new tourist resort on the coast at

Kaluakoi. Despite being home to the world's largest rubber-lined reservoir, Molokai had scarcely enough water for those who lived on the island let alone the wasteful, money-spinning resorts. He said he had been waiting for years to be connected to the mains but now all priority was given over to Kaluakoi. He felt bitter and cheated and he told me that every tourist in Hawaii uses up to ten times more water and electricity than the average resident.

'It's no wonder our crops are suffering,' he said.

Giraffe, ibex, kudu, eland, oryx, aoudad, zebra, sika and Indian black buck have made their homes on the semi-arid, brushy ranchland of Molokai's Tropical Safari Park but I passed it by and camped with a couple from Alaska on Papohoku beach. And what a beach! It was a far cry from cheek-by-jowl Waikiki. Here we had literally mile upon mile of sand and surf to ourselves. In fact Papohoku, Hawaii's largest beach, has so much sand that it used to be dredged during the 1950s and taken to Oahu to make up for what they lacked.

From Molokai's heel I pedalled back along the sole to Kaunakakai, the island's main town where no building rises higher than a coconut tree, and on along the magnificent coastal road flanked on one side by 5,000-foot razor-backed ridges. After climbing the narrow and ribboning road to Puu

O Hoku ('Hill of the Stars'), I plunged down into the toe of Molokai at Halawa Valley.

For hundreds of years, on their geometrically carved field-terraces, Halawa's farmers had grown the islanders' staple food – taro, a plant with heart-shaped leaves whose root is ground to make *poi* (which looks and tastes like wallpapering paste). But in 1946 a 36-foot *tsunami* (tidal wave) swept into the valley and left behind it a plant-killing deposit of salt. Today, a handful of people still live there among the ruins of several wooden houses and Hawaiian burial grounds half hidden beneath a profusion of tropical undergrowth.

From the blue, frothy seas of the bay, Halawa Valley thrusts four miles inland through a deep cleft of dense jungle brimming with wild ginger, avocado and mango trees, orange lilies and tiny strawberries, culminating in 500-foot waterfalls silvered with sunlight.

Returning over the Hill of Stars, I passed through the grey-barked Kalanikaula Grove, full of *kukui* (candlenut) trees, so named because their nuts were once burnt as a source of light. This is one of Hawaii's most sacred spots.

For centuries Molokai was revered as a place where religious rituals were performed by powerful *kahuna*, or priests. The *kahuna* Lanikaula planted the grove of *kukui* trees that, once sheltering his home, now guard his grave. When the Del Monte corporation wanted to clear the land to make way for tropical fruit crops, not a single Hawaiian worker would fell the trees. Ancient tradition holds that the *kukui* tree may only be touched with the intercession of a priest.

Back along the shore the beaches were free of basking *haoles*. In their place were a few families of local Hawaiians picnicking beneath bright blue tarpaulin shade-shelters, surrounded by food and beer and laughter and music that boomed from the open doors of their beefed-up trucks. Boisterous shouts and waves were directed my way as I rolled by. A man who resembled a Sumo wrestler scuttled with surprising agility up some rocks from the beach to hand me an icy Budweiser and a freshly barbecued corn-cob. He slapped me heartily on the back and said he had seen me ride over the mountain a few hours earlier.

'That road is one mean dog,' he said, 'a killer by truck, let alone by bike.'

He shook my hand in an enthusiastic, bone-crunching grip and then returned to his rumbustious beach party. Emblazoned across the back of his T-shirt were the words: HANG LOOSE.

Later a woman who filled up my water bottles from her hose (the water was warm and rubber-tasting) gave me a bagful of freshly picked, sticky-sweet mangoes from her jungle-garden. Further along I passed a sign that marked the site where, on July 14, 1927, Smith and Bronte had crash-landed their plane after completing the first trans-Pacific civilian flight in just over 25 hours. They plunged unceremoniously into the squelchiness of a mangrove swamp but at least they emerged alive.

I carried on along the reef-lined south shore, dodging the occasional mongoose which darted rapidly in front of my wheel, and passed ruined walls of stone and coral rising from the shallow waters. These were the remains of ancient royal fishponds, built between the 15th and 18th centuries to provide a steady stream of fresh fish for the Hawaiian *ali'i*, or chiefs.

The sun was sinking into the sea as I pulled into One Ali'i Beach Park to camp among the coconut-free palms on the shore. I put up my tent in a prize position beside the lapping waves but I didn't get a good feeling. There was no one else around and it was too exposed – not so much to the weather as to prying and unwelcome eyes. I was tired but I couldn't relax. I felt on edge. Once again I had a feeling that I was being watched.

Suddenly a pick-up slammed into the park, the truck's headlights like eyes searching through the encroaching darkness. I hid in the bushes as its occupants skidded and screeched continuously in the dirt, round and round, music blaring, voices screaming. Empty bottles were thrown into the dark and I heard them shatter against rocks. Then with a resounding squealing skid, they left. I decided I would, too, before they returned.

As I was hastily packing my panniers, a man appeared from the shadows. My heart leapt mouthwards. He looked sinister and shifty-eyed. Squatting hunched on his haunches, he relit a moth-eaten cigarette and asked me what I was doing.

'I'm going,' I said.

'But aint-cha just arrived?'

'Oh – maybe I have, maybe I haven't. But I'm going now,' I said in a roundabout, nonsensical fashion.

'Say, lady – you alone?'

'No, no,' I said, as in-built alarm bells started ringing, 'I've got a van-load of friends picking me up any minute.'

I had a nasty sensation he might be about to pounce on my back.

'You wanna take a walk along the beach?' he asked. 'The night's real beautiful.'

Like sure I do, I thought. 'Sorry,' I said, 'I can't. They'll wonder where I've gone.'

'You know, I don't like liars – they kind of piss me off. Yeah?'

'Yeah? Oh yeah. I don't like them either, but some are okay and sometimes you can't blame people,' I said, not at all sure what I was talking about but I knew I just had to keep talking, as I crammed the rest of my kit into my bags. 'Everyone has their ups and downs and . . . ummmm . . . well, nice to meet you,' I lied, as I hurriedly swung my leg over Starcraft and sped like a hot-rod back to the road.

I tore through the night, legs spinning, heart pounding, back towards Kaunakakai but not quite sure where to go. I was certainly in no mood for camping and the island had only

three hotels, all in the $70 range. But I stopped at the first
one I came to: Hotel Molokai.

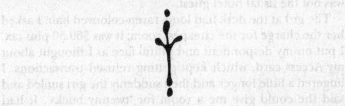

Entering the brightly lit reception area and looking out at
groups of holidaying couples relaxing and laughing at the
poolside bar felt wonderfully safe. It was a world away from
that dark, threatening park where, scared and alone and
clammy-skinned, anything could have happened to me and
no one would have known. Here, the unique twanging sound
of jaunty Hawaiian music bounced out of the background;
glasses chinked and clinked and mingled among happy
voices and the warm, romantic light of candles flickered on
the tables of the open-air beach-side restaurant. I wanted to
be part of this cheering scene. I was afraid to go back out into
the night – a darkness full of shady characters.

I dithered for a while in reception, savouring the safety
and pondering my next move. I ambled around looking at
things and saw a notice pinned to the wall:

Restaurant & Bar

Hotel Molokai has a charming restaurant fronting
the beach where fine American and Jawaiian
food is served.

There was something more than fishy about that, I thought –
Jaws-on-toast, perhaps?

An Australian couple, dressed for dinner in squeaking
shining shoes and smelling of soap and wafting aftershave,
walked into the 'laaaby' arm in arm. They looked at me with
a perplexed expression, glancing from my bike leaning
against the glass doors and back to me. In my agitated and

decidedly scruffy state – dusty shorts and T-shirt, well-worn shoes, and perspiring rivulets running from temple to jaw – I was not the usual hotel guest.

The girl at the desk had long, raven-coloured hair. I asked her the charge for the cheapest room: it was $69.50 plus tax. I put on my despondent and pitiful face as I thought about my Access card, which kept getting refused transactions. I lingered a little longer and then suddenly the girl smiled and said she could give me a room for 'twenny bucks'. It had been that easy! I thanked the workings of the Hawaiian gods and then spent the rest of the evening sitting among the local yokels and a handful of tourists in the sultry night air as voluptuous hula girls swayed and gyrated, expertly wiggling all their wiggly bits in time to hand-pummelled drum beats and twangy strings. A pure tourist set-up but it was fun, and what's more, it was safe.

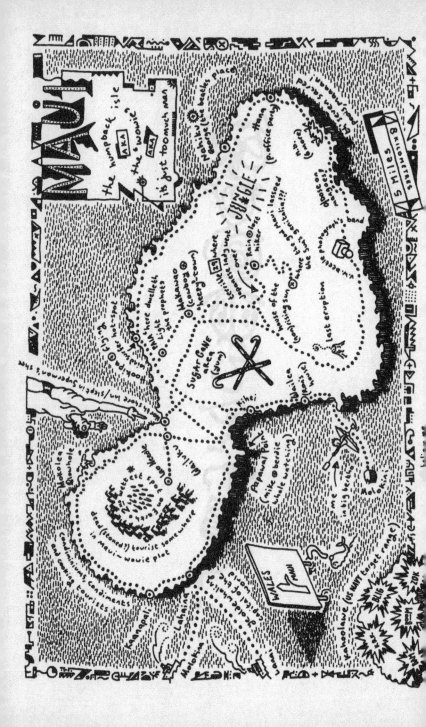

10

Maui Wowie

On the boat to Maui we hit a storm, the rampaging wind churning the waves into walls. The ferry bucked and dipped and corkscrewed its way erratically across Kalohi Channel. Down in the cabin many of the passengers were becoming explosively unwell. I donned my jacket and precariously climbed the ladder-steps to the empty 'sun' deck to do battle with the elements.

Outside I felt immediately better. It was invigorating and fun. The salty spray blew across the deck with water-cannon force, soaking me in seconds. I lassoed myself in the lee of the wheelhouse and settled in to enjoy the ride. My sights focused one moment on the sea and the next on the sky as the boat bounced its way from wave to wave with violent shuddering thuds.

After a while Roger, the Captain, spotted me and invited me into the wheelhouse where Bruce Springsteen was crooning huskily with his Hungry Heart. Outside on the windscreen thousands of seawater droplets swam down the glass like tadpoles. Roger said they looked like sperm.

Samson, the ship's mate, was continuously scanning the mountainous seas with binoculars, on the lookout for whales. Every now and then one would surface and spout spectacularly close by. Roger would suddenly divert course. He told me that a hydrofoil had hit a whale at 45 mph a few years back. There was a real mess, he said.

Cresting the top of one wave, I caught sight of a gigantic floating shoe-box passing way off port (but, there again, it could have been starboard).

'That's a container-platform pulled by a tug,' said Roger, 'full of anything from air-conditioners to cattle.'

If there were cows on that one, my heart went out to them. It was no weather to be ruminating at sea.

The boat entered the Pailolo Channel and it suddenly became calm; the sun even came out as we approached Maui's Lahaina harbour. Whey-faced passengers staggered on to the deck, looking as people tend to look when they have spent the past hour filling a retch-inducing 'motion sickness' bag.

One couple from Colorado had escaped any feelings of nausea and I watched with bemusement as they set about photographic procedures. Bob was trying to take a 'natural' shot of his wife Sandy.

'Honey, how about smiling as though you're having a good time,' he said, in embarrassingly head-turning tones. 'Take your hands out your pockets – try with your hat on – lean real casual on the railing. Nope, that ain't right neither. Don't look at me! Hey! Hold it hon, you got it . . . . that's great.'

At last, as a painfully-fixed grin froze across her features, Bob snapped the shot. I felt like clapping.

Jumping on to the quay, I came face to face with a massive marlin flopped out ignominiously on its side. As I stared at this shark-sized creature, a patch-eyed pirate in an angular hat sidled up to me. He lived on a floating museum, the *Cathagian II* – the only truly square-rigged ship left afloat on the seas – which was imposingly moored up behind me.

'Well, hi there! I'm Wally,' he said, 'and this is Catastrophe, the ship's cat.'

I stroked him and he purred (the cat that is) as Wally said 'That there's a 225lb Pacific Blue Marlin. Pretty much a tiddler.'

A tiddler! It was at least twice my length.

'Marlins are the hawks of the underwater world,' Wally explained. 'They spot their prey with razor-sharp vision a hundred or more feet below and dive on down like stream-lined fighter jets.'

Looking at its huge and deadly spearlike snout, I said, 'I wouldn't fancy being on the receiving end.'

'Come and see my ship,' Wally suggested.

So I did. And very nice it was, too: a gently swaying beauty of old, creaking wood. Below deck I sat transfixed, watching a whale being born. The documentary film on the life of a humpback whale was a memorable one. An hour later, when I climbed back up into the dazzling sunlight, my head was swimming with scintillating whale facts: a humpback's brain is five times larger than a human's; its lungs are the size of a compact car; the tongue weighs two tons; air is exhaled through its blowhole at over 300 mph. I was beginning to feel like a humpback boffin.

Back in the early 1790s, King Kamehameha the Great trapped and slaughtered the defending army of the Maui king and he made the harbour town of Lahaina ('Merciless Sun') his kingdom's capital. Fifty years later it became known the world over as the whaling capital of the Pacific as thousands of whalers plied the warm waters surrounding the islands, searching for sperms and humpbacks. The sailors were on to a good thing in more ways than one. Naked and curvaceous island girls willingly swam out to the ships anchored offshore to trade their favours for knick-knacks and novelties like nails (of all things). When the missionaries arrived and began to curtail the moral chaos, some of the sailors became so peeved at such righteousness that they fired a few cannonballs into the Mission.

I booked into the nostalgic green-and-white, double-veranda Pioneer Inn on the harbour front where, the cleaner proudly told me, the likes of Errol Flynn and Spencer Tracy had once stayed. The original house rules from 1901 (the year the inn was built) were pinned on the back of the door in my $25 room:

> Women is not allow in you room;
> If you wet or burn you bed you going out;
> You are not allow to give you bed to you freand;
> If you freand stay overnight you must see
> the mgr.
> Only on Sunday you can sleep all day.
> You are not allow in the down stears in the
> seating room or in the dinering room or in the
> kitchen when you are drunk.
> If you cant keep this rules please dont take the
> room.

Lahaina, I discovered, has some curiously named streets. As I left the town I pedalled down Kipulu ('Fertilizer Place') and up Niheu ('Fancy Hairstyle Street') before sweeping up and around the northwest coast, past the concrete resort of Kaanapali where a lot of identical tourists zipped past me in their identical hired convertibles, and on until the road turned to dirt. This was perfect for cycling. The traffic ran out (taking the dirt road route was forbidden for rented cars) and I followed the mountainous shore-hugging road through a tiny, undisturbed fishing village full of weather-worn houses and taro fields.

That night I slept on *Superman* sheets at the Northshore Inn in Wailuku ('Water of Slaughter'). Sleeping on *Star Trek* sheets in the bunk opposite was Ted from Texas. With his pointed, dust-scuffed boots, ten-gallon hat and guitar, he looked every bit the wild-west cowboy but in fact he was a sewage works supervisor and had been living on the Big Island for two years. He told me that today was the first time he had left the island in all that time.

'Yeah, today I quit,' he said. 'Quit the dirty work, quit the lousy bunch I worked with. They gave me a real hard time so this morning I said, "You know, you guys, I don't think you're such a great lot. You kind of get up my nose so as from today you won't be seeing me no more."'

Then he had climbed into his truck and driven away from them and his $8-an-hour job. He was now thumbing through the job ads in the local Maui paper and looking a little unsure.

Out on the veranda was Brendan from Auckland who, from what I could gather, had been travelling continuously for the past five years, living off a lot of money he had either made (he had once owned a hi-fi shop and had built a micro-light plane) or inherited (he was a bit cagey on this subject). He had done a four month 'Inner Understanding' course in Sydney which I think might have done him more harm than good: he never seemed to move from the hostel and it was guaranteed he could be found either slumped in front of MTV (a channel that pumped a continuous stream of rock videos) or out on the veranda engrossed in heavy-going, introspective books. He was a 'discover yourself' sort of person who took himself very seriously, questioning life and the meaning of his existence on the planet. It was a waste of time to ask Brendan the usual travelling banalities like: Where're you from? Where've you been? How long have you been here? Where're you going? All he had to say on the matter was, 'I'll leave Maui when it feels right inside. I've got a lot of thinking to do before then.'

I left Brendan to his earnest thoughts and went to muse on inexplicable cosmic oddities while washing my socks. After that, with my head in need of some light entertainment, I flicked through a free tourist magazine. On one page was listed the 'DO AND DON'TS IN HAWAII', among which were:

(1) Don't honk your horn. It's considered to be the height of bad manners in Hawaii.

(2) Do wear glasses or goggles when driving your mo-ped: Helmets are optional, but eye protection is not. It's the law! Wear 'em or the next thing you see will be a ticket.

(3) Do not try to pick up that cute little blue bubble you see floating in the ocean or resting in the sand on the beach: It's a Portuguese Man-of-War.

(What it failed to mention here was what to do if you *did* pick up that cute little blue bubble and got stung. Answer: apply meat tenderizer or urine.)

(4) Do not stick your chopsticks in your rice bowl between bites or courses: This is considered bad luck.

(5) Do not stop in the middle of the highway
     when you see a whale: Tempting as it may
     be, this is more than a little dangerous.

(And what it failed to specify here was just what a whale was
doing on the highway in the first place.)

Then I met Claire and Jaqui from Bristol who had just
'trained it' all over America. They decided they liked Maui
and wanted to stay, but in order to do so they needed some
money. Their attempts at working down the road in the
Banana Hostel turned fruitless when green cards were
demanded. Instead they turned their attention to the hair of
the Northshore Inn's occupants, either cutting it or thread-
ing it through multicoloured beads, as well as hiring out their
'Rent-a-Wreck' hired car as a taxi service. When they were off
duty we would sit together on the sun-soaked balcony, overlooking the formidable hulk of Haleakala Volcano, and eat
other people's pineapples.

Outside the Maui Boy Restaurant I met 36-year-old Craig
Handfinger. Hailing from Philadelphia, he had spent the
past few years travelling round the world in the merchant
navy. Then he came to Hawaii and, lo and behold . . . he liked
what he saw and stayed. That was three years ago. During
that time he had tried his hand (and finger) at several jobs,
the latest one being as a guide to coachloads of American
tourists. He had only lasted three weeks because, he said,
'My dawg has more intelligence than the average American.
They're not interested in culture, just cushy comfort and
whether the food is safe to eat. They ask the dumbest questions too, things like, "Can we watch an avocado grow?" and
"How many restrooms we got on top of the volcano?" But the
question which really made me quit was: "Is this island completely surrounded by water?"'

One day news came through that a tourist had been murdered while hiking up near Iao ('Supreme Light') Valley
where an impressive basaltic needle rises sheer up over 1,200
feet. Rumour had it that the tourist had strayed off the beaten
path and trespassed into a private back-country patch of

marijuana (*pakalolo*) which is viciously guarded by the growers with lethal booby-traps and armed patrols. It seemed they didn't take kindly to snoopers, or lost tourists. *Pakalolo* is big business in Hawaii: it is the largest money-spinning crop in the islands and is looked upon as a major source of agricultural revenue. All sorts of names are given to this 'crazy smoke' weed, the most circulated ones being 'Kona Gold' and 'Puna Butter' on the Big Island and 'Maui Wowie' on Maui.

Wheeling into Paia ('Noisy Town'), it soon struck me that this was a place where *pakalolo* was big business. The colourful store-front town was roamed by hip, windsurfing dudes with bleached hair and Day-Glo, and paradise-seeking hippies with beards and tie-dye.

As I was drinking a drink outside the Mana Store, I was approached by a hirsute and bare-footed sort who sported shortish hair apart from a long, thin, straggly strand that dangled unappealingly down his back with a feather on the end. He was making steady progress through a large tubful of carob-soybean icecream. After enquiring briefly about my wherewithals and whereabouts, he introduced himself as a prophet called Light. Having great difficulty in taking people like this seriously, I naturally laughed. Then I asked him where he was from. Deadpan, he said, 'Nowhere in particular, I just appeared.'

'But you had to appear from somewhere,' I said. 'Where were you born?'

'I wasn't born anywhere. I materialized from a greater spiritual power.'

When I pressed him on this highly debatable point, he finally admitted to having emerged on planet earth in a suburb of Los Angeles. He had gone to Oxford to study law, but gave up that idea when he decided that 'all lawyers are so full of shit'. Instead, he metamorphosed into a travelling prophet.

He invited me down to a grass-shacked dope den on the beach where 'life has new meaning' and 'manic things happen, man'. From what I could gather, he was all for preaching to me about love, peace, harmony and spiritual balance and to let Maui Wowie do the rest. I said that I generally didn't

make a habit of going to curious sounding places with curious sounding people. By way of some colourful language, he
told me exactly what he thought of me and walked off –
which is precisely what I had hoped he would do.

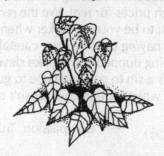

Noisy Town seemed to be full of middle-aged Flower
Children left over from the sixties who, besides other oddities, were into name-changing. In the Mana Store (a huge
health-food shop) near the 'fat-free, sugar-free, crap-free'
granola bin, I met a yoga-teacher-cum-crystal-healer clutching
an armful of alfalfa and mung bean sprouts whose name was
M'ocean, pronounced 'motion'. I came across people with
names like Starlight and Moonshine and Sunbeam who were
all very much into therapies of an alternative nature.

On the wall outside the Mana Store was a big bulletin
board pinned full of hand-written notices about what was
happening and what was on offer in the area. There were
rooms for rent, 'non-smoking, vegan, must possess a positive
outlook on life'; courses, 'yoga, aromatherapy, acupuncture,
spiritual healing . . .'; and a wide medley of other messages:

Birkenstock sandal missing – left foot.

VCR PROBLEMS? Let me take care of them.

PREGNANT MOMMIES NEEDED . . . join the
'Ladies of Informed Birth and Parenting' . . . we
do waterbirths – an experience yer gonna
wanna repeat!

There was also an 'alternative' notice from 'alternative' types who apparently had alternative ideas to rent-paying:

> We hope people are sueing all land owners who charge high prices for rent. We the renters are paying you to be your caretaker when you should be *paying us* to be your caretaker. We are being dupped, acting like slave-ass niggers. It's a sin to pay someone to go to sleep, especially when Mother Earth doesn't charge you to be here.
>
>   Compassion, Truth + Love

But the notice which really caught my attention was a lengthy advertisement for a 'SEXUAL TANTRIC SEMINAR' that asked, for all the town to see:

IS YOUR SEX LIFE AS CONSCIOUS AS THE REST OF YOUR LIFE?

There followed rather wordy but intriguing nonsense about 'tantric wisdom' . . . 'healing planets' . . . 'journeying into the spiritual potential of sexual love' . . . 'esoteric side of Tantra details' . . . and 'the Art of Conscious Loving', before getting down to the nuts and bolts of the matter:

WAYS TO INCREASE ENERGETIC FLOW AND PLEASURE

> These include techniques to harmonize moods and energy fields; esoteric kissing; transformative touching; varied positions; the man learning to use the lingam as an energetic wand of light, as a master artist uses a paint brush; the woman learning to consciously squeeze and play the yoni like a multi-stringed instrument of exquisite beauty.

It ended up by saying: 'Sex is God's invention and it is mankind that corrupted it.' Certainly food for thought if not a lot else, I thought.

This 'Art of Conscious Loving' seminar was run by Chuck and Carol Muir, whose photograph was attached to the notice. This gave me pause for thought. As far as Carol's features were concerned, I have nothing derogatory to say – in fact she looked positively attractive – but as for Chuck . . . well, he resembled a mixture between something from the *Planet of the Apes* and the dog's dinner and the thought of going anywhere near his lingam was, frankly, not pleasant.

Noisy Town's bulletin board had me glued, but whenever somebody came broadside I felt a trifle embarrassed by appearing so engrossed in the likes of 'exquisite multi-stringed yonis' and so I would rapidly divert my attention, pretending to ponder the perplexing whereabouts of the Birkenstock Right-Footed Sandal.

⚬⚬

I pedalled onward: upward. I had headed inland to cycle up Haleakala ('House of the Sun'), the world's highest dormant volcano. Its crater is 3,000 feet deep and a mind-boggling 21 miles in circumference – large enough to contain the whole of Manhattan. It also claims to be the highest elevation gain in the shortest distance in the world: from sea level to 10,023 feet in 38 miles. The ascent held all the agonizingly pointless potential of being something fun to tackle, so up I went. But slowly. Very slowly.

In fact I progressed so slowly (not only because of the incline but also because I kept stopping to refuel on irresistible mango windfalls) that after about four miles I decided to call it a day. With night fast-falling (the tropics don't have a long, drawn-out dawn or twilight: it plunges straight and suddenly from day to dark and dark to day) I needed somewhere to camp. One of the spiritual alfalfa-eating queens from Paia had told me about Rainbow Park, where it was possible to sleep without those perambulating and permit-demanding park rangers rudely awakening you at torch point.

I found the park. It was a paradise for mango addicts but I was not happy with the place – not the location but the company. Over near the stench of the solitary port-a-loo were two dodgy, doddery old men sitting beside a vivid orange camper van. They were both drinking and drunk and they had a brute of a dog that kept pawing the ground like a bull and snarling in my direction. I thought: I'm not going to stay here. So I left. As I did so, one of the men called after me, 'Hell, Hank. There goes one lucky saddle.'

I had passed Makawao Union Church just down the road and decided to see if I could find the local vicar, on the not altogether true assumption that where there is a holy man, there is safe camping.

The church was locked and the house next door had another massive mastiff. I tried the house next door to that instead and I struck lucky. Inside were the Reverend Tom Jackson and his wife Marge, an elderly Canadian couple from Honolulu with 11 children, 23 grandchildren and a number of 'great ones' to boot. The Jacksons had come to help at Makawao's Union Church for a year when the previous reverend had suddenly become 'involved' with a parishioner whom he had been counselling and subsequently moved in with her. The local church-going folk weren't impressed and Tom had been recruited to take his place. Now their year's stint was almost over and they were looking forward to getting back to downtown Honolulu, their friends and family and the heat. Tom found the fresh, cool air of Haleakala's foothills a bit too cold for his 'poor old bones'.

All this small-talk was picked up over tea and cakes in a lounge that overlooked the tall, rustling cane fields. After I had been there a while, I suddenly realized that Marge couldn't really see; blood clots on her retina threatened her with increasing blindness. It was truly something to watch her in action. Her hands were her eyes. Touching was everything. She busied herself in the kitchen, cooking far better than many who can see, but said that she didn't like feeling for things in cupboards and drawers because of the cockroaches. What really amazed me was her incredible ability to make clothes and she showed me a complicated skirt and top with pockets which she had made. But she did admit that the needle on her old hand-operated Singer sewing-machine was a bit tricky to thread!

They kindly offered me the sofa as a bed but I was more than happy to camp in the garden beneath a banana tree. Marge kept the back door unlocked for me at night so that I could use the bathroom if the need arose – which it did. The worst aspect of my nocturnal relief missions was not extracting myself from the cocooned cosiness of my North Face Blue Kazoo sleeping bag, but walking by torchlight through the garage to the back door. Because the house was right beside an expanse of sugar-cane fields, I would find a battalion of cane spiders attached to the ceiling and walls of the garage, jockeying for space with geckos. I didn't mind these suction-footed lizards but the spiders were huge and horrible, with a leg span of colossal proportions and a body the size of a big toe. They were fast movers, too.

The worst moment came when I found a cane spider sitting on the toilet seat looking as though he owned the place. Such was my need to be seated that, in a rare act of bravery, I was poised to swipe him on to the floor with a towel when suddenly back-ups arrived in the form of another two eight-legged monstrosities. One shot down the side of the shower towards my bare flip-flopped feet, with appalling alacrity; the other galloped up the side of the pan and strategically positioned itself to join Corporal Cane on the front line. I got the message and beat a hasty retreat.

I spent quite a few nights with Tom and Marge but not all in one go. As they lived more or less in the centre of Maui, they insisted that I made their home my base, returning to it after cycling off in sporadic bursts for exploratory missions around the island.

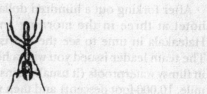

In the morning after my first night there, I continued grinding up the volcano – an ascent which was to last the whole day. Not long after I departed from Tom and Marge and the posse of spiders, I hit Makawao ('Eye of the Dawn'), a place renowned for being a true cowboy town. Cowboys there were but they seemed to be overrun by yet more New Age hippies. Outside the Down to Earth health-food store was another community bulletin board filled with the usual alternative therapies on offer such as 'CRYSTAL DAYS ARE HERE TO STAY – add an ever-lasting sparkle to your life', interspersed with advertisements like:

LOVE BOUTIQUE – PLEASURE PARTIES

Love is a piece of cake and we have all the
frosting. Sensuous lingeries for Him and Her –
UNIQUE ADULT JOYS.
Delights for the Goddess in every woman.

Emerging from the store with an eight-grain tofu and tahini sandwich in hand, an incense-scented couple slowly ambled past me.

'Awesome. Man, am I stoked out? . . . be fasting tomorrow . . . sure 'cos I ate a lotta shit last night . . . gotten myself real bad . . . yeah . . . need some inner cleansing . . .'

As I progressed up to the House of the Sun, I was periodically passed by descending bunches of cyclists – well, more like rotund American tourists topped by full-faced motorcycle helmets and sitting astride buckling, fat-tyred cruisers. They were organized by a group who ran special 'Bike Down A Volcano' tours, namely Maui Downhill or Cruiser Bobs.

After forking out a hundred dollars, you were met at your hotel at three in the morning and driven to the top of Haleakala in time to see the sunrise (weather permitting). The team leader issued you with a hefty helmet, clad you out in flimsy waterproofs (it usually rains at some point on the 40-mile, 10,000-foot descent) and then you followed the leader –

at a painfully slow pace, no overtaking allowed – for one of the longest freewheels in the world. I read that Bob Kiger, or 'Cruiser Bob' as he is better known on Maui, was the one who came up with the original idea for bicycle 'cruisin' ' down what the US Geological Survey claims is the steepest road on earth. This adventure begins at the edge of Haleakala's immense crater, described by Mark Twain as 'the sublimest spectacle I ever saw'.

From what I could gather, the majority of the Maui Downhillers were shapeless people who hadn't been on a bicycle for 40-odd years and who, judging from their pained expressions while descending, wished they had kept it that way. Of course accidents had to happen. Marge told me that recently one unaccustomed rider who failed to negotiate a hairpin bend ended up pancake-fashion beneath the wheels of an ascending tour bus.

As these helmeted freewheelers wheeled past me at their slow pace, I was the object of a hundred predictable shouts; 'Hey kid! You're headin' the wrong way!'

Of all the Polynesian islands, Maui is the only one to be named after a demi-god. This is because Maui was more than Wowie. He was hot stuff. Legend has it that he brought fire, fished up all the 132 Hawaiian islands from the bottom of the sea and pushed up the sky to enable humankind to walk upright. But he produced an even more impressive feat. The sun used to speed so rapidly across the sky that the days were too short for the men to fish or harvest their crops and Hina, Maui's mother, complained that the sun set well before she could finish drying her *tapa* (the Polynesian cloth made from pounded bark). Maui asked the sun to slow down, but in vain. So he ascended Haleakala volcano armed with the jaw bone from his grandmother's grave as a hook. He also had a rope woven from his sister's pubic hair and he lassoed the sun-god by his genitals. Caught with his pants down, so to speak, the sun quickly agreed to cross the skies more slowly. Thus Haleakala became the House of the Sun.

I panted on through a forest of eucalyptus, past paddle-shaped cacti, flowering jacaranda and green ranchland. Then I was upon the Terrible Twenty-nine, a steep sequence of switchbacks corkscrewing up the mountainside. Three days before I tackled them, a Japanese woman in a hired car had taken a deadly plunge over the edge of one of these 'twisters' and thus 'went home' with a crunch before her time.

The temperature steadily dropped 3°F for every thousand feet that I climbed, which meant that it would be 30°F cooler at the summit than at sea level. The sun of the foothills had disappeared all too quickly for my liking and I toiled onwards, first through a cool mist, then through a wet mist and then through a cold, wet, heavy fog. To keep my numb mind off my painfully complaining limbs, I busied myself with riveting data about how many different rains I was experiencing – in all about twelve. It came sideways, diagonally, normally, not normally and upside down. It pattered, it poured, it pissed, it pelted and it came in big bucketfuls of cats and dogs and stair-rods and sheets. In a word it was: wet.

Every now and then a car-load of glum tourists would emerge from the murk, their doleful expressions momentarily turning to surprise as they spotted me glaring glumly back. Then they would vanish into the mist. But one couple broke into smiles and stopped the car. It was Bob and Sandy (the photographer with the natural touch – 'Smile as though you're enjoying yourself . . . put on your hat . . .') from the Maui ferry. Overlooking a precipice, we chatted and joked and compared notes. I said it was wet down there; they said it was sunny and hot on the top: 'We've burnt our noses, but I got a great shot of Sandy smiling as though she's enjoying herself!' Then they gave me their business card ('Talisman Arts and Crafts – handcrafted jewellery, crystal, pottery, pewter') and told me to come and stay if I was passing through Boulder, Colorado.

Their receding tail-lights were quickly swallowed by the mist and I continued crawling forth with numb hands but lifted spirits in the knowledge that the sun was somewhere up there. But I still had 5,000 feet to go and, progressing at a preposterously slow speed, I never did get to see the sun again that day.

On my last legs and last bit of puff, I turned off at Hosmer Grove 'campground' where I could just make out one other tent through the gloom. I clambered into my sleeping bag and ate six of Marge's homegrown bananas before plunging into a comatose slumber.

Later – much later – the three occupants of the other tent woke me up as they emerged from the dark and dripping woods and trudged past, stumbling over my pegs, in heavy boots and sodden waterproofs. They didn't sound too happy.

'Shit. That was some lousy day. Last goddam time I rely on your sense of goddam lousy direction. Jeez!'

I took it that they had got a little bit lost. A cacophony of peeved and angry voices argued deep into the night. Unable to get back to sleep, I tuned into the World Service and heard that in Switzerland a madman had gone on the rampage by ringing people's doorbells and shooting the unfortunate souls who answered the door. The result: six dead and a lot injured. On that cheery night-cap I went to sleep.

At some time during the night it stopped raining and around 3am my neighbours trooped noisily past my tent, back into the blackness of the woods, no doubt to get lost again. Half an hour later I was on my way and panting heavily in the thin air to reach the summit for sunrise.

A pilgrimage of cars passed me and I would soon be mingling with the occupants as they stood swaddled in hotel blankets, shivering violently, cameras at the ready. As I scrambled up the bank to join them, the swirling misted skies burst into a profusion of pale purples and pinks and golds.

I felt odd – an uncanny mix of being half dead, half alive. Dead from the dizzy-making thin air and sweat-chilled struggle of my pre-dawn ascent; alive . . . well, apart from still breathing, what I saw spread out below and above me was, frankly, most impressive. The vast crater was a massive vortex of eddying, swift-moving mists whipped into a kaleidoscope of colour by the elusive sun.

Once I had moved away from a man with dog-breath, the air smelt deliciously sharp and clear. The black volcanic walls of the crater were silhouetted against harlequin skies. Everyone faced the east. Suddenly there was a unanimous intake of breath and a clacketing of clicking shutters as the upper crescent of the sun exploded over the edge of the wavering horizon, sending a rayed brilliance of flickering fire over everything it touched. And then, just as suddenly, a dark malicious mist whirled in, blotting out not only the sun but everything and everyone in seconds. That was it. The show was over. The freezing rain sliced its way down as the wind picked up pace.

There was an air of disappointment among the milling hordes. The sun had risen and been a let-down in one. They thought: What a sham! What a swiz! One woman blamed the park ranger. 'But I've drove *all* the way up here at this god-forsaken hour to *see* the sunrise, not a goddam bowl of mist,' she bawled, 'and now you're telling me that a sunrise cannot be guaranteed. Jesus – it's a bit late!'

'Well, I'm real sorry, ma'am, but we don't have control over the weather, you know,' the ranger said impassively.

Her querulous clamours were ugly. I put up my hood and moved away, buffeted by the strong, wet wind. I felt far from swindled. Despite the weather, I was more than content – I was elated. I had cycled up to the House of the Sun without either expiring or toppling over the edge, and I had had a wondrous sneak-preview of the sunrise. I felt on top of the world in all senses of the word. And I had 40 miles of continuous downhill ahead. What more could I want?

Down in the car park, looking wet and cold and a trifle shell-shocked, was a gathering of Maui Downhillers and Cruiser Bobbers. They looked far from happy: they had paid a hundred dollars to see a sun that hadn't risen and now they were about to embark on a freezing, rain-lashed descent down a volcano they couldn't see. And they had to leave now, whether they liked it or not – the group leader said so.

Feeling suitably smug, I wished them a happy descent and went to warm up in the visitors' centre where I picked up a 'House of the Sun National Park Certificate':

I SURVIVED THE 37 MILE DRIVE UP FROM SEA LEVEL TO THE SUMMIT OF HALEAKALA VOLCANO (10,023 ft/3,055 m). THE GREATEST ELEVATION GAIN IN THE SHORTEST DISTANCE IN THE WORLD!

Later I crossed out the 'DRIVE' and scribbled 'CYCLE RIDE'. They didn't print any certificates for smart-ass oddities who had bicycled.

By the time I had finished wandering around it was sunny and hot, and at that altitude I burnt my lobes in a matter of minutes. After going on a semi-hike down into the crater and ambling close to Science City (a space-age research development manned by the University of Hawaii and the Department of Defense) I decided I had better get going while the going was good.

Down and down I dropped – mile after glorious mile of falling and flying and twisting and turning this way and that. Sometimes I had to slalom around the occasional *nene* goose (the rare state bird found only on Haleakala and the Big Island's volcanoes) which scuttled worriedly across my path. Once, I stopped to marvel at the silverswords, an endangered species of spiky-glinting plant. Had I been cycling a hundred years earlier or more, I might have had other things to swerve around. In Charles Nordhoff's guide book written in the early 1870s he gave some practical advice: 'If you carry a gun you are likely to have a shot at wild turkeys on your way up or down.'

I went like the wind, soaring round corners, prone on the straight, eyes streaming. At one point I came up behind a fat lump of a tourist bus slowly winding its way down, belching out fumes, hogging the road. It is deeply frustrating to belt hell for leather down a mountain on your mount and have to brake because of some motorized monstrosity blocking your way – especially when it has taken two days of major heart palpitations to get up.

The road narrowed, I had entered the Terrible Twenty-Nine and my adrenalin was pumping. I had tasted speed – I was Miguel Indurain in the Tour de France sweeping down the mountainside to cheering crowds and I wasn't going to let this multi-wheeled lump stop my fun. Foolishly I pulled out and, with a thrusting surge, rocketed past the bus at full throttle.

I made it by a hair's breadth. Any later and I would have ended up sandwiched between the bus and an upgoing van or else followed in the tyre tracks of the Japanese woman over the side – the quick way down.

Phew! This was thrilling stuff. I was licking up the tarmac, the miles swooshing by. Then, for a couple of thousand feet, I fell from the sun into a wet wall of mist and it was fun and exciting being not quite sure where the edge was. Just as suddenly I burst back out into the brilliance of day and down past the forest of eucalyptus, the cactus, the ranchland, the hippie cowboy town, the pineapple plantations and the fields of sugar-cane – all streaking past in a colourful blur – and before I knew it I was back with Tom and Marge, windswept, sunburnt and elated.

Suddenly everything was still and quiet and warm. My voyage to the House of the Sun was over. Two days to get up: two hours to get down.

Dozing in my sleeping bag at dawn the next morning, I tuned into the local radio station:

'This is KHEI radio. How're yer doin', folks? We've got a great day for you. The heat is on . . . the beat is good . . . and you wanna know what . . . wanna know somethin' that will really wake you up? Josephine Cochran invented the dishwasher one hundred years ago today. Yes siree. She was from Witt, Illinois.'

It was one of those truly mindboggling facts that stop you dead in your tracks even if you are lying down at the time. America never fails to make you wonder.

I hit the Hana Highway, a narrow and rutted coastal road twisting its helter-skelter way along the north shore from Paia to Hana. In a distance of a mere 30 miles or so, I bounced over 54 one-lane bridges and around 617 hairpin corners. Motorists tend to find it a hellish drive (the Hasegawa Store in Hana sold T-shirts saying 'I survived the road to Hana') but for anyone on a bicycle it was sheer joy.

For a while, though, I got no further than Hookipa Beach Park, where I became transfixed by a dozen windsurfers speed-skimming the surf and literally flying clean over the tumultuous, high frothing waves. This was the spot where the annual O'Neill International Windsurfing Championship took place, and bronzed and brawny types performed for the $10,000 prize.

I pulled myself away and soon I was immersed in jungle as I climbed and dropped down the spiralling road. The deep blue whirling waters of the boisterous Pacific pounded the laval rocks on one side, while sweeping streams and waterfalls gushed and rushed down the mountainside on the other. Chunky ropes of hanging creepers dangled from lush-green, giant-leafed trees in which strange birds whooped and squawked and warbled. I passed through thick forests of bamboo and the amazing technicoloured rainbow eucalyptus, the bark of which resembled a riot of different shades of paint left to drip and mingle the length of the mighty trunk.

It rained on and off – mostly on. I rattled and rolled over bridges with names like Kole'a ('Windborne Joy'), Haipuena ('Glowing Hearts'), Waiohonu ('Water of the Turtle'), Keaaiki ('Burning Star'), Hana-wi Elua ('Second Whistling Wind') and Puaaka'a ('Open laughter'). How could you help but feel happy? At one point I filled up my bottles from a mountain spring that the locals called 'alive' water.

My time watching the windsurfers had been well spent; the early morning rush of tourist traffic to Hana all passed me to make it back along the dead-end road (dead-end for hired cars, that is) before dark. Apart from the local pick-up trucks, the road was mine, as were the fruity pickings along the way. I stuffed both bags and belly full of guavas, mountain apples and papayas. My only highway hazards were the mangoes whose tyre-squidged windfalls produced a slippery slime beneath my wheels.

Round every corner grew the cyclist's best friend – the banana. Hawaii has over seventy species with hundreds of variations. It is hardly surprising, then, that the locals have many a myth about bananas: it is considered bad luck to dream about them; to meet someone who carries them; or to take them on a fishing trip. An old taboo not only prohibited women from eating with men but also forbade them (under penalty of death) to eat bananas along with coconuts.

After I had been on Hawaii a few weeks, I learned that bananas do not actually grow on trees. The plant is a gigantic herb, a member of the grass family like wheat, rye and barley, and has a multitude of uses. The leaves come in handy for house roofs, umbrellas and rain hats, bowl covers, table cloths, cigarette papers, clothing and temporary sandals, cattle feed, dye, packing material, as a truce flag and as a covering of the traditional *imu* (underground oven). The leaf buds are used as a vegetable; the leaf sheaths as water channels in the fields and as containers for leis and plants during transportation; leaf-sheath fibres for thatching, stringing leis, plaiting into clothing, cloth and thread. And the trunks act as rollers for propelling canoes into the sea. Bananas also have medicinal uses and antibiotic properties and it is said they can even bring relief to saddle-sore cyclists:

stuff some peeled ones down your shorts and wonders will supposedly be worked.

I carried on along the coast with undulating green hills on the inland side. Nearby was Puaa Kaa Park ('Place of the Rolling Pigs'), its name dating from days gone by when plump wild pigs were said to have rolled down the slick, steep grassy slopes. At one point I passed a sign nailed to a tree saying: CAUTION, BABY PIGS CROSSING. I kept an eye out in case a rolling porker tumbled across my path, but all I had to contend with was a skid-pan of squashed mangoes.

Nearing Hana, I stopped at a ramshackle fruit stall to buy an enormous coconut from a little old woman called Annie. Her friendly, dark weathered face was crevassed with creases and she became very animated when I said I was from England.

'My great grandfather was from Dartmouth. Would you know it?'

Then she said that George Harrison lived down the road. 'He's from England too. Would you know him?'

I drank the ice-cold milk from the coconut. She took a small hatchet and with a dextrous and forceful whack she cracked it open and piled the sweet nutty flesh into a plastic bag. It would last me for days.

I camped down in Waianapanapa State Park, beside the spray-lashed rocks and a small beach of black sand. Following a trail through a tunnel of thick vines, I came upon a legendary meeting place for lovers – huge tub-like caves, formed from the lava, which could only be reached by diving into a pool and swimming under water. Long ago Popoalaea, a Hawaiian princess, fled from her jealous husband Kakae and hid in a cave. After much searching, he eventually found and killed her. Every now and then the waters of the cave turn red, allegedly from the gory murder, but in reality from millions of tiny red shrimp which invade the caves at certain times of the year.

Back in my tent I ate a banana-and-honey sandwich and tuned into the 7 o'clock news on the local radio station. Buckingham Palace had just announced that Prince Andrew and Fergie were to separate, but of far more interest was a report of a man in Honolulu who gave joggers a hefty clout with an iron bar as he drove past them in his car. He was still at large.

The next morning I rode into Hana ('Rest From Hard Breathing'), a small town which had been destroyed in 1946 when an earthquake in Alaska's Aleutian Islands sent huge tidal waves which washed away hundreds of homes and many people with them.

Everything now seemed very quiet.

Apparently this wasn't unusual. Not a lot ever happened in Hana. Reading the local paper outside the grocery store, I learned that the highlight for the month was a planned 'CEREMONY FOR RENOVATED POST OFFICE'. The public was invited to this spectacular event at which, it was proudly announced: REFRESHMENTS WILL BE SERVED.

I kicked myself for arriving in Hana a week too early as it is not often you get a chance to attend a ceremony for a renovated post office, refreshments included.

The road out of Hana soon turned very narrow, rutted and rocky. I passed a small house with a big sign at the gate that said:

KAPU – KEEP OUT
I MEAN YOU!

I joined a few splashing tourists in the Seven Sacred Pools (there were a lot more than seven) which tumbled down the hillside in giant steps fed by cool mountain water from the many streams and waterfalls.

From here on, the rent-a-car tourists had to do a U-turn and head back the way they had come as the road rapidly deteriorated and it was only advisable to tackle it in a sturdy four-wheel drive. This suited me very nicely as all traces of traffic immediately vanished. The road was bad but not *that* bad. I rattled and rolled over pits and potholes and skidded on yet more mangoes. I also ate more mangoes than I care to mention, but I shall mention it anyway because I think it is a fact worth mentioning. I ate nine – in one sitting. I admit they were not the biggest I had seen but they were still big. I had hoped to make it way past my all-time record of six and hit double figures but the ninth got the better of me. As I waddled back to my bike I ruminated on the fact that I never even used to like mangoes. This fact I found truly amazing.

Fairly suddenly, I passed from lushness into a parched and brittle landscape. Hawaii is like that. Each island is like a miniature continent with extremes of sunshine and rainfall within a very short distance. One moment I would be pedalling in torrential rain through a wildly overgrown tropical rainforest. Then, turning the corner, I would find myself in searing heat among desertscape and cactus. Maui is a prime example of such oddities: Lahaina has a mere 17 inches of annual rainfall, while only seven miles away Mount Puu Kukui receives a very wet 40 feet.

In Hana I had strapped two gallons of water to various parts of my bike to see me through this hot, empty and uphill desert. About once an hour a vehicle would pass. One time a jeep stopped, it was full of four likely lads – bare-backed and baseball-capped. They asked if I wanted a lift.

'You've got over 3,000 feet in this heat ahead of you,' they thoughtfully informed me. 'Come on, jump up here and we'll give you the ride of your life!'

Panting and sweating profusely, I said, 'I'm fine thanks – never felt fitter.'

As soon as they had gone, I sat behind a rock and rested.

Later a bright orange VW Beetle pulled alongside. Behind the wheel was a trumpeter from Toronto (or, as he said it, 'Terranno') who was part of a small orchestra touring Hawaii. He lobbed me an orange and a bottle of pop and then one-handedly took a photograph of me.

'I'm impressed,' he said, 'but you sure gotta be crazy!'

That night back at Tom and Marge's, camped beneath the banana tree, I dreamed that I was in a fast-falling helicopter on crash-course to earth. Like a balloonist throwing out sacks of sand to become more airborne, I started frantically hurling out pannier-loads of mangoes to lighten the load. But it was a fruitless task. After what seemed an eternal fall, we finally crashed and I found myself riding off into the desert on a toddler's tricycle.

spy hop   chin slap   pec slap   tail slap   flukes   breach   blow

I rang Ron, the kayaking masseur from Lanai. He had invited me to stay with him and his friends, John and Bryer, if I was passing through Kihei and said he would take me kayaking.

I had only kayaked once before – well, not so much kayaked as hung on for dear life while being washed down 17 miles of angry rapids in France's Ardèche Gorge. Now I was about to embark on a ten-mile round trip across the whale-infested waters of the Pacific to Molokini, a small, crescent-shaped volcanic island. I felt a trifle ruffled. A group of us went; we were eight altogether. As I was a complete novice, Ron put me in the front of *Big Bertha* (a double kayak) – me up front with pony-tailed John in the rear.

That was fine. Easy. All I had to do was to pretend to paddle. John did the rest – propel and steer.

The sea was calm, the wind at our backs, and we made it to Molokini within the hour. I was surprised to read, months later, that this spectacular crater is visited by as many as a thousand snorkellers and divers every day and that the sheer

volume of visitors not only affects the fish population, but is also said to leave a bath-tub ring of suntan oil around the crater wall.

When our kayaking caravan arrived, we had the place to ourselves. Ron came along broadside and handed me a snorkel. Over the side I went. Below me in the clear, turquoise waters was one of the greatest concentrations of fish in all Hawaii – over 700 species as well as several hundred varieties of seaweed and many thousands of sea creatures and reef coral, all in a small space. It was as if I had dived into a tropical fishtank. In front of my window swam a colourful kaleidoscope of scales and fins and snouted bubbling mouths, all skimming and flitting this way and that. It was a submarine dream.

Back on board a drama was slowly unfolding. One of the group's experienced kayaking girls was doubled up in pain with violent stomach cramps. Groaning, she moaned that there was no way she could paddle the five miles back across a fast-growing chop of waves.

Gallantly (foolishly) I offered to paddle her flimsy, single-seated vessel so that she could take my easy hot seat in *Big Bertha*. She needed no persuading. Ron said I should be able to manage.

The sea was blue but bellicose. As we emerged past the headland, the swell had risen dramatically. The wind had blown up out of nowhere and hefty waves buffeted me around like polystyrene. Flailing wildly, I realized I was well out of control and was being swept towards the ragged rocks of Molokini's backside. Just as an alarming vision of shipwreck flashed across my mind, Ron shouted above the roar of the crashing surf: 'You've gotcha paddle upside down!' and then, 'Try steering with your feet!'

Struggling in the surf in a sudden Pacific squall is not the ideal place for your first kayaking lesson. This thought struck me as the menacing rocks loomed ever closer. I also thought: Surely there are more attractive/sensible/safe locations to be doing this – perhaps in a toddler's paddling pool?

For the sake of self-preservation I had to do something, and fast. It was news to me that in these highly sophisticated craft there was a foot-operated rudder and it did seem a little late in the day to grasp this rather crucial fact. So that my short legs could reach the rudder-pedal, I had to adopt a prostrate position along the floor of the boat which rather hindered my ability to navigate, let alone paddle. In fact the only useful thing I could accomplish in this position was to pray. To confound matters, I suddenly felt seasick, but I think it was more sick with fright than sick of the sea.

The thought of my life ending without my ever eating another mango galvanized me into action. With a determined burst of adrenalin and in a bizarre supine paddling position, I managed to propel myself away from impending disaster to . . . well, possibly impending death. It suddenly dawned on me that I was crossing humpback territory.

Seeing a 50-foot whale catapulting itself clean out of the ocean when you are securely planted on dry land is fine, but witnessing it when you are out there with them is fantastically frightening: fantastic to see such a massive and venerable creature rearing from the depths – to hear the awesome noise of the exhaled air gushing through the blowhole and to see the tail splash-slapping the surface with such a force that it would crush you in seconds – and frightening to think that one of these whales could quite easily rear its mighty form from beneath the bobbing, flimsy craft at any moment.

Just as I was thinking I might end up like Jonah, I made it back to shore. I felt like a dead Portuguese man-o'-war – all jelly, and minus the sting. Fighting for nearly two hours into the wind, my arm and neck muscles were a complaining combination of aches and pains. Ron said that, although I was the first novice he had taken to Molokini, he hadn't been worried about me; he knew I would make it.

'I figured that if you were crazy enough to bike to the House of the Sun, you would come out of this one OK.'

I was glad that it was after this sea-faring excursion and not before it that he said, 'A couple of kayakers recently drowned out there. They hit a heavy swell, became weak and gave up.'

It felt good to be back in the saddle.

That night, back at Ron's house, I read in the *Maui Times* about a 'Syringe Bandit' spreading a message of fear:

> Los Angeles bicycle shop owner Bill Ledgerwood always worried about being held up at gunpoint, but never dreamed he would be threatened at needlepoint. Ledgerwood was the first victim last week of the man who L.A. police dubbed the 'Syringe Bandit' after he threatened people eight times with a needle he claims is loaded with his AIDS-infected blood.

The other front page headline was closer to 'home': it was about a recent rash of mystery dog deaths. The dogs had been intentionally poisoned with a strong pesticide.

The next day I was sitting on a bench outside a church having a rest and a read when a side door opened and a matronly woman sporting a corrugated bouffant hairdo and horn-rimmed glasses said, 'Well, you sure gotta be hungry – you're three hours early.'

'Early?' I said, with a look of confusion.

'You're homeless, right? Tonight's the weekly cook-up we do for you guys.'

'Oh, I see,' I said. 'Well, no, I haven't got a home here but I'm not homeless.'

'My – that's a kind of cute accent you got yourself there. Where you from?'

'England.'

'You are? Well, bless you. Tell me – what are you doing here, where're you staying?'

So I told her I was cycling round the islands, camping in cane fields and people's gardens and she said 'bless you' again and then she invited me to stay for the free meal that the church cooked on a weekly basis for the homeless. With an uncharacteristically Christian spirit, I thanked her and said I was fine for food and that I wouldn't want to deprive the needy of their supper, but that I would love to stay to meet the people.

They were an interesting bunch, mostly just disillusioned dropouts and druggies and drunkards – mainlanders who had come to Hawaii looking for a better life and fallen through the nets of society. Greg was a scrawny 26-year-old with straggly hair and big, empty eyes. He was a born-again Christian and reformed alcoholic and lived in a makeshift shelter in some woods out of town. Since he had bumped into Jesus he felt a contentment in his life. At least, he had until last week. He'd had a dog to which he devoted as much love as to his newly found faith. One morning he had woken up and found his dog dead – a victim of the elusive pesticide poisoner.

'Maestro was my baby,' said Greg. 'I tell you – if I find the killer I'll strangle the bastard. Jesus might not like it but this is serious – my baby's gone.'

Across the table was a man known as Johnny S. Only ten days ago he had found himself on the streets when his girl-friend had kicked him out of their home. One of the cooks who helped at the church later told me that Johnny S. had beaten his girlfriend.

'He was in a heavy metal band,' the cook said disdainfully, as if that explained things.

Waipio Valley, Hawaii, which I plunged head-long into.

Beneath the falling waters of Waipio Valley, Hawaii.

The tantalising types found frolicking beneath the palm fronds in Pu'uhonua o Honaunau, Hawaii.

Overlooking Diamond Head with the locals in Honolulu, Oahu.

Amid the land of (gulp) gulches on Lanai – the Happiest of Isles.

The happiest of camp spots, until I was fined. Anini Beach, Kauai.

En route to the Garden of the Gods, Lanai.

The masked paper bag painter, Hanalei Valley, Kauai.

Traditional Hawaiian fishing, Honaunau.

Beneath the land of live lava flows – Chain of Craters Road, Hawaii.

The cloaked wonder of
Waikiki, Oahu.

Waianapanapa, Maui, where a Beatle lives nearby.

A Buddha and a bicycle in Maui.

Life's a struggle (uphill all the way) and then you die – the Sunniest of Houses, Maui.

Light, fruity refreshments in Honokohau, Maui.

Trying not to look fit for nothing after two days of 'upness' –
on top of the House of the Sun, Maui.

The poppy fields, California, 'but watch out for them there rattlers'.

Walkies,
California-style.

Like mistress, like
pet. LA suburbs.

'Shoo-bap-a-doo-da, she's my baby'.
California, of course.

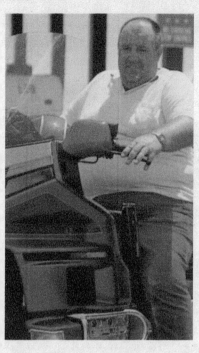

Cutting a fine figure on a (Gold) Wing and a prayer – Santa Cruzin', California.

Dwarfed by the towering copper-coloured cliffs of Zion Canyon, Utah, which I rode up... and down... and up again. It was that good.

Bryce Canyon, Utah. One heck of a place to lose a cow.

Uh-oh! About to be sucked up by another monstrous storm, and with no place to lay my weary, worried head. Far from anywhere, Arizona.

Framed by the Mittens of Monument Valley, Arizona.

Snap! Durango, Colorado.

Flashers' Paradise, U.S.A.

Below: Helmeted but light-headed, high in the Rockies.

The place that didn't pass me by. The mighty Rockies again.

Comparing machines with the Amish in Indiana.

Later that evening, lying in my tent after flicking an invasion of slugs, cockroaches, moths, earwigs, geckos and fat, red ants off my fly-sheet, I read the free *Maui Bulletin* by torchlight. Perusing the personal columns, I suddenly spotted:

DRAMA QUEEN

Take the house, the kids and the inheritance but please . . . leave the band gear. Johnny S.

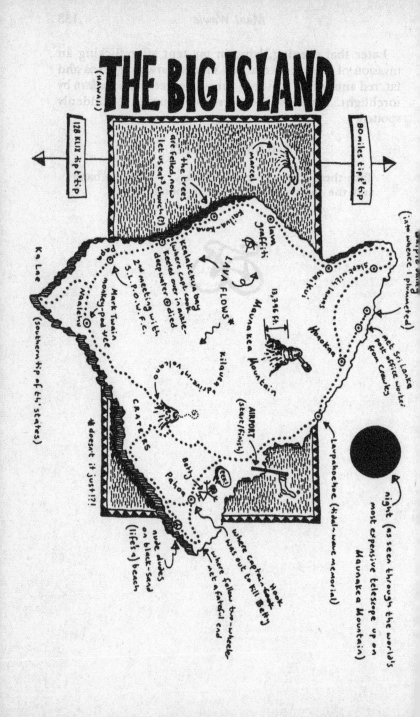

11

Cook's Lump
of Lava

![bicycle] America is home to the 'drive thru' and the 'drive in'. To avoid the physical exertion of getting out of their cars, Americans can remain comfortably seated while motoring through cinemas, restaurants, theatres, banks, mortuaries, post offices, dry cleaners and even trees. But Hawaii has the only drive-in volcano.

Elsewhere in the world, people flee when volcanoes erupt; in Hawaii, they flock in their thousands for a close-up view of the spectacle. Local airline and helicopter companies cash in on the tempestuous workings of Pele, the fire goddess, by offering fly-by excursions as Kilauea ('The Spewing'), one of the most active volcanoes in the world, spews fountains of raging fire into the sky.

The island of Hawaii is known as the Volcano Island or the Orchid Isle but more commonly as just the Big Island because, compared to the other islands in the chain, it is just that – big. It is already some 4,000 square miles in area and, being a mere stripling in geological terms, it continues to grow, like any adolescent. Its mountain peaks emerged from the ocean a mere million years ago (most of the world's land masses date back 300 million years).

Mark Twain captured the diversity of this eventful isle when he said he could 'see all the climes of the world at a single glance of the eye'. An impressive 17 climatic zones are found on the Big Island, where the scenery ranges from dense, lush rainforests to trees jacketed in solid lava and parched, barren laval deserts. At the island's heart is Mauna Kea ('White Mountain'), rising to a height of 13,796 feet above sea-level – but there is more to it than that. It pushes straight up from the ocean floor and its full height is 31,796 feet which, they say, makes it the tallest mountain mass on earth.

In Hilo, the island's capital city, a continuous cloudburst drummed upon the corrugated roofs, bounced off giant-leafed plants and turned rough roads into quagmires. Such weather was normal for Hilo, where it rains an average eleven feet a year. I took shelter in a hostel run by a friendly English girl from Newcastle who had arrived in Hawaii a year before for eight days' holiday and ended up marrying the hostel owner.

'England's a dump,' she said. 'I'm never going back.'

I shared my clean, cramped room with middle-aged Donna from San Jose who was very much into 'love healing', whatever that entailed. She seemed a bit shocked that I was travelling alone.

'And biking too – it's so dangerous. You know, there's a lot of animosity on these islands. There are a lot of local Hawaiians who despise the *haoles* – they can get real violent. Did you hear about the girl who was recently pulled off her bike, raped and murdered just down the road in Puna?'

It was impossible not to have heard about it. Talk of this atrocity was constantly in the local news and posters were pinned up everywhere offering a reward for information on her murder.

Then Donna asked me some curious questions. Did I fantasize when cycling? What colour was my mother's hair? What size were my feet? Did I read my daily starsign? She read it to me out of the local paper, whether I liked it or not:

| **CAPRICORN:** This week you will win a trip to Europe, you will find a | Rolex watch & the IRS sends you a refund cheque for $8,658. |

'That's why I don't read them,' I said.

'You're a pessimist,' she told me. 'You need a certain belief, like me, and then you'll see that life has more meaning. I can see that you need to open yourself up.'

The thought of lying on an operating table with a massive incision inflicted from head to toe flashed across my mind. I didn't like the idea of that and so I went to wash my socks.

When I headed out into the rain the next morning, Donna said, 'I'll be thinking of you and sending you my blessings. Remember, love heals all pain.'

My horoscope turned out to be true – to a certain degree. Instead of winning a trip to Europe, I was given a free hotel room in Honokaa; riding towards Pee Pee Falls I found a Rolex substitute in the form of a small adjustable spanner (which was of far more use); and at the Tidal Wave Memorial I found 25 cents on the ground. Maybe there was more to Donna than met the eye.

Imposing precipitous valleys (known locally as gulches) awash with waterfalls and exuberant rivers punctuated mile upon mile of rustling green sugar-cane seas. This was the coast for cane: the rain, and lots of it, could be relied upon and the cane lapped it up thirstily, needing a ton of water to produce a pound of sugar.

At Waipio Valley ('Valley of the Kings') the narrow road dropped over a thousand-foot cliff as an outrageously steep 25% slope and I was not surprised to learn that since the early 1970s, when people started driving it, more than 20 hapless souls had dropped off before their time. This does not sound a lot of deaths until you realize that only about two vehicles a day attempt the road.

I stood astride Starcraft at the top of this formidable incline. I was in pensive mood, cogitating my impending drop like a first-time diver teetering on the edge of a very high board.

It was at this point that I met Noel and Wiltrud Wickramasinghe who told me not to do it if I valued my life. Wiltrud was German, but her spry and convivial husband Noel was a Sri Lankan who had worked for the post office in Crawley for 27 years before going to live in Germany. He became even more animated when he learnt that I was a country bumpkin from Sussex. We sat for a while on this exotic island in the middle of the Pacific comparing notes on the likes of Crawley, Horsham, Midhurst, Didling and Iping. Then, like long-lost friends we took photographs of each other grinning inanely with a thousand foot *pali* (cliff) and Hawaii's longest black sand beach as backdrop before we parted.

Cautiously, I embarked upon my startlingly severe mile-long descent. Within seconds, gravity got the better of me. Brakes were of no use whatsoever: if I applied them I shot over the 'bars as if bucked from a bronco. I didn't roll downwards. I fell – with all the panache and speed of a sack of concrete. Free-falling. My stomach was left half a mile up the road wondering where the rest of me had gone. The rest of me, stomachless, realized that my only chance of survival was to take preventative action by colliding with the bank and clinging to some roots – which, surprisingly, I did without difficulty or injury.

I continued cautiously down the hill on foot, realizing too late that, once you started down, you couldn't guarantee to stop. Small, tentative footsteps rapidly turned to ten-foot strides which in themselves turned to a frantic out-of-control, graceless flight. I dropped like an overweight ostrich pushed off a cliff, landing in a sprawl like a cartoon character, all arms and legs.

Slowly I came to my senses and was promptly picked up off the ground by Syd Akman, a photographer from Seattle. For want of something better to do, he took a picture of my dazed, dishevelled state and handed me his business card. A quote by Jennifer James was written along the bottom: 'Success is the quality of your journey.' Were there, I ruminated ruefully, any qualities to my journeying?

Once I had dispensed with Syd, it soon became apparent that I had stumbled upon (or rather fallen into) the proverbial Garden of Eden. I found myself in the midst of an overgrown and edible jungle, surrounded by stomach-filling succulence just asking to be plucked from trees and bushes. There were mangoes, bananas, lemons, limes, passionfruit, grapefruit, breadfruit, mountain apples, coconuts, pumpkins and avocado pears. Wild pigs crashed through the undergrowth, and the fishponds and streams were prolific with prawns. There was coffee, too. The place was a gastronomic paradise just waiting to be eaten.

A silver-glinting waterfall gushed with thunderous force over the cliff face, crashing in a crescendo into the sea. I dropped my bike and flopped down on the hot, black sand beach as my body was tantalizingly cooled by spectral clouds of spray gliding gently from the waterfall's wind-blown mists.

On the Big Island, the ratio of men to women is 8:1. I picked up this promising piece of information in North Kohala (the home of King Kamehameha the Great) from Lisa, an ebullient half-American, half-Iranian who worked at the local Realty office, and Steve, a swarthy bandanna-headed baritone from San Francisco, who were both in their late twenties and freshly in love. They were inseparable and co-existed in perpetual, interlocked entwinement.

I had met them in 'downtown' Hawi, which was merely a

crossroads and a couple of blocks of ramshackle wooden and paint-worn false-fronted buildings leaning lazily upon each other. They had seemed surprised to see me. No tourists ever stopped in Hawi apart from lost ones, they said. It was an out-of-the-way, not-a-lot-to-do town which made me like it all the more. It had a certain cowboy charm to it, which was only to be expected as one of America's largest privately owned ranches, the Parker Ranch, was just over the mountain. I had passed *paniolos* – Hawaiian cowboys – on and off for most of the day as they herded and lassoed and tended to more than 60,000 cattle that ran on the ranchland's quarter of a million acres.

Lisa and Steve invited me to a party in Lisa's house, a huge, dark wooden building in the midst of a llama farm. All their friends were mainland Americans and they all had the same story: 'Came to Hawaii for a two-week holiday and never went home.' The intriguing assortment included a Montessori teacher, a scuba diver who worked the tourist boats, a fireman, an artist, a flautist, a florist and an ex-cruiseline baker called Sam who had just won a baking competition on Hawaii for devising a macadamia nut and chocolate-chip cookie. When I was first introduced to Sam, he struck me as a bit of a complex 'carbohydrate' – rather demure, unfathomable and intense. He spoke in riddles, swinging erratically from one subject to another, one moment earnestly debating the cosmic role in Armageddon and the next pontificating about the pros and cons of a good rough-puff pastry.

He became highly excitable when he heard that I, too, was a cook and we spent a high-spirited time comparing culinary notes. Later, out somewhere near the llamas under a thin sliver of silver moon, Sam became a bit fresh and tried to introduce me to his *coq* (*au vin.*)

It was time to make a move. As I did so, I bumped into Carmelita, a juggler from Massachusetts, who had once set up a juggling workshop for some of Boston's inner city children. She said it helped them to focus their attention away from the life of violent crime and armed street gangs.

Carmelita was a vivacious half-hippie, half-entrepreneur. She invited me into her customized chocolate-brown camper van which she had recently driven across America with her boyfriend, John. The most arresting feature of this van was the wood-burning stove fitted behind the driver's seat, with a chimney leading out of the roof.

'Man, is it manic,' said Carmelita. 'I would cook breakfast as John was drivin'.'

Perplexed, I asked, 'Weren't you afraid of going up in flames?'

'Why, no,' she said, 'it were safe as hell – only had one slight incident when cruisin' 'cross Texas. I was tossin' pancakes at the time when the cops came up behind and pulled us over – said did we know we had smoke comin' out the roof!'

I rode southwards down the coast through an expansive and dramatically desolate lava desert. In places, people had written their names or formed messages of love with brilliant white coral rocks on the black lava:

ALOHA MOM AND DAD LOVE JADE

MARRY ME PEGGY? PASSIONATELY DAN X

Off to my left, Mauna Kea reared its sun-streaked hulk high into the sky. Above its coronet of clouds, the atmosphere atop this monolithic mountain is the purest and most rarefied in the world and the summit is so clear of pollutants that an internationally manned astronomical observatory complex has based itself there, providing data to scientists all over the world.

*

Hitting the Gold Coast of Kona, I was soon into the heavy-duty tourist town of Kailua-Kona – miles of concrete condos and sumptuous hotels. I rode along the front to the church of Mokuaikaua ('The Trees Are Felled, Now Let Us Eat'), the walls of which were fashioned from massive, rough-hewn lava stone plastered together with a mortar of crushed and burned coral bound with koa-wood oil.

I was about to set off up the hill to Captain Cook when I was set upon by Esther, an Israeli, and her husband Digby, a freelance photographer from 'Noo Yawk'. They were a flamboyantly comical couple in their late fifties, one little and the other large, and both sporting shorts that were totally the wrong dimensions for their opposite physiques. Digby's were so big and baggy that he could quite easily have accommodated a friend or two: they flapped forlornly like a ship's sails around his pallid, knobbly knee caps and were hoisted so high up his spindly trunk that they almost impeded his vision.

Esther's shorts almost defied description. They were skimpy and tight enough to threaten more than her circulation. In fact, judging from her body's two-toned coloration, she had cut that off long ago: anything below her waist had the pasty appearance of having died, while the blood in her upper region was pumping and pulsating so furiously beneath her puckered, puce skin that the prospect of internal combustion looked a distinct possibility. I felt she was living on borrowed time.

Esther and Digby let it be known that they wished to take a photograph of me for some 'sporty magazine'. Would I mind? Thinking this would entail a quick snapshot, I readily obliged, little knowing what a farcical palaver was about to take place.

Digby was intent on photographing me on my bike on the beach with 'the traa-pical backdrop of a palm tree as company'. To reach the beach entailed the tricky operation of lowering my heavily laden mount down a ten-foot stone wall. I said it would be much easier if I removed my bags first but Digby wouldn't hear of it, mumbling something about 'good exercise for the old muscles'. Who was I to argue? Under Esther's orders, I jumped down to the beach so that they could lower my bike down to me. Simple as that – but in reality things are never as simple as that. Neither Digby nor Esther had ever handled a fully laden bike before and fully laden bikes don't handle like you think bikes should.

For one thing, the weight takes you unawares. Esther enthusiastically presumed she could simply carry out our choreographed manoeuvre single-handedly. This was to be her downfall in more ways than one. With a 'let-me-handle-this-Digby' look, she gripped the top tube and hoisted my bike all of a good 2cm off the ground. Realizing she was lifting the equivalent of a small car, she staggered with a pained expression on her face before dropping the bike on her toes.

Fortunately for my bike, it fell inwards; but unfortunately for Esther, she stumbled, entangled a flip-flopped foot in the rear wheel spokes and tumbled partly over the wall, threatening to crush the life out of me. She was suspended upside-down in a rather spectacular nose-dive, with flimsy Digby clinging to one of his wife's mighty flailing feet for all he was worth. Somehow I resisted the urge to grab the camera and take a fetching centre-spread picture for their 'sporty magazine'. Instead I scuttled back up the wall, hastily rounded up a small task force of bemused passers-by and together we sweated and strained and hauled elephantine Esther back upright again.

I thought Operation Tropical Desert Storm would be aborted there but, oh no – having regained composure, the formidable Esther and Digby weren't that easily defeated. I was directed back to my former front-line position while they rehearsed stringent elevation manoeuvres. My visibly worried Starcraft was clasped by clammy hands fore and aft.

'Okay, Esther sweetheart,' commanded Colonel Digby, 'let's try lifting to practise . . . now, take it easy . . . that's great, real nice and slow . . . remember to bend those knees . . . swell . . . Okay . . . so on three. One . . . two . . . threeeeeeeeerrrgheeee!'

By now quite a sizeable crowd had gathered to watch this unusual seaside spectacle.

'Okay, Esther sweetheart. You ready, honey? I think we've got the feel for it so the next lift – let's go for it. Deep

breath . . . brace yourself . . . one . . . two . . . and . . . three-
eeeeee.'

My bike finally made it down to the beach, swiftly followed
by Esther, whose forceful landing virtually triggered off a
series of major earth tremors.

Digby extricated photographic paraphernalia from his
bags while Esther commandeered the light-reflecting
department. Three hours later, the deed was done. I
wheeled my bike back up to the road through something
which had escaped our notice on the downward journey – a
gap in the wall – and cycled off up the hill with thoughts of
bemused disbelief in my head and a New York address in my
pocket.

At Captain Cook I booked into the 70-year-old Manago
Hotel where Dwight Manago, the manager, gave me a big,
airy room for $15. Although the bed looked as though a
beached whale had been the last occupant, it was a lovely
room – old creaking floor boards smelling of polish, and
three walls of windows. Stretched out in the distance 2,000
feet below, past the higgledy-piggledy roofs of colourful corrugated iron and the thick jungle-gardens, lay the wide,
sweeping Pacific, drawing down the melting fire-ball of the
sinking evening sun.

I swept down the magnificent mountain switchback past the
famous Kona coffee plantations (the only commercially
grown coffee in America) to the lavatorial-sounding village of
Napoopoo ('Holes'). Here by the sea, beneath a palm tree
and sitting on a rock in the lotus position, was a woman from
Alaska. She had been living for a year up the mountain in
Kainaliu ('Bail the Bilge'), working as a landscape gardener,
and was about to fly back to Anchorage to sell off possessions
still in a small flat there.

'Don't you miss Alaska,' I asked her, 'the snow, the emptiness, the bigness, the bears?'

'I've never felt so happy, so free, so in control of myself as
here,' she replied. 'Sure I miss my folks, but there's no way I
could live up there again – it's full of guys out of their heads,
massive depressants, drunks. You know what? In one year I
knew six people who committed suicide, one of which was my
brother. You think I miss that?'

With spirits momentarily lowered, I wandered off down
the road to Kealakekua ('Road of the God') Bay where more
death-thoughts awaited me. It was here, on February 4th,
1778, that the great sea-girdling explorer Captain James Cook
was bludgeoned to death by natives after terrible cultural
misunderstandings.

In short, the Hawaiians had mistaken Captain Cook for
Lono, the fertility god of the earth, believing that the billowing white sails of Cook's ships (*HMS Discovery* and *Revolution*)
were Lono's sacred, floating tapa-sheeted *heiau* (temple).
Encounters were overwhelmingly friendly for a while. Natives
throughout the land came to worship the very ground where
Cook stood, reverently prostrating themselves in front of
their returned 'god'. For over a month, they readily replen-
ished the ships' stocks with provisions, stretching their own
supplies to the limit. But during this time one of Cook's sea-
men died, proving to the by now suspicious Hawaiians that
these white newcomers were indeed mortals and not gods.

Things turned sour when some locals stole a small boat.
Cook, together with nine armed sailors, went ashore with the
plan of luring their king, Kalaniopuu, back to the ship where
he would be held ransom in return for the stolen cutter. A
skirmish broke out, a few shots were fired, clubs were wielded
and Lieutenant Philips lay wounded. Cook and his remaining
mates were overpowered by sheer numbers (an estimated
crowd of 20,000 angry warriors) and they retreated into the
sea to make for their offshore ships.

The problem for Captain Cook, the greatest seaman ever
to ply the Pacific, was that he couldn't swim. While his companions literally swam for their lives, Cook was left to face a
humiliating end. A forlorn figure standing knee-deep in

water, he was soon hit on the head and that was that: the stalwart sailor keeled over and died.

I sat for a long time on a rock trailing my legs in the warm, clear sea while reading and trying to imagine that scene of confusion and the thoughts that must have flashed through Cook's mind when he realized that the sea, once his friend, had gone and done the dirty on him – thoughts like how he wished he had listened to his mother and tried for his 20-metre doggy-paddle certificate before venturing across miles of unpredictable open ocean.

I was reading Mark Twain's *Letters From Hawaii* and was astonished to note that, when Captain Cook and his men came ashore on Hawaii for the first time, 'no one in the party had had any movements of his bowels for eighteen days, several not for twenty-five or thirty, one not for thirty-seven, and one not for forty-four days.'

I continued reading and losing myself in unproductive reverie while dreamily dangling my legs in the sea until a local in a loin cloth, and not a lot besides, kindly informed me that if I valued my limbs he would advise me to lift them clear out of the sea because of the sharks that come into the bay during the evening to feed. Losing no time, I shot from the rock back into the saddle.

I rolled on. Pinned to a tree beside Bong Brothers grocery store was a notice that took a bit of digesting:

WANTED

77 people. We will pay *you* to eat anything *you* want & lose 10–29 lbs THIS month.

Certainly food for thought, I thought. I wondered if it had anything to do with Project LEAN (Low-fat Eating for America Now). It was impossible to travel in Hawaii and not be aware of this campaign, which was hitting the state by storm with advertising on TV, radio, in papers and restaurants and free supermarket handouts and even on the packaging of fatty foods. Once in Sure Save I picked up a tub of chocolate chip ice-cream on which was written: 'Put me back you fat bastard and watch that waistline.' Or words to that effect.

But such vigorous campaigning didn't seem to be having much impact on its Chubby Checker citizens. People resembling inflated burgers still waddled around in their sea of cellulite, hungrily engulfing an inexhaustible supply of pure-grease take-aways. As if to emphasize the tragic problem of obesity, I spotted a front-page headline in America's version of the *Sun*:

340lb GIRL SITS ON MOM AND KILLS HER

But she was a mere featherweight compared to a woman I read about in the *Evening Standard* a few months later:

WOMAN LOSES 900lb

A woman who once claimed to be the world's fattest has set a new record. Rosealie Bradford, of Pennsylvania, now 150lb, has lost more weight than any other woman, 900lb. She credited a diet programme by US exercise guru Richard Simmons but said that she began by simply clapping her hands. 'That might not sound much to you but it was a major feat for me,' she said. 'My heart rate was elevated just from doing that.'

At her peak weight of 75 stone she had been confined to bed for 12 years and lorry scales were needed to estimate her weight.

Her next goal is to write her own diet book.

I sallied forth through the world's largest macadamia nut farm before going for a swim in a lava field. And very odd it was too. Keeping to Màmalahoa Highway, I had entered an area that was marked on my map like wire mesh. It was called Hawaiian Ocean View Estates but in reality it was one big solidified lava flow criss-crossed with an endless assortment of dirt roads on which an occasional house stood looking lost and forlorn in the curiously hostile landscape.

I was perplexed to learn that the lava land of Ocean View Estates was being sold as fast as hot cakes. How could anybody want to build a house in an area that resembled the aftermath of a nuclear holocaust – a black, lumpy lavascape where nothing grew and where no water ran? What possessed people to live in such an eerie wilderness?

I wanted to know and so I stopped at the only gas station beside the only grocery store, a brand new construction which looked as though it had just reared its ugly head from the depths of the earth to surface upon a sea of choppy, petrified lava.

Martie-Jean ran the gas station and, as chance would have it, she also ran the only bed and breakfast in this whole expansive lunar land. Fancying the idea of laying my weary head to rest on a lava flow, I expressed murmurings of interest. Martie-Jean handed me her card:

BOUGANVILLE BED & BREAKFAST

Learn the secrets of Hawaii and share the friendly, healing atmosphere of owners Don and Martie-Jean.

Breakfasts to remember!

'Good morning,' I could hear them say, 'do help yourself to a bowl of Crunchy Crushed Volcanic Rock 'n' Raisins. How do you like your free-range lavas – scrambled, fried, boiled, sunnyside up or rocky-bottom down?'

Printed on the bottom of the card was:

CTC Air/Car/Room Arrangements – all islands,
'Your home to our home'.

To me CTC meant only one thing: Cyclists' Touring Club. The thought of having chanced upon a B & B in the back of beyond run by a CTC couple momentarily struck me as supremely exciting. But I should have known better: never count your chickens before the horse has bolted. In Hawaii, where cyclists are about as rare as the *nene* goose, CTC stood for Certified Travel Consultant. Not quite what I had in mind.

Nonetheless, I followed Martie-Jean's directions to her Bouganville Bed & Breakfast. It was an optimistic name, I thought: the nearest bougainvillaea (or, for that matter, living plant) was at least 40 miles up the road. A more apt and realistic name might have been Bowels of the Earth Bed & Breakfast – but I suppose that doesn't have quite the same ring to it.

The house looked as if it had just been beamed from space, falling from the skies to land at random in the middle of a lava field. A Martian would probably have felt quite at home but for a human it was as good as finding yourself on an alien planet.

The building perched precariously on top of sharp laval rocks. Around it was a wooden veranda, patrolled by fierce-fanged guard dogs. The view from my window was of lava and more lava; apart from a moth-eaten plant that had been potted in earth imported from more fertile climes, there was nothing photosynthesizing within sight. All was black and rocky and deathly quiet, with neither the hum of traffic nor chirping country sounds. There was only a strong, moaning wind.

Behind the house lay a small swimming pool sunk into the lava. After hoiking out the crusty forms of at least 20 drowned cockroaches (the only living species that appeared to thrive here) I swam around the circular pool until I felt dizzy. Then I swam around the other way to undo my dizziness and ended up feeling even dizzier. As I bobbed around on the surface, looking out on the rocky lava outcrop which surrounded me, I thought: What an odd place to be having a swim.

Later that evening Martie-Jean and her husband Don invited me into their living room for a cup of tea and a potful of macadamia nuts. They were both from Seattle but Don's job as a ski-lift installer had brought them to Hawaii. Skiing doesn't spring to mind as being big business on a tropical isle – indeed it isn't big business but it is still business. Between December and May you can leave the surf and sand behind and an hour or two later be skimming down the snowy slopes of Mauna Kea.

When I bid Martie-Jean and Don goodnight, they replied, 'Sleep loose!' – presumably the laid-back version of 'sleep tight'. I returned to my quarters where, with toothbrush in mouth, I heard on the radio that a child molester in Texas had agreed to undergo castration.

All night the wind whipped across the barren volcanic expanse and clawed at the windows like a man trying to get in.

By mid-morning I had reached fertile lands again; fields and trees and cascading bushes of violet-flowered jacaranda and wild clumps of orchids and lilies that crowded the side of the road.

Everything suddenly seemed so green – even the sandy beaches. This was no optical illusion: the sand really was green. In the past, ancient lava flows frequently broke open veins of olivine, a clear green semi-precious mineral. In the case of the green beach, a whole undercone of olivine had collapsed into a small bay, where it had been weathered to sand.

Apart from a couple of local fishermen, there was nothing around – no people, no vehicles, no houses, no tourist booths, no tourists; only the rocks, the sea and the green sand beach. I was pleasantly surprised that Hawaii's tourist industry had not cashed in on this natural phenomenon by filling test-tubes with the sand and selling them to credulous tourists, as the English do at tantalizing Alum Bay on the Isle of Wight.

Feeling professorial I decided to take my own sample (as it were) and stooped to fill an empty film canister with the olivine mineral. I was so intrigued with the oddities of this land and particularly with this unusual sand that I stuck some in my diary and on the back of every postcard I wrote during the next two weeks. I still have half a canister to this day which I have contemplated putting into a glass tube and selling for an astronomical price. Any takers?

I stood at Ka Lae ('South Point'), the southernmost point in the United States, and was filled with that inexplicable feeling of satisfaction which comes from having reached an extremity of land, whether it be the highest, the lowest, the westernmost or the whatever-most. No one is impressed but yourself, which adds to the pointless thrill of it all.

With a complacent air and a smug smirk, I surveyed the mighty Pacific and considered the fact that the closest continental landfall was almighty Antartica, some 7,500 miles (or half a year's cycle ride) to the south.

On the dead-end road down to South Point I had passed the strangely impressive Kamoa Wind Farm, where 37 massive white windmills beat their blades against the cloud-scudding sky. Cycling back past the farm, I stopped for closer inspection.

A sign on the gate said 'Private – No Trespassing' and another informed me that the Kamoa Wind Farm was non-polluting and helped to decrease the Big Island's dependence on oil to produce electricity. It said its 37 generators could produce '18,000,000 kw of electricity per year – enough to take care of the electrical needs of 3,000 families'. I'm not too hot on my kilowatts but 18 million sounded suitably impressive.

There was no one else around. As I was debating whether to trespass for a closer look, a white pick-up truck pulled up and out jumped pure Hawaiian-blooded Roy.

'Hi there!' he said. 'I'm the chief technician. Like a look around?'

Roy took me inside one of the towering 85-foot windmills, made in Japan by Mitsubishi. The workings were a far cry from the nostalgic old wooden ones of Holland, which basically operate if there is wind and don't if there isn't. Roy unlocked the doors to a computerized box full of buttons and switches, flashing lights and digital screens. He flicked and beeped and tapped away at this control panel in order to shut down the power. All fell silent.

Back outside in the hot, dazzling sun Roy told me that he had recently called the police to evict a bunch of hippies who persisted in climbing over the fence to sit in a yoga-like, spaced-out trance at the foot of the whirring machines. With plenty of Maui Wowie at hand, they swore that they could hear the windmills talking to them.

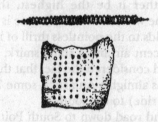

I toiled slowly upwards as I climbed a flank of active Mauna Loa ('Long Mountain') which, at 60 miles long and 30 miles wide, is the most massive volcanic mountain on earth in terms of cubic capacity. I had joined the Hawaiian Belt Road and pedalled past petroglyphs, more tasty macadamia nut orchards and something that my map described as '1790 footprints in ash'.

In the small jungle village of Volcano, I stopped and pulled out a well crumpled piece of paper which I had picked up in Hilo. On it were some faded photocopied directions to the 'Holo In', a 'Basic No Frill Accommodation' run by a Japanese electrician called Satoshi Yabuki.

I found the hostel without any trouble down a series of narrow, overgrown back roads, but problems arose when I pulled into the front yard: I was greeted by a hostile gaggle of free-range guard geese. With long, outstretched necks, they doggedly pursued me at terrifying speed around the 'In'. It was impossible to get near the door as it was persistently patrolled by one particularly unpleasant specimen which hissed and spat and launched into vicious attack if I overstepped my mark into its ten-foot guard zone. At one stage, while I was in hasty retreat, it took me unawares and ruthlessly plunged its beak into my lower left 'cheek', clinging on painfully. I was in this humiliating position of having a bill up my bottom when the door burst open and a woman appeared.

'Hi there,' she said breezily, 'the geese aren't giving you any trouble, are they?'

With a grimace and my eyes watering, I said, 'Ooooohouuuuch, hello. No, they're fine.'

The woman called the offending goose to heel. It finally unleashed my rear-end from its vice-like beak and scuttled obediently to its owner.

Apart from three geologists (an Italian and two Americans), I was the only one staying at the hostel and had a room to myself. The woman who had saved my behind from ending up as foie gras was Susan, Satoshi's girlfriend, who taught English down in Hilo.

That evening some friends of theirs came round for supper, Japanese Yoko and American John. He said, 'I know what you're thinking but don't say it,' before I did. Which I didn't. I was invited to join them and we all sat down to chunks of raw tuna dunked in a dip, a starchy soup, tofu with soy sauce, ginger and horseradish, rice and green tea. Later the geologists arrived on the scene and the Italian kept trying to cajole me into going on a nocturnal hike with him to Puu O'o vent where we could sleep (more likely expire) beside a live lava flow.

The next morning I cycled into the drive-in volcano of Kilauea, home of the fire goddess Pele. Over the past thousand years residents of the island have tried to appease her fiery temperament by sacrificing berries, animals or men, or by appealing to her more recent tastes with bottles of gin.

Visitors are warned not to remove rocks off Kilauea for souvenirs because of Pele's revengeful nature – anyone who chips lava samples from the sacred site will be cursed by the tempestuous fire goddess. It is said that the authorities came up with this idea to preserve the natural rock, but many a tourist, having scoffed at the superstition, seemingly pays the price: every year scores of packages containing lumps of lava are sent back to the National Parks Service with notes imploring the officials to return the rocks to Pele because the senders have suffered bouts of bad luck.

It seemed that bad luck could strike even before Pele's victims had set foot on the volcano. The day before I arrived at the crater, a judge's daughter from Colorado had been boiled alive like a lobster when she slipped and fell into a fuming, steam-vented fumarole. She must have been planning to export a whole lorry-load of lava for a death like that.

Down in the district of Puna, I was hoping to camp for a few days on the beach while I explored local villages which had been completely engulfed by recent lava flows. But I was put off when I realized that this was where a girl had been knocked off her bike, raped and brutally murdered two months ago. No one had yet been caught. On top of this, a local policeman told me that the highest proportion of people out of prison on parole lived in Puna.

'The place is full of crazy Vietnam Vets, too,' he said, 'so go easy out there.'

I read later that in the jungles of Hawaii (which are almost identical to those in South East Asia) live 350–400 Vietnam veterans ('Bush Vets') – enough to make a small army. 'Saigon John', living in a makeshift tree house, is heavily armed and not to be messed with. Nearly 30 years on, he is still living his Rambo war. In the past, those who came out to get help were told by doctors that there was nothing wrong with them and they were given drugs instead of psychological help.

Playing safe, I checked into the Village Inn in Pahoa where Bill, the owner, gave me a room called Robert Louis Stevenson for half price. Built in 1910, it was an attractive old (ancient by American standards) wooden building with creaking open gangways overlooking an inner courtyard filled with flowers and an abundance of tumbling Japanese creepers. A sign on the wall of my room said:

PLEASE *DO NOT* STEAL THE LINENS AS IT WILL BE A DETRIMENT TO OTHER GUESTS

Living in a room a few doors down from me was Ed and his pregnant wife, Kathy, from Tucson, Arizona. Ed was on the Big Island for a few months' training for the mighty Ironman, an impossible race, starting from Kamakahonu ('Eye of the Turtle') Beach, which involves a 2-mile ocean swim, a 100-mile cycle and running a marathon. As if that isn't exhausting enough Hawaii also stages a biennial Ultrathon – two Ironmans rolled into one, which involves over three days of continuous racing.

Also living at the Village Inn was Richard, a fireman and ex-lifeguard who had known the murdered girl well for over 20 years. When I told him I was heading for a day's cycle along the coast, he wouldn't let me go unless he came too as my bodyguard. I was touched by his concern but how did I know he was not an unsavoury character behind a false front? Maybe he would do the dirty on me out in the middle of nowhere. I spent a day sizing him up, chatting to Bill and Ed and Kathy and some of the locals who had known him for months, and in some cases years, after which I decided he was a pretty safe bet.

Ed and Kathy said they would drive round and meet us

halfway and off we went. Although my map had been published recently, it was already out of date. The town of Kalapana was still present in print but in reality it had been completely destroyed by a monster tongue of black lava that had spewed down the hillside, engulfing more than 200 homes before crossing and entirely blocking the coastal road and spilling into the sea. Where a few months before there had been a beautiful black sand beach with happy people swimming and surfing and Richard lifeguarding, there was now a solidified mass of blackness.

We climbed on to the lava and walked around for a while. Richard said, 'Somewhere under our feet is my best buddy's house.' We clambered on and then he said, 'Where we're standing now used to be sea – some of the best surf along the coast.'

Down on the other side of the road was a small cafe which had narrowly missed being swallowed by the lava flow. It used to have a thriving trade from the locals, the surfers and the tourists but now it was closed down and eerily empty. A lonely breakfast menu in the window bore witness to its former life.

Further along the coast, Richard showed me the spot where the 23-year-old girl had been followed by two men in a pick-up truck. They waited for their moment before deliberately driving into her, knocking her off the bike. Then they threw her injured body into the back of the truck and drove to some isolated woods, where she was raped, beaten and left for dead, covered with rocks. By chance, a woman walking in the area heard her moaning and alerted the emergency services. Because of a mix-up over the location, they went the wrong way and ruined her faint chance of survival – they found her eventually but she died a few hours later in hospital. Richard had known her since she was a toddler.

That night, back in Pahoa, I switched on Sky News and was startled to recognize the face looking back at me. It was my local London fishmonger being interviewed because an IRA bomb had just exploded outside his Soho shop. It felt odd to be sitting in the middle of the Pacific, having seen no one I knew for months, and suddenly seeing a familiar face in familiar surroundings – a place that meant home.

Then I watched cocksure Neil Kinnock being interviewed prior to the General Election and saw John Major stunned by an airborne egg attack.

The night that followed was not a peaceful one. Pahoa lived up to its name as a wild-west town. It was all action outside my window and I watched the movie unfurl with my nose pressed to the pane. A loud rumpus emerged from the bar across the road and then, just like the westerns, a man was punched through the saloon doors and lay sprawled and grovelling on the dusty road. A fight erupted between a few more bar-dwellers resulting in a man being stabbed by a Filipino. Then a gang of meaty, murderous Hells Angels arrived, roaring into town on their growling Harley Davidsons to add to the fun in the bar.

A woman in the car park below, evidently far from sober, crawled into her station wagon and started ramming back and forth, bumper-car fashion, into any vehicle in her way amid shrieks of demented laughter. When she finally tired of that game, she accelerated away and crashed with force into the front of the post office.

At last peace, of sorts, prevailed. Flaking out on my Robert Louis Stevenson bed, I drifted into eventful dreams but my rest was short-lived. An hour later I had a hairy moment when a hirsute intruder attempted to suffocate me in my sleep by smothering a furry cushion over my face. At least, that is what happened in my dream. In reality, some stray moggie had leapt through the window and pounced on my head.

Outside there were more nocturnal activities down in the parking lot. It was no night to be a car: one moment they were being rammed and ruined by an out-of-control station wagon and the next a woman called Betty was enthusiastically smashing car windows with her handbag, screaming in colourful language that Captain Hook was out to kill her.

And so the night passed.

❀

Back in Oahu, I landed at Honolulu to the British news that
the Labour party and the Tories were neck and neck and
that a hung parliament looked likely. The *Honolulu Advertiser*
was more interested in who else was up for the running, with
its eye-catching headline:

BRITONS CAMPAIGN ON MARS, RAIL
PLATFORMS

A 'lord' in a tiger-print suit and top hat, a portly brothel-keeper and 300 low-flying followers of a maharishi are making wild pitches for votes in Britain's national election.

Eighty-four parties are putting up 2,903 candidates in 651 constituencies in today's vote.

There is the Forward to Mars Party, campaigning to put a Briton on the red planet; the unashamedly hedonist Funstermentalists and the Up the Creek Have a Party; and the Justice from British Rail Party, fighting for prompt train services.

. . . 'All those on that No. 11 bus, vote for the loonies,' Sutch and his yellow-and-green-clad followers in the Official Monster Raving Loony Party bellowed through megaphones. Later, he appeared on an Australian talk show, sharing a hospitality van with brothel-keeper Lindi St. Clair, alias Miss Whiplash, who heads the Corrective Party and campaigns for legalized prostitution.

. . . . The Leighton Buzzard based Natural Law Party, an offshoot of the World Government of the Age of Enlightenment founded by Maharishi Mahesh Yogi, modestly promises 'a disease-free, crime-free, problem-free country that will move towards heaven on Earth'. George Harrison gave a concert for the party. 'I don't really know what they stand for,' former Beatles' drummer Ringo Starr told reporters Monday. 'I saw George this morning and he wasn't really sure what they stood for either. But he didn't like what the others stood for.'

And I thought: What a wonderfully cocked-up country.

*

The day before I flew back to Los Angeles, I sold my bike – not back to the bike shop, as I had planned, but to Leylá Zeyrek, an effervescent Turkish girl who worked at the Interclub hostel. Leylá wanted my bike badly; I wanted a ticket to Los Angeles, and who was I to refuse when ready cash was waved in my face? She offered me just $7 less than I had paid originally – not a bad loss for two months of solid use. The sale done, I footed it down Ala Wai Canal from the hostel to 'Cheap Tickets' travel agency in buoyant mood and I ate my last Hawaiian banana to celebrate.

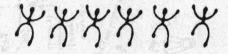

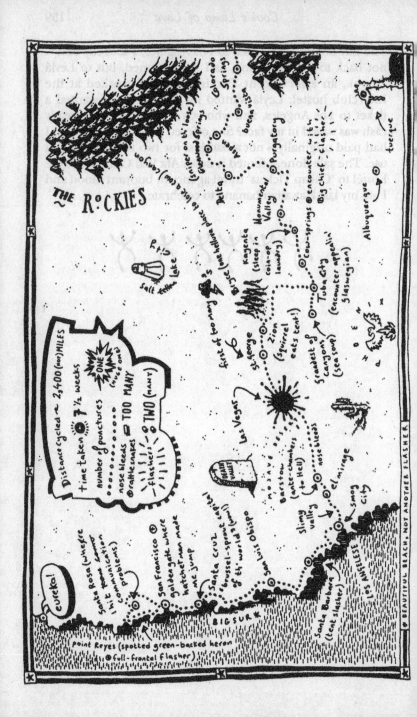

12

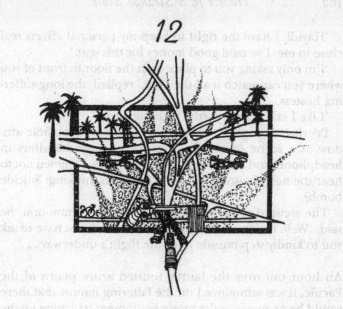

The Angels are Burning!

Overflowing in the seat beside me on the flight to Los Angeles sat a wide, disconsolate-looking woman dressed in a *muumuu* – a garment like a nightdress, introduced by the missionaries to cover up the 'shocking' nakedness of the Hawaiian women. She caused a bit of a stir when she refused to remove her handbag from her lap prior to take-off.

'Why, no!' she said, clutching the bag firmly to her voluminous midriff. 'You ain't getting me puttin' my purse on the ground.'

'It's for your own safety,' said the Hawaiian hostess, whose raven-headed mane of hair was sprouting two plumeria flowers.

'Hayull, I have the right to keep my personal effects real close to me. I've paid good money for this seat.'

'I'm only asking you to place it on the floor in front of you where you can watch it all the time,' replied the long-suffering hostess.

'Like I said, I ain't partin' with my purse.'

Peering through the clawed perspex of my peep-hole window at a scene of middle-distance baggage handlers in headphones and a runway that ran to the sea, I feigned not to hear the neighbouring skirmish. But I was thinking: Suicide bomb?

The steward arrived. Finding a brewing commotion, he said, 'Well, ma'am, if you fail to comply we'll just have to ask you to kindly step outside once the flight's underway . . .'

An hour out over the faintly tousled azure plains of the Pacific, it was announced on the faltering tannoy that there would be no movie as the movie equipment had gone up the creek, and a tinny apology was made for the silence in our head-sets because the sound system had also broken. I sincerely hoped the engines were made of sturdier stuff.

'. . . but we will be providing our own form of on-board entertainment, as Shirleen here has volunteered to sing and dance for you. Haven't you, Shirl?'

Evidently this was news to hostess Shirl: there was a squeal of protest somewhere mid-cabin amid much stifled sniggering. This was becoming a very odd flight.

The sing-song never materialized but a spontaneous trivia quiz did in which passengers were asked such brain-taxing questions as:

1. What is the wing span of this aircraft?
2. What is the total combined age of the flight crew?
3. What is the most frequently asked question from boarding passengers?*

* Answer: 'What's for dinner?' followed closely by, 'What's the movie?'

4. How many passengers look around them and think: I might die with these people?

(Actually, I just made up that last one. But I'm sure lots of people do.)

The tannoy said: 'Answers should be scribbled on a small piece of folded paper and they will be collected in half an hour and the winner gets to land the plane. Only joking . . . the winner gets a free drink as long as they're over eighteen.'

Surprisingly, there was plenty of audience participation and a jovial air prevailed. Even the purse-clasping *muumuu* beside me issued a watery smile.

When we touched down in LAX, the plane taxied and then stopped in the middle of nowhere in particular. Still in fairly festive mood, we all trundled down the steps in the dark and boarded a concertinaed airport bus that transported us everywhere apart from where we wanted to go. As the driver grappled with a racketing-static walkie-talkie, it was obvious he was having a spot of difficulty in locating our terminal.

A flowery-shorted passenger with mottled turkey legs and ebbing patience remarked, 'Jeez! I've had enough bus tours in Hawaii to last me a lifetime – I don't need another!'

'Well, it ain't my goddam fault!' hollered the driver, adding *sotto voce* out the side of his mouth, 'it's this fuckin' goddam lousy good-for-nothin' radio!'

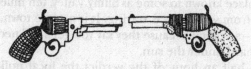

Los Angeles was burning. I was serving chocolate mousse at the time back at the Bartlett Base Camp. The dinner party was interrupted by the querulous shrill of the telephone. It was Lee, Kermit's son, who broke the news that riots were running riot downtown.

'Turn on the TV,' he said.

In Moorpark, all remained calm. Dinner party chatter continued unaffected by downtown happenings and I continued to dollop out rich spoonfuls of chocolate mousse.

Lee rang back. He was standing outside his house and could see South Central LA on fire. Rioters had taken the city by storm. This time we acted. Anxiously, we climbed the thickly white-carpeted stairs to the bedroom and turned on the TV. Everyone gasped. Everyone was shocked. Every channel looked the same – flames covered the screen.

The violence had begun within hours of the jury verdict acquitting four white police officers caught beating Rodney King, a black motorist, on 81 seconds of amateur video film. The footage showed 56 blows delivered with hard wood batons as he writhed on the ground in the chilling glare of the squad car's headlights. One officer was seen rushing to kick him in the head. King received nearly a dozen fractures and later told investigators:

'The first blow was enough to make me feel my jawbone move. My face got rearranged.'

Computer messages and audio tapes recorded the officers involved laughing and boasting about the thrashing they had given King. Police officer Powell, a particularly nasty piece of work, was heard to taunt him by saying, 'We had a pretty good hard-ball game tonight. You lost, we won.' His computer message said, 'I haven't beaten anyone this bad in a long time.'

Rodney King's trial took place in Simi (pronounced *See-me*) Valley, a place known to some as Slimy Valley, ten miles down the road from where I was staying. It is a white town, full of rednecks – so called because they say you get a red neck from working hard under the sun.

Within half an hour of the verdict the local police had posted units on each of the four roads leading into the valley and warned everyone to stay indoors. People panicked. Simi Valley had over 10,000 known gun owners, and 500,000 rounds of ammunition had been sold in one gun shop alone in the four hours that immediately followed the verdict. As a result, the city ironically had more protection from its gun-toting citizens than from the police and the sheriff's department.

But Simi Valley remained relatively calm. It was South Central Los Angeles, epicentre of the riots, that erupted into a war zone. The nation and the world were shocked and rocked by scenes that made London's recent poll tax riots look like a tea party. The protests sparked off racial anarchy far worse than even the notorious Watts riots nearly three decades before. People went wild. Arsonists raged through the city, burning businesses and homes and looting and shooting their neighbours.

The police lost control from the start and watched helplessly as swarms of people stormed supermarkets and superstores and liquor stores, going on what the media called 'looting free-for-alls'. Hungry hands grabbed anything they could get. And it wasn't just individuals. Whole families were swept along with the fiery flow and could be seen laughing and larking around as they casually loaded looted booty into their cars and pick-ups – televisions and videos, liquor and lamps, beds and rugs, suits and T-shirts and tools. It was a fun day out shopping with the kids, with the only requirement that the wallet be left at home.

It felt strange to be sitting in the suburbs watching television scenes of total anarchy that were taking place just down the road – like watching *Miami Vice* and *Thunderball* and *Terminator* all rolled into one, only for real. The statistics were devastating. In all, 5,383 fires ate through the city; 55 people died and nearly 2,500 were injured, many of them critically and many of them police and firefighters who were shot or attacked with knives and axes.

Helicopters clacketed over the burning city through growing clouds of thick, black-billowing smoke, filming the flames and the live, rubber-burning car chases, the shell-shocked cops and Korean community shoot-outs, the innocent truck-drivers set upon by murderous gangs and beaten to head-smashed pulps with bricks and boots, the 'do-gooders' with their trickling garden hoses trying to tackle raging infernos as overstretched and undermanned firefighters fought a losing battle elsewhere. As I watched, half of me wanted to walk straight through that violent TV screen scene and be there in that Hollywood movie, proving to my disbelieving eyes that what I saw was fact not fiction. When the camera panned in on a bike shop being broken into and excited youngsters riding away on $2,000 Marins and shining Schwinns, I admit to thinking momentarily that maybe I *was* missing out on something here . . .

Everyone had something different to say. 'Revolution is the hope of the hopeless'; 'It's right to rebel'; 'Look what you create'; 'Fuck Police', ran some of the more printable graffiti I saw scrawled on walls and gutted buildings when I took to the streets with Kermit a few days later. As I stood around the stench-smouldering ruins of a shopping centre where the charred steel girders lay and hung in twisted and tortured shapes, a harrowed and hollow-eyed black man shuffled past me wearing a T-shirt with LOVE KNOWS NO COLOUR across the front.

'I sure am pleased that things have calmed down, and I think our actions helped,' said President Bush, somewhat shallowly.

Governor Bill Clinton had a different thought: 'We must not stay on the road we are on. We must not permit this country to drift apart further by race and income.'

I had not realized that America had such a huge racial chasm. It is a country where blacks have a three times greater chance than whites of dying from a policeman's bullet, a country full of black ghettos where frustration, shame, rage and despair are fuelled by drugs and violence.

Today two out of three Americans think immigration is now detrimental for America. They don't agree that their taxes should go towards those whom they see as an ungrateful underclass. They dislike even more having to pay for the damage when that underclass rises up, as it does from time to time.

America can no longer peacefully assimilate all the immigrants who want to live there and blend them into one big, happy and multi-cultural nation. One of the most alarming crime developments to date is how black youths are now killing one another in a sort of self-inflicted genocide that reflects both bravado and hopeless despair.

Time magazine reported that 510,000 people 'escaped' from California in 1990–91 – an exodus which is still smaller than the continuing migration to California from other states of about 570,000 a year. Los Angeles, America's richest and most troubled city, has more Mexicans than any other city outside Mexico City, more Koreans than any other city outside Seoul and more Filipinos than any other city outside the Philippines. It is now contemplating teaching Spanish as a first language in schools instead of English.

Within the next couple of generations the white English-speaking American will be in a minority. And as I travelled through America I couldn't help hearing and reading about something else that was disappearing, albeit not quite as fast: the traditional family unit, and with it a quality that the politicians and preachers are forever inserting into their rhetoric. They call it 'family values'.

❦

The sound of rain woke me in the night but, in an area where there had been a drought for over six years, it was an artificial rain. Every night phantom sprinklers, elusively embedded in people's gardens and carpet-cropped lawns, fountained into action. This made me wonder how it was that in England, a country renown for its leaden-sky dampness, hose-pipe bans are imposed after what seems little more than a six-day dry spell, galvanizing squads of helicopters to swoop in for a snoop and catch pooh-poohing drought offenders hand-hosing their cars.

I lay awake in perplexed mood and then set about pondering my next plan of action. Should I cycle south to Mexico or north to Alaska? Did I want to see sombreros or bears, cactus or firs? Did I want to sweat or shiver? Like a spoilt child, I decided I wanted it *all*. I wanted to go everywhere at once.

The pipelined rain pattered on. A distant woo-wooing of a siren pierced through the night. I thought: Up or down?

North or south? Jet engines throttled back high overhead. Baron, the neighbour's brute of a pet, growled and barked below. His bark seemed to echo the spine-chilling howl of coyotes in distant hills.

The snarls reminded me of something I had read somewhere about noisy dogs: in the US dogs may not bark for more than two minutes every hour during daylight and not at all between 8pm and 8am – a sort of programmed pooch. Sadly this unlikely law didn't seem to be enforced in puppydawg lover's Moorpark. A French company at Crufts recently launched a special collar which, its makers claimed, stops dogs from barking by emitting a sweet-smelling perfume. It sounds too good to be true, but then I suppose a mute and smooching pooch is no use as a rowdy, mean-mooded guard dog.

The sun, a blurry disc of light, lay on the other side of a jaundiced blanket of cloud. The infamous smog of Los Angeles was so thick that I almost carved my way through it. 'Never trust air you can't see,' say the LA Smog Cops. The nauseous taste penetrated everything but then, in an area which is home to 25 million constantly used vehicles, an area where 1,246 tons of noxious gases are spewed into the atmosphere daily from over 3,000 businesses, what could I expect?

My eyes stung and the sweat poured, making my T-shirt stick thick and heavy across my back as I fought my way by bike through the urban mania of north Los Angeles. Cars as big as boats and as numerous as a nightmarish army of ants gunned through the maze of wild, wide streets. The drivers were all drug-crazed psychos, of that there was no doubt. They bulleted towards me from every angle, aggressive and determined. I needed eyes like a centipede does legs. I needed crystal-sharp reflexes. I needed a head that swivelled 360°. I needed an air-conditioned suit of armour and a sub-machine gun. I needed to be aggressive, too, which is not easy while perched on an open-to-everything bicycle in Los Angeles – a city designed on the assumption that everyone has a car. It was easy to see how cars were California's biggest industry. The streets were mean and hostile places where drivers glared at you with death threats in their eyes.

It was Sunday, a day when the chances of escaping alive from the mayhem of LA suburbia would be higher. Or so I thought. If it was like this on the 'day of rest', what was it like on the other six? Urban anarchy.

But being a Sunday meant that I wasn't entirely alone in negotiating the frenzied streets on a bicycle. In five hours of city riding I came across one other rider, passing on the other side of the street. A shimmering lycra-clad racer. He slalom-shot across the traffic and came alongside. Walter Jnr hailed from Houston, Texas, and had lived in Los Angeles for 20 years. In the back pocket of his cycling jersey, where most cyclists store a resuscitating Mars Bar or banana, Walter had a .45 semi-automatic.

'Sure, everybody gottem,' he said. 'Head out without a gun and you're in deep shit, man. Rely on the cops for protection and you're dead. It's each for his own out here, you know. I tell you – anybody try some goddam lousy trick on me and they'll end up the sorry ones. I wish you luck, kid; you're gonna need it.'

With that, he turned and swerved and was swallowed by the traffic.

I would never have made it out of Los Angeles had it not been for the expansive knowledge of Norty Stewart, a master route-planner who for 37 years has designed custom-made trips for people travelling throughout America on bicycles, motorbikes, horse-carts, chariots, covered wagons or on foot. Working out of the American Automobile Association club from its Los Angeles office he will, free of cost to members and charity organizations, plan and advise a route, avoiding all freeways where possible, and provide you with maps and

Bike Tiks (a series of strip maps) and lorry-loads of guide books.

Compact and bespectacled Norty was eager to help. All during the riots his office on Figueroa Street had been closed due to 'civil unrest', so the answering machine told me. I finally met him three days after the fires and lootings had subsided. Entering downtown had been a shock - the place looked bombed out and was virtually empty. Small huddles of blacks loitered uneasily on street corners, or beside charred remains of what only days before had been their local convenience store or gas station or home, looking disbelieving or angry or shell-shocked. A terrible feeling of tension and distrust hung heavily in the smouldering, putrid air. The National Guard patrolled the streets in jeeps and small armoured tanks with sleek, black, wicked-looking guns at the ready. One group patrolled outside McDonald's, as if they were guarding the welfare of their stomachs. But there was nothing cooking today. The burger bar was dead. The windows were smashed, a fire had partially eaten through the side wall and furious scrawls of graffiti covered another.

Everywhere smelt of recent war, as if a lull in fighting had come to town. It was how I imagined a war-torn city to feel – Beirut, Baghdad, Sarajevo. I had to remind myself that this was a 'civilized' American city. Just up the road from where I was standing spread the green oasis of Beverly Hills where, merely hours before, movie queens had looked down from their multi-dollar mansions towards Rodeo Drive to see flames inching towards them.

About 90 per cent of the 2,000 routes that Norty plans annually are for cyclists. His detailed map zig-zagged me north of the city, over and under thundering bumper-to-bumper freeways. Before I left he assured me, 'I've never lost anybody yet. Nor have any of my customers had a fatal accident.'

I said I was glad to hear it, sincerely hoping that I wasn't going to be the first to break his record. In only half a day's cross-city cycling, I had experienced enough near-fatal misses to last me a lifetime. I hate to imagine where I would have found myself without Norty's directions – probably in gang-land territory with a bullet through my head.

But so far so good. The heat-baked San Gabriel Mountains were upon me and I felt that the angels of Los Angeles were on my side.

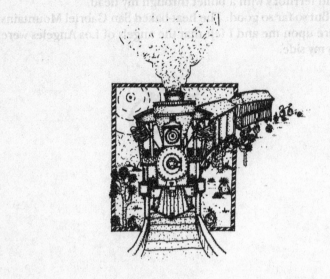

13

Wheels in
the Wild West

Late afternoon. The climb up the San Fernando
Pass was not coming easy. It was hot and humid,
and salty sweat stung my eyes. Suddenly I thought
I was hallucinating. I wiped the back of a glistening hand
across my brow and looked again. No, I wasn't seeing things:
it really was a clown sticking out his thumb. No one else was
around. Just me and a peregrinating clown. Droplets of sweat
dripped from chin to top-tube to road. The clown was shuf-
fling down my side of the road, his back to me, his arm
stretched out. All was quiet – just the soft, smooth running of
my transmission and my heavy, regular breathing filled the air.

A sudden, hair-bristling din rang out, rebounding off the rocks. It was the clown. He had turned round, seen me and laughed – a blood-chilling cackle. I felt scared. Who was this clot-head? Who the hell goes hitching dressed as a clown? But there again, why shouldn't they? After all, this was California, prime nutter country. Could this be, I wondered, a psychopathic crazy in disguise? Would I soon be just another American statistic in a body bag?

'Hey, babe!' he called. 'Got room for me?'

My fears were unfounded. The clown was an art student from Pasadena on his way to work. He was off towards Palmdale to stand in the road and hand out leaflets advertising a newly built community of model houses on view to the public. For a five-hour stint of standing in the sun and pulling in the passers-by, he earned $20 an hour – $200 for a weekend's work. Not bad for acting a clown.

❧

The sun sank into the radiating mountains as I turned into Soledad Canyon and I came across a studded expanse of cactus, standing to attention like a battalion of soldiers guarding their lengthening shadows.

I found a lakeside campsite, full of colour and noise. Rolling down a steep driveway, I stopped in front of a small, dusty office. A dark fortress of a woman wearing a surly expression barrelled out of the door, shouting, 'Zee exit eeze zat vay!'

'Oh . . . thank you,' I said, 'but I'm not looking for the exit – I've only just arrived.'

The old bat didn't beat around the bush.

'Yar, yar. You must go. You are not velcome.'

I had stumbled upon a Polish holiday camp, though it didn't look like much of a place for a holiday. Crushed cans and empty beer bottles and wind-blown litter covered the ground; radios pumped out full-volume distortion; dogs at stool were depositing where the urge took them – beside barbecues, tents and sandpits – while other scraggy beasts were howling and biting and fighting, much like the scrums of screaming children. Most of the men seemed to be staggering around blind drunk. The air smelt heavy and rank. I was all for leaving.

A few miles up the road I came to the Oasis Campground, though 'Junkyard' would have been a more appropriate name. Slum-like trailer homes wallowed among mounds of scrap: picked-over engines, oil drums, tyres and ripped-up car seats. This wasn't the sort of place to which fat-cat Americans retreated. Those who lived here were on welfare or they were poorly paid city dwellers who drove up for a weekend of barbecues and boozy inertia.

I rode slowly down the stone dirt track that led between the shouldering trailers. Glazed faces fell silent, their jaws dropping open as they turned to stare at me – just like in the westerns when a spur-spinning, gun-hipped stranger swaggers into town. Evidently these trailer troglodytes were not used to cyclists appearing out of the cloudless blue on a Sunday evening.

Approaching one group, I asked if it was okay to camp for the night. The ice was broken.

'Why, sure, I guess. Where ya from?'

'England,' I said and was promptly handed a foot-long hot dog and a beer.

'Shoot! We don't get many of you guys round here,' said one man in a grimy, gut-hugging T-shirt.

I asked who owned the place. At the Junk-Oasis entrance I had passed a small, shoddy shed with peeling paint and the sun-faded word 'OFFICE' barely visible on the side. It was dusty and rusty-padlocked and didn't look as though it had been opened for years.

I was pointed towards a dilapidated mobile home like a big, dog-eared shoe box. I knocked three times on a dirty-splayed door which left my knuckles stained and sore. There was no answer. I walked round the back and found a few wood-splintered steps leading to an open screen door. I called. Still no answer. Gingerly, I took a peep.

The place was crawling with cats and choking with trash but it was the smell that hit me first – of stale sweat and smoke and rotting dead. Cat crap lay everywhere: on the sordid thick-pile puce-coloured carpet, on the table and even on the sink beside a half-eaten sandwich. The compact, twisting tubes of some cat-caught rodent's innards glistened unappetisingly on an open newspaper in front of the TV. Drained beer cans everywhere added to the filth and clutter; piles of dirt-encrusted plates covered the sideboards. It was a dark and fetid place and hard to believe that somebody actually lived here.

I met the owner outside. He was chugging along in a bull-dozer, with a wilting cigarette hanging from his lips. A tight scar ran across the edge of his eye and his stubble-covered jaw looked dented on its left side. Over the noise of the engine, I asked if I could camp the night.

'This ain't no campground,' he said. And then, 'How many buddies you got with you?'

I told him it was just me. When he asked what I thought I was doing on my ownsome lonesome, I told him I was planning on riding across America.

'Boy, you gotta be kiddin',' he said. 'What the hell d'ya wanna do *that* for? You gotta be nuts.'

Then he paused, scratched his stubble, spat and said, 'Sure you can stay here – you that crazy you stay here for free.'

I put my tent up among a lifeless load of mechanical debris. The cold concrete toilet block was a health hazard: I came face to faeces; broken glass covered the floor of the mould-slimy shower; suspect blood-brown stains splattered the walls. Thick spider-web traps spun-stuck to the corners; the toilets didn't flush and ominous insects scuttled everywhere. As I was trying to get the tap to work, a gaunt woman shuffled in wearing a threadbare dressing-gown and worn toeless slippers. In one hand she held a can of Bud (from which she took perfunctory slurps) with a nearly burnt-out fag between her jaundiced fingers; with the other she pushed long, lank hair back from her eyes.

'Hey, you be kinda careful when you take a shower – we gotta Peeping Tom round here.'

The water pipes shuddered unhealthily. When I turned the tap full on, a fat cockroach fell out on to my toothbrush. I aborted my ablutions after that.

Showers and smelly cyclists should go well together but they don't always work. It should be bliss to douse yourself liberally after a bit of a pedal and to wash away all that stickiness, sweatiness and grime, especially that cyclist's trade mark of an oil chain-ring slime on the rear shin, but from my experience the cleansing ritual is not always that simple.

Baths are out because I rarely come across them unless I have splashed out for a hotel, or perhaps a bed-and-breakfast. You might be confronted with the popular, but fiddly, bath-and-shower combination which involves a good bit of tap-twiddling and knob-tugging. Such actions unfailingly produce a sudden and violent jet which ignominiously hits you fully clothed on the back, pinning you to the porcelain with all the thrusting power of a water cannon. I fall for this one every time. It is generally far less hazardous to forgo the shower for a soak. That said, in penny-saving places, you discover that there is no plug. A plastic bag with a wet sock in it works well for a time but crafty cyclists of a bathing nature never leave home without an adaptable plug.

Whereas troublesome baths can momentarily dampen the spirits, showers can be veritably stressful. Rolling wearily into a campsite after an energetic and exhausting day of pedal-pushing, you often find that you have been issued with the last tent space – a lengthy hike away from the toilet block. You arrive out of breath only to find yourself at the wrong end of an unruly queue of screaming, soap-hurling adolescents. Having waited for what seems like hours, you finally lock the cubicle door, remove your clammy clothes and shivering, poise for action on the slimy, mud-sludged floor. Then – eureka! You discover that this is a coin-operated shower and, of course, you have no change.

After a half-naked dash to the campground office for some coins, you are back in business and that is when the fun really starts. With a coin-op shower, time is never on your side. Don't be fooled. Although the instructions may say that you have a full five minutes, they invariably lie. The water stops abruptly after what seems merely 25 seconds leaving you fully lathered, with soap in your eyes. Then, fumbling blindly, you discover that you have left your towel in the tent.

You should consider yourself lucky if you have managed to get that far. One of my major gripes about modern showers is that the control panel is so darned complicated. Why it was ever necessary to replace the easy-to-figure-out-and-turn-on individual hot and cold taps with some state-of-the-art single lever device is beyond me, especially as in order to activate it you need the mind of a cryptanalyst and the ambidexterity of a bomb disposal expert: the first to work out how the blessed thing works and the second to oh-so-gingerly strike the temperamental thin line between searing hot and perishing cold.

Shower curtains are another problem. They are infuriatingly flappy things which constantly try to seize you in their mildewed and clammy embrace. Then there are the drains that don't, and the occasional unsavoury leavings of a previous occupant who has either inconveniently mistaken the shower for a convenience, or been suffering from one of those debilitating bowel complaints for which time and place mean nothing.

Then there is the shower wildlife. I have met a family of frogs in Morocco, a dead chicken in Romania, some assertive rats in India, an assortment of hairy-legged poisonous spiders in a variety of places, and more evil-looking, heavily armoured and apparently indestructible cockroaches than I care to remember.

Never mind the cycling, this cleansing business can prove to be far more exhausting and potentially life threatening than the actual pedalling.

❧

I crossed the San Andreas Rift Zone without a shake or a shudder and was into Antelope Valley where the soft, curving hills looked as if they had been sprinkled from the heavens with pot-loads of powder paint. Miles and miles of wild poppies (California's state flower) had exploded into a multi-hued magic carpet. Forces of small Painted Lady butterflies fluttered amidst a spectacular floral patchwork of poppies, brilliant deep-lilac cones of lupins, green and yellow fiddlenecks, brodiaea, lavender blooms, thistle sage and tidy tips as dainty as daisies. Curious-sounding horned toads and not-nice-to-meet rattlesnakes were just two of the many creatures who had made the poppy fields their home.

The Spanish called the poppy *copa de oro* (cup of gold), and Gold Rush miners pressed its blossoms in their letters home. Doing likewise today is not such a good idea: picking a poppy now results in a hefty $1,000 fine and six months in jail.

I was heading into what John Steinbeck had called a 'terrestrial hell': the Mojave Desert, scorching and silent and desolate. Prickly bulbs of Joshua trees defied the frying heat, scattering themselves here and there among the occasional abandoned miners' sheds – doors banging, worn metal signs clanging eerily in the life-sapping wind. Tumbleweeds like giant hedgehogs bowled across the road in front of me, just like in the movies. Off to my left was the preposterously named Lovejoy Buttes and, beyond that, Edwards Air Force base, home for space-shuttle landings. I had hit the High Desert, a deadly flat 2,000-foot plateau. The name of the sun-broiled land rising upwards to my right accurately summed up the heat of the place: Fry Mountains.

On my map, El Mirage had a blob that indicated it was of town-size proportions. In reality it was just a spanking new, ill-stocked grocery store. Nothing more. I couldn't understand what it was doing there. It looked as if it had just fallen off the back of a truck en route to some far-off mega-mall and landed in drained, silent Nowhere. And then one day a water-starved cowboy, dragging himself along on his knees through the wind-whipped desert and feeling the Death Devil crawling up close behind, looked up listlessly, wiping the sand-stuck sweat from his eyes, and saw a shimmering grocery store and it saved his life and he rejoiced and he praised his Lord and he called it El Mirage. Or so I thought.

Pushing through the swing doors into the air-conditioned interior, it felt as if I had just fallen through ice. The difference in temperature between out there and in here was not much short of 40 degrees. Teeth chattered, arms turned to 'chicken skin' and I had to go back out to wrap up before I came back in. That is what the modern inside-out, back-to-front world does for you: turns you topsy-turvy.

The only other customer was a bearded, baseball-capped, pot-bellied man with a pyramid nose. I asked him how many miles it was to Adelanto.

'Seven,' he said.

The bottle-blonde at the till disagreed.

'Hell, Lew – you ain't know what'cha talkin' 'bout. It's seventeen.'

Lew tugged at his thicket of beard and said, 'It's seven miles from *my* place.'

Nearing the end of an 80-mile day in head-dazing, blistering heat, a matter of ten miles can make a big difference on a bicycle. It can feel like you are doing the day all over again, only on legs like wilted celery stalks.

'But we're not *at* your place, Lew,' protested the till girl.

Lew said, 'Whale . . . I'm just down the road.'

Ah – but this was jumbo-land America where 'just down the road' can be translated to mean mighty more, like anything up to 50 miles – a *very* long way by compact-island British standards. I opted to settle the dispute by consulting my Mirage-blobbed map and calculating the exact distance, which I suppose I could have done before really except that it's not as much fun as taking a general involve-a-local consensus.

'It's neither seven nor 17,' I proclaimed. 'It's 12.'

In the event it was 13.

I undressed to a degree, took a deep breath of artificial air and stepped back into the furnace, the heat mugging me the moment I hit it. I swilled back my remaining ice-chilled V8 and ate a banana to acclimatise.

Climbing into his dust-covered flat-back truck, Lew said, 'Been here since '58 and I tell you this ain't no place for a young girl be travellin' alone. Shit, I don't wanna scare you.

Like the lady says, it can be a kinda freaky place in the day but it's the nights that turn real wild. I've seen some crazy guys on the highway in my time and I wouldn't go nowhere without my Smith 'n' Wesson. Say, just don't be out after dark, huh?'

The unfeeling Santa Ana wind bared its teeth and did everything it could to prevent me from reaching Adelanto before dark. Feeling like an over-broiled chicken and with energy long since left, I at last pulled into town – a strip of highway with a few fast-foods, motels and gas stations flashing neon to the motorists.

A mini-blob on my map marked a campsite, something that my European mind interpreted as a big, green and grassy field with dandelions and thick shady trees. But it turned out to be a gravel parking lot full of monster RVs shouldering each other's bulk for space.

'No tents allowed,' said the man behind the desk. I put on my pitiful look which, considering the circumstances, came quite easily and I was led to a postage-stamp square of grass (outside the jacuzzi and toilets) upon which I lay.

In the night it did something strange for the desert: it rained. In the morning I discovered that the man behind the desk had forgotten to turn off the postage-stamp sprinklers.

By 10.30am the temperature had already hit 100°F (or 'a century', as the locals called it) and was still climbing. It was head-hurtingly hot. The desert stretched out around me, brittle and barren.

Entering the honky-tonk town of Lenwood, I passed a high chain-link fence incarcerating a mountainous pile of skeletal junk and car corpses. On a gate crowned with barbed-wire was a sign:

WARNING

If there is anything in this yard worth your life
BE MY GUEST

I spent the night in Barstow (where the temperature stays over 90°F for a hundred days in a row) in a seedy $12-a-night motel run by an Indian woman in a curry-coloured sari eating a McDonald's. My room was dark and fetid: it was like entering a dungeon where something had died. Blood-brown plastic curtains hung heavily like body-bags across a small, unopenable window. The thick magenta carpet was carpeted with age-old ash, dirt and stains. The concave bed looked and felt as if the last occupant had been a ten-ton Sumo wrestler. It took me a while to muster enough courage to venture into the bathroom. It was the sort of place where I could quite easily imagine finding a slumped and naked form, its throat cut by some drug-crazed psycho.

But there was no body. Instead I found a transparent surgical glove behind the toilet and a dandruff-ridden comb down the side of the sink. When I started up the motor of the bulky air-conditioning box eating its way through to the outside wall, it growled and shuddered and yelped like a dog run over by a lawn-mower. My $12 cell rattled and trembled as if in an earthquake.

But I was happy: I'd found shade.

Revitalized after a long and gaspingly glorious cold shower, I turned off the dying dog so that I could hear the news on a monochrome TV which needed a kick-start. Ten thousand jobs had been lost, it said, as a result of the LA riots. And 'Princess Di's suicide attempt' was causing a sensation: supposedly she had walked in on 'Chuck' (as the flamboyantly tied newscaster called him) doing up his flies after a quick bit of behind-the-couch humpy-bumpy.

Switching channels, I learned that a man with AIDS in Oklahoma was bedding as many people as possible in order to spread the disease. Then an investigatory documentary came on: in front of a wall pinned with posters of topless, balloon-chested women, a salivating and goofy-eyed presenter asked, 'Why is America obsessed with big breasts?'

Without waiting for an answer, I kick-turned it off and climbed into my Sumo-dipped bed with Jack Kerouac and his *Lonesome Traveller.*

In a futile attempt to beat the heat, I hit Interstate 15 early the next morning to begin crossing one of California's most isolated and hostile stretches of land: the Devil's Playground cauldron was waiting for me.

To avoid the fat-laned freeway for a while, I left the god-forsaken town of Barstow and its desert jumble of junctions by turning off on to a rough dirt road and rattling along through the grit and dust beside the railway.

Nothing came down the road; nothing came down the track. I had the big, hot emptiness all to myself. Much later, I had to cross the tracks. As I stopped, looked and listened, Greencross Code fashion, I saw in the distance the nebulous headlight-eyes of a far-off freight train liquid-shimmering down the rails.

I flopped back down the shaly bank into the sand to wait and watch it trundle past. There is something hypnotic about sitting in a flat expanse of hot desert beside a hazy horizon-to-horizon American railroad and waiting for the manifestation of a monstrous snub-nosed Sante Fé engine hauling over 140 box cars.

Distances are deceptive in the desert. It seemed my sit-squat shadow moved faster than the approaching freight, as if the morning had been burnt alive by the sun before the racketing-clacketing was even within striking distance. But then, American trains are not renowned for speed. Which is odd. Comparatively tiny countries like home, Japan or France have fast-flying 125s or Bullets or TGVs that scream through the countryside, sending the outside world into one green or built-up blur.

In America, trains are built more on the lines of Thomas the Tank Engine; they are friendly, unsleek plodders, feeling their way, taking their time as if they know that there is no point getting into a tizzy and all out of breath and hot and bothered in order to cross a vastness that seems never to end. It is a vastness where no one is waiting to jump on or jump off them because those metal elongated flying eggs have won an easy war in passenger transport. And that is sad. It is the trains, not the planes, that have feeling and character and sneakily show you terrestrial wonders which you would never otherwise see.

At last the train was almost upon me, slowly, like a giant concertinaed caterpillar crawling down the tracks. As it shuddered cautiously, unhurriedly, along the burning hot rails it let out a shrill and mournful cry. I thought of that madman Jonathan Raban (Trav). in his *Hunt for Mr Heartbreak* whose description no one could better: 'The sound of its whistle – that long low oboe-chord of the American railroad, a sound perfectly contrived to strike a note at once imperious and deeply wounded.'

But then it stopped. First the whistle, then the engine. I was waiting – I had been waiting surely hours – for this never-ending train to pass me by and now, among a cacophony of ululating spits and hisses and wheezes and sputters, it ground to a halt in front of me.

The driver looked down at me through his far-up caterpillar eyes and then swung out of its high-rise head, jumping down into the gritty railside sand. I watched big, heavy, steel-toed boots scuffing towards me and it suddenly dawned on me that this would be a perfect place to be shot.

'Well, hi there!' he said in a friendly, twangy tone. 'My cousin does a lot of that in Europe.'

What, loitering with intent beside railway tracks?

'A lot of what?' I asked.

'Biking,' twanged the driver. 'Thought I just gotta stop to say hi. Don't see too many of you sorts out here.'

So the caterpillar driver and I sat until our shadows were eaten by the rapacious midday sun, talking about trains and bikes and destinations in a faintly unreal set-up in the middle of the wide, silent desert sand on the edge of the Devil's Playground.

And I thought: No wonder American trains are so slow.

14

Fry Till Yer Die

Out of the 50 American states, the only ones which permit bicycles on freeways are Arizona, Wyoming, Washington, Montana, Nevada, Idaho, Utah, Colorado and California. The latter limits you to a certain one thousand miles and this included part of Interstate 15. I was now on it, heading for Las Vegas.

People had told me it would be hell, literally. I had said, 'maybe.'

Although it might not sound much fun cycling on a truck-and-trailer fast-flowing freeway for 160 miles across the heat frizzled desert, with Death Valley on one side and the Devil Playing on the other and not a lot else in between, it *was* fun – in a peculiar sort of way. Certainly it wasn't half as bad as they said it would be. I had a hard shoulder all to myself – a shoulder as wide as a lane on the M25 and far better maintained.

Carrying enough water was a bit of a problem but my major concern was a toiletry one – namely, where to go? It was a painful, fretful time. There was nothing whatsoever to lurk behind; no rocks, no hillocks, no welcome foliage to obstruct the view between me and a thousand inquisitive motoring eyes staring at me zoo-like from behind a speeding, sealed-window world. But even if there had been, I was somewhat reluctant to leap from saddle to sand, no matter how bursting my bladder. The thought of being taken unawares by a rattlesnake bite or a scorpion sting in sensitive areas was not particularly attractive. No, this was no pee-stop paradise, for sure.

At one point, with internal water levels rising dangerously high, and just as I was envying the efficient practicalities of the male appendage, I was mercifully relieved by the heavenly appearance of a roadside rest-stop. Apart from the toilet block there was a water fountain, shade and a bevy of yawning and limb-stretching motorists who thought me something of an odd species.

One was a passenger from a sinister black-windowed tourist bus. He was Alan Blundon from near Camberley, Surrey.

'You must be getting a bit hot out there,' he said. 'Would you mind if I took a photo of you? I'll be home in a few days. I could send your mum a copy if you like – show her you're still alive.'

Nearby, an elderly white-haired woman said to her husband, 'Hey, honey, there's that biker we passed way back. Gee – she musta been moving.'

The woman shuffled over, handed me a bag of oranges and said, 'Mercy me! Why, bless your heart. How did you make it here so fast?'

I said it was surprising the speeds you could reach when there was nowhere to pee.

Another white-haired woman had been hovering in the background. She suddenly strode up to me, thrust a $10 bill into my surprised but far from reticent hand and said, 'Hon, I'm Dorothy and I'll be praying for you.'

'Well, thank you . . . Dorothy,' I said awkwardly, 'that's awfully kind of you.'

Then Dorothy clambered into her Buick Century and promptly drove away.

I took a last deep, shady breath and rode on into the grilling and weighty wind. Off to the north of the Interstate were places like Bicycle Lake, Pilot Knob Valley and Cowhole Mountain. Near the turning for Zzyzx (pronounced Zigh-Zix), a car pulled on to the shoulder and an outstretched arm attached to an ice-cold can of Budweiser appeared out of the window. The arm (and the beer) belonged to spiky-cropped Rex.

'Hey, hi! You travelling cross-country? Wow man, that's a killer idea.'

The previous year Rex had done the same sort of thing but on a recumbent from Washington to Maine.

'A whole bunch of us did the Bike-centennial route,' he said. 'It's real swell once you hit the rhythm. Right? Boy, I didn't half have a sore butt though. My girl, Linda says I've never been the same since.'

We laughed – me, standing there in the desert in the sun on the shoulder with a beer, and Rex, a stranger, in his car, telling me about the state of his butt beneath the Zzyzx sign. Then he wished me luck and gunned off into the heat haze and I was left there holding a beer on the shoulder, torched by searing winds, and I thought: Is this real? Then I looked up, saw the sign and decided to call my bike Zzyzx the Starcraft.

I continued riding in a torrid zombie state, mile after sweltering mile, when I saw what I took to be an old fanbelt or a piece of rope or an old shredded piece of tyre in my path ahead. Too heat-weary even to divert course a foot, it was only when I was practically upon this shoulder-debris that I realized with horror it was a rattlesnake pausing for thought in the road. Suddenly my roasted and torpid body snapped into full alert. My heart shot out of my head; my legs shot up to my handlebars at the same time as the basking snake-belt woke up and speed-slithered down the bank.

Twelve miles from Baker, I pulled off at a dingy gas station to use the loo, buy an orange juice and sit outside on a plank of wood in the shade to recuperate from that heart-palpitating moment. There was no business doing and the owner, who looked like a weather-beaten Jack the Ripper, came out to talk to me.

'Tell you what,' he said, 'jump in the truck and I'll take you for a ride into the desert and show you where the rattlers hang out.'

'I appreciate the thought,' I said, 'but not today.'

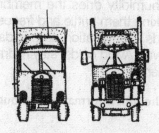

By the time I reached Baker, I felt fried. Rolling down the dusty, shimmering strip I saw the big digital temperature readout on top of a 40-foot pole near Bun Boy. It flashed 117°F. If I had wanted my pulsating perspiring to end in expiring, I could have 'hung' a left here and headed into Death Valley, the hottest place on earth. Feeling quite sweaty enough already, I opted for the straight and a shade cooler road – the road to 'Vegas.

Although it was early in the day, I still felt as if I was being baked alive in a fan-assisted oven. Occasionally wind-devils whipped up swirls of sand, sending them whirling across the highway and stinging into my skin. Then, to add to the fun, I had sixteen nose bleeds within the space of three hours. All I could do was pull into the side of the shoulder, stand astride my mount and, with valuable toilet paper pinned to nose, throw back my head and stare into blistering skies, listening to the constant whoosh-whooshing of the flying freeway traffic.

It was at times like these that I thought how utterly odd I must look. Motorists' eyes would have picked up a curious passing vision of a stationary bicycle person with helmeted head tilted heavenwards. Hell, it's one of those crazy guys, they would have said, and probably presumed I was performing a desperate religious ritual by turning to some godly wonder who could remove me from such scorching purgatory.

Later I read in a confidence-boosting 'DON'T DIE IN THE DESERT' leaflet:

> The low humidity dries the membranes of the nose, making them brittle and frequently causing nosebleeds. Dehydration and colds may cause them as well. Avoid colds, stay hydrated and use a humidifier.

Particularly helpful information, I thought.

The desert was red and desolate and infinite. Sometimes scrawny sagebrush and the odd cactus studded the nigh lifeless ground. The occasional rocks were always eroded into weird and tortured shapes.

At one point the road rose up slightly over a fair-sized hillock. As I crested the brow, I was faced with a bullet-straight 15-mile stretch of fat freeway carving itself across the desert floor. Far in the indistinct distance, the road was eaten by the burning, purple-pink rocky lineations of the Clark Mountains – mountains that I seemed to be cycling forever towards but never getting any closer, as if the further I travelled forwards, the further they slipped away. As I sweat-struggled onwards in a daze, the sheer size of the country suddenly hit me like a bolt from the blue. In my head I looked down upon a map of America, a massive and meaty bulk, and I thought: Where am I? Who am I? I felt like a peanut on the planet, an insignificant pin-prick crawling across a monster nation. Where else but America could you join a double ribbon of highway that runs for nearly 3,000 miles and never encounter a traffic light?

The implacable sun seeped through my skull, filtering its fiery feelers into my brain, and I knew I had flipped, with both paddles out of the water, when dubious wordings like this entered my mind:

> I met a vegan in Vegas
> Leon was his name,
> Leon liked the neon
> And because of that he came.
> Leon ate no meat
> Nor dairy products too,
> His diet was that of gambling
> With an occasional bamboo-
> Shoot.

A massive chromium bull-nosed truck with a UFO attached to its hulk brought me back down to earth when it pulled into the shoulder, *my* shoulder, ahead. The brawny driver jumped down and said, 'Hey, I know a crazy person when I see one and I'm looking at one here and now – right? Betcha thinking that sun sucks, huh? What d'ya say to a ride and a beer out the chill-box?'

Playing safe, I said, 'Sounds like a nice idea but I'm fine thanks,' while inside I thought: Yes please! You Wonder! You Saviour! But I was taking no risks.

As if reading my thoughts, he said, 'It's okay – I'm just transporting this airport satellite to Denver. You worried, huh? You'll be in good hands.' And he added, 'Hey, relax . . . I'm real safe. I'm a christian.'

Thanks, but no thanks.

Panting onward and upward to 4775 feet took me up and over the innovatively-named Mountain Pass. After calling surrounding places things like Mohawk Hill, Searchlight, Devil's Hole Hills, Pilot Knob Valley, Squaw Tit and Zzyzx, maybe the anonymous namers had run out of imagination.

The road fell away from me on the other side and I

dropped down, feeling deliriously joyful, towards the stateline of Nevada, the Silver State. After passing nothing for miles and miles, the uncanny mirage of a monolithic, multi-coloured fairy-tale castle loomed shimmering and sudden from the desert.

'Surely this can not be?' I said to myself, half expecting it to evaporate into the blue. But no, this was real all right, in an unreal sort of way. Only in America could you come across something so wonderfully unexpected; something so utterly unbelievable; something so ridiculously absurd. In the midst of all the dessication of this bleached and tortuously thirsty land, there grew, with all the capricious colour and vigour of a cactus flower, the money-spinning Prima Donna resort and casino. Its lurid sign flashed:

WE'LL TREAT YOU BETTER ON THE BORDER

Merry-go-rounds and ferris wheels whirled and perfectly positioned palm trees topped with giant mock pineapples stood uniform and erect like a battalion of soldiers. Luminescent neon bled light into the burning desert sky. A space-aged monorail carried money-hungry passengers from the Prima Donna over the freeway to neighbouring Whiskey Pete's Hotel Casino.

'The first ever monorail to cross an interstate highway while linking two casino resorts,' were self-congratulatory words I later read in the glossy brochure.

A massive overhead digital neon screen, raised high on vivid orange and pink-striped pillars, faced towards the freeway. It dazzled the drivers with its flashing messages and lured them to part with big bucks:

$$$$$$$ CRAPS! $$$$$$$
1000 SLOTS!
50c HOTDOGS – THE BEST IN THE WEST!
$1,000,000 TO BE WON!
$2.99 ALL-YOU-CAN-EAT ALL-DAY
BREAKFASTS!

Hypnotized, I felt myself drawn towards this alluringly osten-
tatious monstrosity, not just because I was in desperate need
of a toilet but because I wanted to stay there – I wanted to get
out of the heat and sleep in that gaudy fairytale castle sprouting from the desert.

I rolled up to the grandiose entrance along with a dazzling white overstretched limo and leaned my Zzyzxed
Starcraft against the wall. My system was in for a shock.
Having spent hour upon mesmerizing hour alone, talking to
no one but myself, I suddenly stepped from a lonesome heat-
hell into a dark, airconditioned monetary mayhem.
Surrounding me were hundreds of dimly glowing slot
machines, the crunching crank of one-armed bandits, the
shrill head-crunching ringing of bells and buzzers and fast-
filling buckets, the din of clattering coins and the raucous
shrieks and winning whoops of joyful delirium. Plunging into
crepuscular surroundings beneath the transcendental lights,
I found baccarat and bingo and blackjack, craps and keno
and poker, roulette and racing and sport bets.

The players looked mesmerized by their Dalek machines,
forever feeding coin after coin after coin into the dollar slots,
some winning, some not, most smoking and most holding
inexhaustible supplies of drinks offered for free by scantily
clad women in fishnets and Crimplene.

I wound my way through the crowded ranks of fruit
machines, through the winking gloom and up to the frantic
comings and goings at reception. Despite the mêlée, the
girl behind the desk looked fresh of face and genuinely
happy to see me. Whereas in England I would probably have
been greeted with a scowl and a curt bark, here it was a
fixed-grin smile and an ingratiating, 'Well hi there! How're
ya doin'?'

With head pulsating I said, 'Errr . . . fine I think, thanks.
How much is your cheapest room?'

'D'ya have a reservation?'

The sinking feeling struck. 'No, I don't.' And I knew what
was coming.

'Well, I'm real sorry but we're full. Have a nice day
now.'

Have a nice day! What did she mean, 'have a nice day,' when she was sending me to cycle a further 50 miles into a stiff furnace head-wind? My spinning head was telling my wilting legs and my wilting legs were telling my spinning head that I could go no further: they were striking, they were staying put. All I wanted was a tiny bit of shade; a corner, a cellar, somewhere to put my tent. Somewhere to lie down.

Stubbornly irrational, I said, 'You can't be full. I've just cycled across the desert and I've had sixteen nosebleeds in three hours and I need to lie down.' And then, as a grovelling afterthought and because Americans 'just lurv the Brits', I added, 'I'm English.'

What the girl should have replied was, 'Bike across the desert? You gotta be crazy. And then you turn up at the Prima Donna all sunburnt and sweaty with no money and expect a room? You people drive me nuts. Be okay if you turned up in a plastic, gas-guzzling, electricity-generating, waste-ejecting, 40-foot motorized Recreational beast of a Vehicle and show me big bucks . . . then we're talking business. But on a bike? Get serious!'

Instead she said, 'Why – is that so? I thought your accent was kinda cute.'

Then I heard myself saying, 'I'd like to see the manager, please.'

Still smiling, she told me I would have to contact the executive offices, which were located in the basement among a maze of corridors and doors. After much sly perseverance, I finally wheedled my way into the office of the marketing director and proceeded to butter him up with a barrage of nonsensical adulation.

The price I paid for such smarmy unctuousness was . . . precious little. For $12 I wheeled my bike past the bemused spick 'n' span doorman through the main entrance, weaving my way through the mayhem of heavily bejewelled bodies magnetized to the ever-open jaws of the money-gobbling monster machines, into a glass-sided lift that rose up above the sea of gambling razzle-dazzle light and noise, and down miles of identical corridors into an ultra-plush, cockroach-free room overlooking the jacuzzi and the bridged, kidney-shaped, oh-so-blue swimming pool.

Bliss. . . .

free room overlooking the ...... and the oddest kidney-
shaped, off-sky-blue swimming pool.
Bbss ...

15

Virgin on
the Ridiculous

The average American walks around with eight
credit cards in his pocket. Entering Las Vegas
prepares you for the fact that those cards will be
spending a lot more time out than in. As I rode into the outskirts of the sprawling desert metropolis, the city's welcoming
words emblazoned on a giant hoarding over the highway
were:

MEGA LOTTA MONEY MEGA BUCKS

The Spanish name of Las Vegas means 'The Meadows'. This
seems something of a misnomer when you are confronted
with an endless expanse of blinding neon, monolithic hotels
and casinos, and prodigiously wide boulevards grid-locked
with traffic. But of course it wasn't always like this. When

Spanish traders first came upon the area in 1829, they found acres of lush oasis in an otherwise dry and desolate region. It was the only place capable of supporting vegetation.

A few decades later, $18 bought The Meadows for the Mormons. 'All you need to know about the Mormons,' said a man outside the gas station, 'is that in the twenties they forced Hopi Indians into disinfectant-filled sheep dips.'

Until 1931, the place remained a humble mining town. With the Great Depression, Las Vegas faced economic catastrophe but it was saved by Nevada's legislature: legalized gambling and the construction of the Hoover Dam (the blockbusting hydroelectric project on the Colorado River which brings an abundant source of power) both helped to create the famous and flamboyant city of glitter and neon and razzmatazz.

Even then things remained fairly low key until 1940, when the first combined casino and hotel opened on what was to become The Strip. It was overwhelmed with success and others followed hot on its heels – including the Fabulous Flamingo, built by the infamous mobster Bugsy Siegal who established Las Vegas links with organized crime and instigated the wily method of enticing people to the gambling tables with the bribe of bargain accommodation, food, drink, and flashy shows, a system that still brings them in today.

Nevadans have made state industries out of the twin attractions of gambling and marriage licensing. Known as the City of Sinners, it draws flocks of people with big hopes and hungry eyes (more than 20 million in 1992, which is more than all the foreign visitors to London, a major capital city) who come for the glitter and the intoxicating razzle-dazzle;

for the insatiable thrill of gambling; for the all-you-can-eat, stuff-yourself-sick buffets; for the round-the-clock show-girls and the never dull Strip.

Where else but in Sin City can you get a 'drive-thru' divorce, or a wedding in a 'Kwik-Chapel' for $49 plus tax, or buy chocolate by the yard or the bucket?

'If it's worth doing, it's worth overdoing,' goes a Las Vegas maxim. It is a place which is, simultaneously, wonderfully awful and awfully wonderful. Gaudiness and money-guzzlers are everywhere. Rows of slot machines stand like sentries in most establishments – restaurants, drugstores, gas stations, supermarkets and even laundromats.

But not everyone gets rich quick. Inevitably most people lose money many more times than they win. Many don't care; for them, gambling is an addiction and they remain ever hopeful for their lucky strike. Sometimes the 'mega lotta money, mega bucks' shower their way and those who show restraint return home with heavy pockets. But those types are few. More often than not, those big bucks are fed back into the system again and that once-in-a-blue moon winner returns home a loser.

'If you wanna make money in a casino, own one,' said aptly-named Steve Wynn, founder of the Mirage, the Golden Nugget and others. In the City of Sin, many of the casinos make profits of $100 million a year.

I didn't do any of the things that people usually go to Las Vegas to do. I didn't stay at any of the garish hotels like the 4,032-room Excalibur (the world's largest), modelled on a gigantic medieval castle with red, blue and gold spire turrets and a moat, drawbridge and minstrels, jugglers and jousting knights to boot; or the Mirage, with its white Siberian tigers and built-in 'volcano' erupting fire and smoke every 15 minutes. I didn't win any money, I didn't lose any money – in short, I scarce spent a cent. I didn't eat at any 'stuff-yourself-nauseous' buffets; I didn't see any show-girls or shows, or the infamous red-eyed dealers in white leather shoes with jackets slung over their shoulders as they climbed into black-windowed stretch Cadillacs.

I didn't get married or divorced either.

Instead I slept in a cheap and sleazy motel on the ragged outskirts of town and spent my two-day stay with throngs of Mexicans in the US Department of Justice Immigration and Naturalization Service on Las Vegas Boulevard South, trying to extend my six-month visa – a simple task that is made as complicated as possible.

I had been unable to apply for an extension in Los Angeles because of the riots but the immigration office there had told me I could apply for one when I reached Las Vegas. In Las Vegas I was told that I was applying too early before my visa expiry date: I had to apply within two weeks of its expiring but not more than six days before it turned void. I said that, because I was travelling by bicycle, it was highly inconvenient and most unlikely that I would be anywhere near a major city with an immigration department between those specific dates and so I would appreciate it very much if they could do a bit of premature form-stamping while I was here.

For two days, I sat in a small, boxed-in, windowless room hearing peeved and anxious Spanish all around me.

Hundreds of sweaty fingers fidgeted with allotted numbered tickets, waiting for them to tally with a wall-mounted number machine that seemed to click backwards. By the end of those two days I had filled out more forms than was healthy and finally left befuddled as to whether my requested extension had been granted or not. Frankly, I no longer really cared.

Because the LA riots had overspilled into Las Vegas, I spent the evenings barricaded as best I could in my $10 motel cell rather than hit the mean neon streets. The local news was constantly reporting slap-bang shoot-outs by rampaging street gangs and the sultry night air was filled with wailing police sirens.

Peeping through a slit in the blinds, I espied an ugly brawl below in the dark and trashy motel parking lot. A group of white lads with what looked like bandannas tied round their heads were beating up a couple of black guys, bashing them with sickening force against the back of a pick-up. No one was shot (as far as I could tell) but, having read and heard so much about violence of late, it wouldn't have surprised me to see a lifeless form slumped down among the wheels in a pool of blood.

It wasn't just the street gangs that were to be feared. Apparently some children had to be wary of trigger-happy parents. Browsing through Las Vegas's *Review-Journal*, I read how a mother had shot her 12-year-old son in an argument over the TV remote control. She had become angry with him about changing channels and, pulling out a gun, threatened to shoot the television. When her son told her to go ahead, she cursed and shot him in the stomach.

I rode onwards, eastwards, across more and more desert. I had more nosebleeds and saw more snakes, some slithering, some squashed. It was hot. Sweat sheeted down my back. Vehicles melted into the distance. Just when I was beginning to think I was on an endless road through an endless desert, the magnificent bulk of the sharply ridged Virgin Mountains loomed across my path like a giant dragon's tail. The purple-red wall of rock grew steadily higher and higher, until I began to fret that the Virgins were not quite as wonderful after all if I had to climb over them in this heat. Despite scanning their alluring flanks, I couldn't detect any trace of the highway snaking up the side, nor any mouth in the mountains through which the road could pass.

It was only when I was merging with the Virgins that they suddenly revealed a hidden kink and I was plunged into the twisting and gorgeous gorge of the roaring Virgin River.

Stopping at a popular toilet and picnic spot up the road, I was told by flat-topped Fleetwood, the rest area manager, that this stretch of highway was one of the most notorious in the country.

'Folks hauling ass for hours down the dead-straight Interstate fall into a kind of desert trance,' he said. 'They switch into cruise control, steer with a finger on the wheel and start dreaming. When they hit the gorge they're taken by surprise real bad and forget how to drive – tend to end up on the wrong side of the road crushed beneath a semi. Jeez, what a mess. Twenny-two been killed just these last few weeks. Guess that's got something to do with why Nevada's got the highest highway fatality rate in the States. Know something else? It's got the highest rape rate, too.'

'Oh,' I said, 'That's nice to know.'

Fleetwood resembled a mixture of a fork-lift truck and a pit-bull terrier – short and stocky with curious jutting-out bits and mean as a hound dog. An ex-marine, he now earned $8 an hour supervising the rest area and keeping it clean. He lived with his wife in a small house on site.

'Can be a real freaky job,' he said. 'You get to meet the real crazies of this land. Shit, man, just the other day I asked some guy to walk his dog in the dog-walking area rather than letting it piss on the leg of the picnic table and he looked at me as if I'd just asked him to kiss my ass, then pulled a .38 on me. Said he'd blow my balls off if I didn't get the fuck out of here. Nobody, he said, told him where to walk *his* dog. Jeez – guy had flipped all right, but I told him he'd sure as hell picked on the wrong man to try and play big boys' games. I ain't in them marines for nothing, yer know – I had my knife to his throat before he even knew it. Told him if he ever showed his goddam lousy face round here again I'd blow his fucking head to Kingdom fucking Come. Guy knew I meant it too. Man, did I shit-scare the pants off him! There've been worse though.'

As I prepared to go, somewhat shaken, Pitbull Fleetwood said, 'Hey, try and stay off the bike this weekend – it's Memorial Holiday. The roads are a nightmare – full of crazy guys from the city racing to the mountains. We call them the Weekend Warriors.'

16

Sucked in
and Spat Out

The first raindrops for weeks fell fat and heavy and hard as I nipped across the corner of Arizona and entered Utah at St George, a city most famed for its year-round golf (so Fleetwood had said). In no time the skies had turned from burning blue to coal-dust and the wind kicked up pace. Marching over the distant mountains, an ominous drum-rolling storm thundered in and the temperature at last plunged into the blissfully cool low 80s.

The *Sun* newspaper in America is even more of a farcical read than its British namesake. As I waited at the checkout after stocking up on edible supplies at one of St George's mega-marts, I saw the headline:

'PENGUIN STAMPEDE IN ANTARTICA KILLS 11'

❀

I hit the land of the Canyons. The 20-odd miles through the pink and copper-coloured walls of sheer cliff in Zion's National Park were so outlandish that I immediately turned round and rode them again . . . and again. Towering, sky-scraping rocks shouldered the road in such fantastic sculptured shapes and designs and unlikely formations that it was like riding through an extravagant landscape by Henry Moore and Gaudi gone berserk.

At one point I turned off to wander around Zion's visitor centre where, I was intrigued (and somewhat dismayed) to learn:

HOW LONG WILL LITTER LAST?

Cigarette butts	1–5 years
Wool socks	1–5 years
Orange and banana peels	up to 2 years
Plastic-coated paper	5 years
Plastic bags	10–20 years
Plastic film containers	20–30 years
Nylon fabric	30–40 years
Leather	up to 50 years
Tin cans	50 years
Plastic six-pack holders	100 years
Aluminium cans and tabs	500 years
Glass bottles	1,000 years
Plastic bottles and styrofoam	indefinitely

Up the road, round the bend and up the mountain, the splendour of Bryce Canyon awaited me. A multicoloured maze of columns, pinnacles and spires, it is not so much a canyon as an amphitheatre of sculptured sandstone – a massive cathedral of weather-eroded ravines carved into the edge of the giant Paunsaugunt Plateau. The Paiute Indian word for Bryce described it fairly accurately as 'red rocks standing like men in a bowl-shaped canyon'.

In the late 1800s, the pioneering Mormon cattle-rancher Ebenezer Bryce grazed his herds in the shadows of the spectacular and unearthly red-glowing, gold and purple-pink rock formations that now bear his name. His only surviving comment about this phenomenal region is: 'One heck of a place to lose a cow.'

I dropped into the convoluted vermilion cliffs of real cowboy country. That night I slept in the Crazy Horse Campground in Kenab, a wooden saloon-barred Wild West town where more than a hundred film and TV companies had once based themselves to shoot Hollywood movies like *Butch Cassidy and the Sundance Kid*.

The weather had taken a melodramatic tumble out of the blue. Every day for the past week I had been hit mid-afternoon by lengthy and violent thunderstorms. In the mornings I would ride through sweltering heat, only to watch with growing agitation as threatening masses of black billowing cloud built up on the horizon. Creeping, and eerily silent, the distant sky would cloud-burst into life with constant flashes of sheet lightning. It was like watching, with sealed ears, an advancing army of enthusiastic welders at work.

They never passed me by.

As the ground rolled away beneath me, so the intimidating skies rolled and roared ever closer, soon to enmesh me among the fire-flashing tentacles. It was hairy and highly hazardous to be caught in the teeth of such bellowing monsters with nowhere to hide.

The top-heavy sky would fall to earth as it whipped itself into a combustive frenzy, picking up furious strength as it sheeted down in diagonal bolts across the desert wilds. Day after day I spent racing against the voracious maws of these storms, frantic to reach cover before being engulfed in their tempestuous midst. But on a bicycle it is not so easy when distances between towns, or even signs of habitation, can be a hundred miles or more. Nor was it a comforting thought that being caught in a storm on a pile of electric-attracting metal tubes on a flat expanse of emptiness was one of the most dangerous places to be.

One day, as lightning cracked all around, a local sheriff pulled over and wound down his window to shout through the deafening inclement elements.

'Well, hi there! I guess it ain't such a great day to be out. Know what, kid? More than 80 Americans die a year from lightning strikes – twice as many as from bee stings.'

Feeling more than lily-livered, I thanked him for such confidence-boosting information. He smiled a sort of cocksure smile, wound up his window and drove away.

I was facing one such tempest as it stormed hot on my tail, desperately trying to reach some shelter at Big Water when, with only five miles to go, my back tyre considerably let me down by puncturing in explosive style. Like a satisfied caterwauling witch hurling live prey into a bubbling cauldron, the ear-shattering storm cackle-cracked upon me – the rain knifing me so hard it hurt, and blotting out the land in seconds.

The surrounding skyscape crashed and detonated as the life-zapping lightning ripped its violent and shocking path to earth. I threw my bike aside and dived for the shallow ditch, all worries of rattlesnakes and scorpions cast to the wind. Scared and sprawled, I quickly curled foetal-tight on the ground with my face pinned to the reverberating fire-coloured sands, waiting with rattled nerves and breath abated for that fork of death to strike my exposed and cowering form.

*

Feeling like a wasted wader, I finally made it to the aptly named community of Big Water, where a flash flood was raging through Wahweap Creek. When I had asked a checkout girl at a supermarket in Kenab whether she knew if there was a grocery store in Big Water, she had said, 'All I know 'bout that place is it's a polygamist colony. Say . . . you better go careful – seems they get anybody who stays too long!'

I stayed just long enough to sit dripping at a table in the combined gas station and grocery store, where I bought a loaf of bread and made a sandwich. I was about to leave when the door burst open and in strode an enormous, square-jawed Desperate Dan of a man. He looked from me to my bike, leaning up against the window, and back to me and said, 'One of those, huh?' I said yes, I was one of them. I wondered if he was Big Chief Polygamist.

'Guess what?' he said. 'We've had more rain in two days than in two years.'

I said that I'd noticed. When he discovered my nationality, he told me that his father had been in England during the war and had constantly complained about the hornets.

'They stick your ass against your hide and yer scream like a wounded pig,' he said, inexplicably.

I winged past Nipple Bench and Last Chance Smoky Mountain Junction to Page, home of the massive, concrete-arched Glen Canyon Dam and powerplant which, in its making, required 5.1 million cubic yards of concrete poured around the clock for more than three years.

I had entered the Navajo Indian Reservation and rolled on beside the Echo Cliffs. The road was sporadically lined with shanty Indian stalls selling Navajo trinkets – jewellery and leather and carvings and cloth and vibrant, traditional, geometrically weaved wool blankets. It is said that every Navajo weaver deliberately makes a mistake in each blanket, since the Indians believe that perfection marks the end of a weaver's life. It's a nice tale, but I suspect this could be just a crafty ploy to sell off a bodged job.

Shoddily painted roadside signs cried out for custom with slogans to lure a possible purchaser from the heavy-duty Grand Canyon tourist trail traffic:

HOT SALE: COOL PRICE

and

66% OFF-SALE

painted on signs so sun-faded and peeling that the sale had obviously been on-going since the last of the Mohicans.

CHIEF YELLOW HORSE stalls seemed to be the ones doing hot business. Maybe 'PLASTIC MONEY OK YES' had something to do with it, along with signs that advised passers-by who had passed them by to:

TURN ROUND NOW . . . .

FRIENDLY INDIANS BEHIND YOU!

Another storm chased me to Cameron and I arrived bedraggled, exhausted and with nowhere to sleep. The 'campsite' turned out to be an open gravel RV park-cum-canine WC. I ended up pitching tent behind the gas station Gents, which did not waft the most pleasant of bouquets to send me to sleep but at least it provided a windbreak and brief respite from the storm.

*

I spent a day battling against the thundering elements as I oh-so-slowly scaled the heights of the mighty Grand Canyon. At each 'scenic overlook' I would wearily dismount and dutifully trudge to the edge to peer into a thick mist of grey, soupy sea. And I'd think to myself: Somewhere out there up there down there is a sight to be seen but right now that somewhere could be anywhere and nowhere.

So I put up my tent in the Desert View Campground (huh, some view!) among the swirling murk and the juniper trees and crawled inside to perform my daily ritual:

1. Construct supper of banana-goo-and-anything-else-that's-going sandwiches and consume astronomical non-gastronomic amounts with a good book (*Nine Stories* by J.D. Salinger, or *The Remains of the Day* by Kazuo Ishiguro, or any Raban) propped open in front of me with Swiss Army Knife.

2. Clamber into sleeping bag to lie on v. full stomach, head propped in hand, and diary-write by fast-fading torchlight.

3. Resurface to wield toothbrush and to disappear momentarily behind convenient shrubbery.

4. Return to bag. Flop on to back and sigh a long body-shuddering sigh of happy drugged fatigue.

5. Highlight of night: Reach for radio, twiddle knobs and tune into station of interest – usually . . . crackle . . . crackle . . . crackle . . . 'This is London' . . . crackle . . . crackle . . . crackle . . . BBC World Service or Voice of America or Radio Moscow or Radio China, but halfway up the canyon it happened to be America's NPR (National Public Radio) and the noteworthy news tonight was a

report that, in the US, radio listeners are more
interested in the traffic reports than the news,
because the traffic is what actually affects
them.

6. Voices close to ear wake me up sometime in
the ink-pitch black and realize that, once again,
have fallen asleep with radio on.

Dawn broke as unpromising as the day before and so I spent
the morning under canvas doing what I had done the night
before – eating, reading, writing and trannie-tuning.

Noon arrived and, from within, things sounded more
promising. The pummelling patter abated, albeit the mists
still swirled. I decided to give the Grandest of Canyons
another try and rode up to the top. As if on cue, shafts of
watery sunlight burnt through the layers of covering cloud
and within an hour the Canyon was clear.

The Grand Canyon, the world's largest gorge, is improba-
bly huge – up to 18 miles wide, one mile deep and extending
for 277 miles along the silt-carrying Colorado River.

As I sat alone in contemplation, soaking up the scene and
slowly digesting the Canyon's raw and awesome beauty, I suddenly heard, 'Pretty neat, huh?' coming from a fat, suet-faced
form beside me, while a whirring camcorder scanned the
yawning great chasm from rim to rim.

'Hurry, Herb dear,' called a perturbed voice from behind,
'or else you's gonna miss dinner.' The meaty form flabber-
scuttled back in to the fume-billowing tour bus.

Outside Bashers Supermarket in Tuba City, while trying to
cram 47 shopping bags of food into my panniers, I met a
rare specimen: a cycle tourer, the first I had seen since
Hawaii. And he wasn't even an American; he was Scottish –
an immediately appealing Glaswegian with the unpronoun-
cable name (for someone who hasn't quite come to grips
with her R's) of Ruairidh. He was also so tall that I spent
most of my time making conversation with his kneecaps. We

compared notes and discovered that we were both heading the same way for a while.

That night I booked into the Grey Hills Hostel in Tuba City where Ruairidh was staying. He had flown into Albuquerque ten days earlier and a part of his bike (his bottom bracket) and body (his left knee) had already disintegrated. It wasn't as if he was on any short-term tour: he was heading for the bear-infested wastes of Alaska and was leaving Tuba City the next day. As I had planned on taking a day off to catch up on crucial washing and well-behind letter-writing, we agreed to meet at Monument Valley some 80 miles up the road.

A weighty wind blew stiffly across the desert, doing its best to blow me back to Tuba City. It was a hot, hard ride along the long, straight, loping highway past Wild Cat Peak, Red Lake and Elephant Feet. At Cow Springs my map marked a Trading Post (a type of small, ill-stocked, Indian-run grocery store) but when I arrived, red-faced and fit to expire, I found it derelict and boarded up with just the sounds of rat-like scurrying and a broken metal sign scraping in the wind. But at least it provided rare and welcome shade. I sat on the dust-blown wooden porch that overlooked the road.

No sooner had I taken a bite of banana and read a mere two lines of Salinger than a dented, dilapidated, brown pick-up truck, trailing its exhaust on the ground, clunked towards me and pulled up a short distance from the non-Trading Post.

My internal sirens started to ring. Uh-oh, I thought, here comes trouble. I could feel it in my water.

The driver, a cowboy-hatted Indian, turned off his clanking engine and remained behind the wheel. Through the open window I could see that he had a fat face with a big, droopy moustache and he slurped a bottle of beer. I pretended to ignore him. I kept my head tilted down towards my book, but my eyes were wide and alert, surreptitiously watching his every move though the camouflage of my fringe (or what the Americans call 'bangs').

There was an intense, shifty-eyed look about him and I detected his right hand was up to no good. Cautiously, I substituted my uneaten banana for my trusty bicycle pump.

I didn't feel frightened so much as annoyed. Cow Springs was the only shade I had come across for miles. All I asked was to be left in peace for half an hour so that I could have my lunch and lose myself in the world of Salinger. Instead, this silly dick was depriving me of that rest just so that he could gain a moment of self-stimulating satisfaction.

Occasionally a vehicle shot past on the highway in front, oblivious to the Cow Spring Charade that had sprung on me. I longed for an RV containing a holidaying couple to pull in and park – an action which would immediately dispel any inkling of threatened fear within me.

Instead, it was just me and him. Alone. The grit and sand swirled playfully around me in unfathomable eddies and the sign continued to clang eerily in the wind. I knew that he was staring at me. I started to fret. What did he want? To frighten me, intimidate me, rape me or murder me? Would he suddenly step out of his truck and simply blow my head off? He could more or less do anything he wanted to me. Who would try to stop him, apart from me? There was just the wind, the dust and the clanging sign. And him.

Sometimes words can be the best weapon. What better way than to belittle him, humiliate him, shrivel him? If he were to shout, 'Do you want to know what I've got in my hand?', maybe I could retaliate with the handy standby, 'If it's only in one hand, I'm not interested.'

But of course he didn't say anything like that. He didn't say anything at all. As I saddled my steed and warily made to leave, he suddenly flung the truck door open and stood looking ridiculous – his football-fat round head topped in a wide-brimmed hat; his short, squat, stocky legs crammed into pointed, scuffed, calf-length boots; his trousers fallen forlornly around his knees and that right hand pumping furiously. Boy, could I have bazooka'd him in the balls! I think he thought he was Big Chief Thunderclap. But to me he was chiefly just One Big Dickhead.

After a fitful night camped in the tyre-squealing, engine-revving parking lot of Kayenta's rumbustious 24-hour Coin-Op Laundrette (not a night to recommend), I rode off past the rocky outcrops of Half Dome and Owl Rock and passed from Arizona into Utah and back into Arizona within the space of about ten seconds when the road flipped back on itself, leading me into the wonders of Monument Valley.

Towering cathedrals of rock stood proud, dotting a desert landscape that epitomized the stark beauty of the Old Wild West. John Wayne hoofed his way among these buttes in *Stagecoach*, as did countless other galloping gun-toters in epics like *She Wore A Yellow Ribbon* and *My Darling Clementine*.

Rising to heights of 1,000 feet or more and blushing with all the blood tones in the spectrum, some of these massive, eroded monoliths of red sandstone resembled man-made buildings, crumbling castle, pillars and spires, soaring sky-scrapers or ancient temples, all of which have inspired fanciful and appropriate names: Castle Rock, The Alhambra, Grey Whiskers, Setting Hen, Rooster Rock, the Bear's Ears, the Stagecoach and Thunderbird Mesa. The latter immediately stirred up visions of Mr Tracey, Brains, Parker and 'Yes merlady', all string-dancing in my head.

The most photographed lumps of the lot have to be The Mittens: two massive massifs – sheer-walled formations towering from their conical bases, each with a narrow column of rock (the thumb) beside a solid block of rock (the mittened fingers).

I found Ruairidh in the Mitten View Campground, where he had set up base in prize position: a high, albeit exposed, rocky prow overlooking the extensive Valley of Monuments. I joined him in the shade beneath the picnic table weather-shelter where we chatted for hours and the Monuments turned from glowing fire in full sunlight to dark, stark silhouettes as the growing shadows crept across the crusty, burnt-orange floor of the valley.

We spent a stimulating half-hour comparing equipment – camping equipment, that is. Ruairidh appeared suitably impressed by my Dog Dazer, while I was equally absorbed by his Ever-Lasting Match. His Leatherman knife, which included intriguing fold-away pliers, also grabbed my fancy and although my mini Minnox tripod was aesthetically more pleasing (a sort of James Bond, secretly-screwed-together device) I had to admit Ruairidh's was even more ingenious as it included a clamp.

That evening I had a strange encounter in the toilet block with an Indian cleaner who stared intensely at me as I washed my undies in the basin. He edged closer and stood motion-less with mop in hand at the neighbouring sink, his wide molasses-black eyes moving back and forth from my face to my knickers. As I was still feeling a bit sensitive from the Big Chief Dickhead episode, I turned and said in no uncertain terms, 'Excuse me, but do you have a problem?'

'No,' he said, 'Do you?'

'Yes. I don't like being stared at.'

'Why not?' said he, staring.

'Because I don't, thanks. I find it off-putting.' And with that I picked up my washing and walked out.

Sleep was spasmodic during the night as the wind whined with a vengeance through the tent's riggings, flapping and billowing the canvas like a loose ship's sail and threatening to blow me from my moorings. When I did manage to sleep, I dreamt I was in a plane taxiing up a switchback mountain road. At the top we came to a vertical three-mile drop which, the captain informed us, was the intended method of take-off.

'Hold tight!' he called through the intercom as he turned to full throttle, and we jettisoned over the edge without further ado. A phenomenal sinking feeling followed as we plummeted interminably towards the ground. Needless to say, we crashed, and ended up on the runway at the bottom of the mountain with chunks of shattered plane all around. Curiously, everyone climbed out unscathed and we were all ordered to walk back to the terminal where, decidedly rattled, I announced to a waiting passenger: 'Guess what? I've just been in a plane crash.'

'So what?' came the reply. 'You survived, didn't you, so what's the big deal?'

Just what, I reflected uneasily, was this dream trying to tell me?

As Ruairidh and I saddled up and headed off for Mexican Hat and the Goosenecks of the San Juan River, we met a couple of serious, heavy-duty touring cyclists going the opposite way. Steve, an Ozzie, and Emmie, a Japanese, had been cycling for three years, starting in Australia, and had just rolled down from Alaska en route to South America. Steve, who used to 'push trolleys in Safeway', looked particularly travel-worn. Weight was obviously of no concern to him as he had attached a pair of moose's antlers to his front rack and was dangling a few dog-eared compact discs which he had picked up from the side of the road for no other reason than ornamental. He had drawn a rough map of the world on the top of his handlebar bag and said, 'It reminds me which continent I'm on.'

We rode on, first in rain across land reminiscent of Scottish moorland (so Ruairidh said) and then in searing heat across undulating desert where the parched and brittle hills had been eroded into perfectly jagged red and purple zig-zags.

In Mexican Hat we dismounted at the small Trading Post grocery store to take on board a bit of sustenance. Pinned to the wall was a notice announcing the forthcoming 'MEXICAN HAT WATER FIELD RACES' which included watermelon-eating foot races, pole bending, saddle-up races, potato races, barrel racing, sheep-herding races and shoe scrambles.

Mid-afternoon, I had a lucky find. Halfway down the roadside bank a patch of blue caught my eye and on investigation I discovered a box containing half a brand new tent, which I proceeded to salvage with great excitement, much to the baffled bemusement of Ruairidh – especially when I generously offered part of the catch to him.

'What are you going to do with that?' he asked, perplexed.

'Well,' I said, 'it might be useful,' and proceeded to hack off bits which just 'might be useful' with the hacksaw on my trusty Swiss Army knife.

Finding a lot of very useful rubbish at the roadside which motorists miss is one of the many advantages of travelling by bicycle. I admit I leave things like cracked compact discs, antlers and dog skulls for the likes of Steve to dangle off their bicycles but riding across America I had a field day. In fact I had a field few months, despite the 'LITTERING IS unLAW-FUL' signs and the omnipresent ADOPT-A-HIGHWAY schemes where all over the country thousands of civic and social organisations agreed to keep thousands and thousands of miles of state highway clear of litter. At least four times a year they donned orange vests and picked up 'trash' along a consigned two-mile stretch of roadside. In return, a sign noting their good deeds would be erected along the highway for all to see. Judging from the amount of booty I came across, I always arrived on the scene just prior to their clean-up stints and had pick of the pickings.

The amount of money people threw out of their windows baffled me – I always stopped to scoop up sun-glinting dimes and quarters and even dollar bills. My biggest monetary find, scattered among the kerbside grit, amounted to $8.50. I came across maps and books (one was Evelyn Waugh's, aptly named *A Handful of Dust* which, after a bit of a washdown and a dry out, proved a 'jolly' good read); bungee cords were always useful, and once I found a big magnalite torch in fully operable order, batteries included, which I thought was a considerate gesture. There was jewellery, too. But tools have to be the most abundant roadside find. Had I picked up every tool that I passed, I could have started my own line in trade. Nothing is more upsetting than coming across something like a good two-foot monkey wrench, turning it over in my hands, and finally and agonizingly deciding that it is just *too* heavy.

Once I found the contents of a whole tool kit, including a toolbox, littered along the verge. I presume they just bounced out of the back of a pick-up truck. Unable to bear the thought of adjustable spanners, box spanners, philips screwdrivers, pliers, chisels, hammers and the like going to waste, I bungeed the lot on board and heaved and hauled it nearly 20 miles up the road to the first signs of habitation, which happened to be a motel. I staggered into the reception with my weighty find and rang the bell. A check-shirted and ginger-bearded man appeared.

'I know this is a bit of an odd question,' I said, 'but could you provide a caring home for a box of tools?'

At first he thought I was some sort of foreign weirdo, but after I had explained the whys and wherefores of my offerings the outcome proved most pleasing. I was given a complimentary night in his motel, pancakes the size of satellite dishes included.

Just when I was beginning to think I could get used to travelling with Ruairidh, we came to a junction and went our separate ways. He took the high road to Alaska while I took the low road and continued cycling sideways towards the east coast.

I rode on through Indian territory along quiet and sometimes dirt-dusty roads. I saw more snakes, especially on my pee stops (which was a bit alarming), as well as troupes of crimson-chested turquoise lizards who were either scrurrying around in a demented state or basking in the sun doing sporadic bursts of press-ups.

There were prairie dogs, too – squirrel-like creatures minus the bushy tail – which barked and lived in elaborately engineered underground burrows. These 'mice-dogs' (which is the translation of the Greek word for them) would rise on hind legs in alertness as I silently appeared on the scene. They would snap to attention and then one animal would bark a warning. As if orchestrated by some unseen maestro, a whole phalanx of prairie dogs would vanish amid a chattering chorus of alarmed chirpings, diving for safety into their intricate network of burrows.

'Barking Squirrels' was the name the explorers Meriwether Lewis and William Clark called these curious creatures during their dramatic westward expedition of 1804–06, which was the first sighting of the prairie dog known to science. 'Those little animals Set erect make a Whistleing noise and whin allarmed Step into their hole,' wrote Clark in his journal. In an attempt to capture one, 'we por'd into one of the holes 5 barrels of Water without filling it.'

Woody Allen once said, 'Money is better than poverty, if only for financial reasons.' Riding through Arizona I had been surprised at the number of people living below the poverty line. Ugly, ramshackle trailer parks or prefabricated shanty lean-tos with barricades of corrugated iron blemished many parts of the landscape. Some Indians still live in hogans – traditional mud-and-wood dwellings with 'gardens' resembling junkyards of twisted metal, vehicle shells, dissected engines, refrigerators and tyres. There was no order, no grass, no flowers, no fences – nothing to separate them from the dust-blown desert.

Indians have always had a hard time. The land is rightfully theirs, after all; they were here hundreds of years before the head-West-young man American. In Kayenta's Coin-Op laundrette I had met an old Navajo with a sun-crevassed face called Chee Ramirez who told me that the government had not treated his tribe kindly. Indian life, he said, was full of humiliation, exploitation, unemployment, depression, alcoholism and self-destruction.

I read later that the native people have an annual income of $1500, which is 25% of the national average; a 40% unemployment rate, which is more than ten times the national average; an infant mortality rate twice the national average and a life expectancy of 44 years (65 for other Americans). Having cycled through part of the Indian reservations of Utah and Arizona's Painted Desert, these figures came as no surprise to me.

17

Love, Peace and Snipers

Colorado loomed in the form of the lofty, leg-quivering Rockies. After weeks of desert and heat and no foliage, it was wonderful to hit the mountains, the clear raging rivers, the invigorating cool June air. And the green: everything looked so *green* – so alive, so fresh, so clean. No longer was the land brittle and baked and ennervating. Plump, contented cows grazed phlegmatically in lush, verdant pastures crowded with wild flowers. As I climbed steadily upwards the dazzling, snow-capped and sharply chiselled peaks appeared awesomely huge. Every night I camped to the sound of rushing rivers.

Eagles wheeled high in the chill mountain skies, while marmots (the alpine version of prairie dogs) chatted and darted as I passed. Blackbirds displaying radiant scarlet patches when in flight, like a splash of fresh blood, fussed and noisily chack-chack-chack-chacked above my head as I threatened their nesting territory with my silently prying two-wheeled presence.

As I lay in my tent at dawn with the door open, hummingbirds would hover inches from my face and the iridescent brilliance of their powerfully vibrating flight made me marvel and inwardly whoop with joy. When I wore my bright, reflective-stickered cycling helmet, the hummingbirds would mistake me for some curious new flowering species and would flit and spin suspended in space, helicopter-fashion, so close that the supersonic speed of their hovering wings sent a gentle breeze kissing across my cheeks.

Near Hotchkiss, I met a horde of hippies – the Rainbow People – sitting outside a Conoco gas station. They were barefooted and matted and dishevelled and looked in need of a good shower. As they all chomped listlessly into a large communal bag of crisps, a boy with a head of greasy rat-tails and a curtain ring through his nose said, 'This chemically covered shit is crap.'

'Yeah,' said another, stuffing a big handful into his mouth, 'but tasty crap.'

They offered me some and said they were gathering 25 miles up the road in Overland Reservoir. Here, high up the mountain in wooded pastures, 50,000 hippies from all over the country would be gathered for weeks of 'spiritual harmony' in July.

'We're like one big happy family,' said a girl called Magnolia, swathed in cheese-cloth, 'closer to each other than to our own blood relations.'

Most of these wayfaring Rainbow warriors hailed from the west coast. A boy called Blazer had recently spent six months in Hawaii, 'hanging real loose, man'. From there he had flown to Jamaica, where no doubt he had hung even looser. After the 'family' get-together next month, they were heading off to Florida to follow the Grateful Dead on tour.

'Do you ever work?' I asked.

Blazer laughed derisively. 'Shit, man. What would I wanna do *that* for?'

'How can you afford to do so much travelling?'

'Hey, I have my means. I play it cool, right?'

Play it cool? This sounded sinister to me. I wanted to ask more but I opted to change the subject lest I found myself on a 'spiritually-lacking-in-harmony' death-list.

'How do the locals like you? I mean, 50,000 is a fair sized family to have turn up in their back yards. Do you get any trouble?'

'They can get real shitty,' said the Chemically-Covered-Crap boy. 'A coupla years back a gang of rednecks pissed outta their brains burst into camp one night in their truck and drove like crazy into a crowd. Killed a girl and two guys. Jesus, what a mess.'

As I made ready to leave, Blazer said, 'Hey, yer know yer real welcome to come up and meet the family. See how the other side of America lives, huh?'

Later that afternoon I stopped at a house to fill up on water. An elderly woman with a heavily peach-powdered face answered the door. She said, 'Why, sure,' to my watery request and then invited me into her kitchen as she filled my bottles. When I told her that I was trying to cycle across the country, her jaw dropped and she said, 'My – all on your lonesome? May Gad bless you, hon.' Then she made me a cup of tea.

Peachy-faced Crystal complained bitterly to me about the Rainbow People. They were a true eyesore, she said. They were soiling the land.

'They have no sanitation. They've tapped into the farmers' irrigation water supplies, leaving them with nothing to water their crops. They can't be evicted because they're living on public land and, you know what? They cost the local community $30,000 for more park rangers and policing. So much for all their love and peace pomp – they're professional shoplifters. They have no consideration. Us folks round here would just love to see the back of them. They smell real bad too.'

I was hoping to reach Redstone that night but it grew dark

and cold fast once the sun had been swallowed by the Elk Mountains. When the road was clear, I dragged my bike up a bank into a thicket of aspens and went to sleep.

I know many who cycle at night and love it, but increasing the risk of riding off the edge of a mountain precipice or being mown down by a motorist is not really my scene. In a *Bicycle USA* magazine, I read: 'Highway safety officials report that between the hours of 11pm and 2am every third driver on certain roads is illegally intoxicated.' I would rather be in a sleeping bag than a body bag.

Six o'clock in the morning. I threw back my tent door, scared a hare and then turned on the radio. It wasn't the sort of news that makes you happy. A 16-year-old boy had been shot dead in a Los Angeles classroom by another boy who carried a .357 Magnum pistol to protect himself from the gang warfare which had been plaguing the school campus of Fairfax High (where Michael Jackson went to school). The boy had accidentally let off a round of bullets when he placed his school bag (containing the gun) on his desk, killing the boy in front of him and critically injuring another.

Only the day before I had read in *Time* that in America 135,000 children brought their guns to school every day. The article was full of flabbergasting facts and figures:

The US is one of only four countries – with Iran, Iraq and Bangladesh – that still executes juvenile offenders. And nearly 1 in 4 American children under age six lives in poverty. . . . Forget the next century. Just consider for a moment a single day's worth of destiny for American children. Every 8 seconds of the school day, a child drops out. Every 26 seconds, a child runs away from home. Every 47 seconds, a child is abused or neglected. Every 67 seconds, a teenager has a baby. Every 7 minutes, a child is arrested for a drug offence. Every 36 minutes, a child is killed or injured by a gun.

Eight o'clock in the morning. The news was full of even more despair. A 7-year-old boy had been shot in the head as he walked to school by a 33-year-old ex-convict, an expert marksman, who told police he was deliberately aiming at a group of children. The boy was the 110th child under 17 killed that year (1992) in Chicago, the City of Crime, and the fifth under 10 to be shot in a month.

All these devastating horrors seemed so far from me. The air was crisp and clear, the sun was shining, the birds were singing. I packed up my tent with that happy camper's air of satisfaction at having survived a night undiscovered, undisturbed, by dissolving into the land. On that small, body-flattened patch of leaves I had had everything I wanted: food, water, cover, sleeping-bag comfort, books and music – a compact, self-sufficient, self-contained unit. And as I strapped the last bag to my bike I cast a final eye over my vacated leaf-rustling sleep-spot, where I had merged with the trembling and squawking forest, where only the animals, the birds and the scuttling insects had discovered my home.

I swooped down the sun-warmed picture-postcard mountainside, past thick-limbed log cabins and a snaking, swirling river that boisterously joined me on a rushing descent. And as I dropped amid such beauty I wondered if I really was in the same country as all those gun-shot atrocities. It seemed so hard to believe.

I stopped in Carbondale to reload my stomach and panniers with provisions before heading towards Snowmass. That evening, I was talking to some local climbers sitting in a gas station cafe. We discussed avalanches, steam trains, bear attacks, the IRA and Colorado's state motto: *Nil Sine Numine* (Nothing Without Providence). When they enquired which route I had taken over the mountains, one asked if I had heard about the girl in Carbondale. I hadn't. It appeared that about half an hour after I'd cycled through the town, thinking that the glories of Colorado seemed like another world away from street gangs and shootings and horrific news, a 16-year-old girl in the passenger seat of her boyfriend's car was shot dead by a sniper as they were about to drive up the very same wondrous mountain road down which I had swooped to Redstone.

I rolled steadily upwards beside the Roaring Fork and Frying Pan rivers, passing through the 120-year-old town of Aspen, which represented everything commercial and unaffordable to everyone except the Aspen Après-Ski Set. It looked like a cross between the set of a Hollywood frontier western and *Dynasty* at high altitude.

I stayed just long enough to buy some bread, bananas, honey and porridge at City Market before heading out of town to find somewhere to lay my weary head. That night I slept in Difficult Campsite, a slightly inauspicious-sounding base from which I embarked on a 12,095-foot ascent of Independence Pass the following morning. The ride proved to be breathtaking in all senses of the word. There were spectacular views of snow-jagged peaks like iced needles piercing deep blue skies, while my heart pounded resoundingly as I rode higher in the ever thinning air.

It was Monday, a good day to ride the narrow ribboning pass as the road was devoid of the heavy weekend traffic which would have threatened to nudge me over the vertical, unbarriered edge of mountainside.

I had been wheezing and heavily panting for hours when, nearing the top, I stopped in a small layby overlooking a vast, deeply cleft valley. I hadn't been there long when a red Cadillac pulled up and three hip young dudes climbed out, all sporting lurid pink-and-green checked jackets and teddy-boy quiffs. In total silence they opened the 'trunk', pulled out three golf clubs and lined themselves up on the edge of the vertiginous drop.

One by one, in time to the crooning sixties beat bursting from the motor, each took an almighty swipe which sent their balls shooting up towards distant ice-clouds before dropping far down into the valley below.

'Magic!'

'Swell!'

'Radical!'

That was all that they said before piling back into the convertible and gunning off up the mountain, the Cadillac's fins sharking from the rear. Perplexed by such behaviour, I decided to eat a banana, feeling sorry for any hikers' heads that may have been conked by fast free-falling golfballs way down below.

By the time I reached the top after nearly seven hours of upness, I felt fighting fit – fighting for breath and fit for nothing. An ice-wind froze my features and cut through me like a knife. Cherry-cheeked, I crested the Continental Divide, the watershed that separates west-flowing rivers in America from those flowing east; where a panorama of peak after snowy peak soared into majestic skyscapes of tumbling cumulus cloud, solid as snow-mountains.

From now on it was all downhill.

Apart from three fairly minor passes, I fell continuously for two days. And then suddenly the mountains just stopped. Colorado Springs was perched right on the edge and it was from that city that I caught my first sight of what lay ahead: the endless pancake flatness of the Great Plains.

'Boy, I sure don't envy you,' people kept saying when I told them where I was headed. 'Gets mighty boring with nothing to see.'

I spent the weekend in 'the Springs' with a family I had met briefly on a steam train the other side of Colorado, where we had boarded in Durango – famous as a place from where you could catch the train to Silverton on the 110-year-old Narrow Gauge Railroad. You could also ski outside town in a resort called Purgatory.

It was while staying with Steve and Barbara and their two young sons, Josh and Daniel, that the weather turned *really* bad. I was used to the daily violent thunderstorms by now but they were nothing compared to what was coming. Tornado warnings abounded. Hail, the size of golfballs, fell with such ferocity that within an hour there were hail-drifts four feet high and millions of dollars' worth of damage. Houses were smashed, cars were smashed, trees were smashed. Floods torrented through the streets like rampant rivers.

Barbara and Steve had some neighbours to tea. Being originally from Kansas, they were used to tornados and storms like I had never seen and I asked for some tips. What should I do if I was caught out on a long, lonely stretch with a tornado on my tail? They told me 'drive like hell' to the nearest bridge that crossed the Interstate, to climb up into the recess underneath and to 'hold on real tight'. In theory, when a tornado hits a bridge it causes a vacuum, thus momentarily losing its life-sucking power. But it would not be too easy for me to put the tip to test. For a start, I wouldn't be cycling on an Interstate freeway; even if I were, distances between convenient bridges could be an unhelpful 50 miles or more. I told the Kansas couple I was planning on keeping to quiet country roads. Any suggestions?

'Well, the best you can do,' they said, 'is jump in a ditch and pray.'

Little did I know then that I was about to cross the Midwest during its most stormy summer for 104 years.

18

Swallowed
by the Sky

After weeks of devious zig-zagging, I headed due
east along a dead straight road. All day I watched
uneasily as ominous storm clouds built up
around me and flashes of lightning streaked on distant hori-
zons. I was aiming to spend the night in Punkin Center
which, on my map, looked like a fair-sized town.

When I arrived there in the early evening, I discovered
that Punkin Center was no more than a small diner, a trailer
home and a compound full of roadworks equipment surrounding a quiet crossroads. There was no one around.

The diner was closed. I knocked on the screen-door round
the back and a girl answered, wiping her hands on her food-
encrusted apron. Michelle did the waitressing and lived with
her grandpop across the road in the trailer yard, where I

ended up camping – much to the consternation of their motley three-legged dog, which tried its utmost to devour me.

That night the sky cracked and crashed around me in deafening explosions, the wind whipping the driving rain into a ferocious frenzy as it sheeted across the plains.

The morning dawned clear and calm but it was only a furtive ploy to trick me and catch me unawares out in the shelterless open. More storms were forecast and there were copious tornado warnings. I decided to make a rush for it and pedal-pelted along like wildfire towards Wild Horse near the Kansas border. On the way I came across road repairs and a woman with a STOP/GO sign called out, 'Hey, well hi there! I guess you gotta be Josie.'

Word travels fast in these flat, friendly parts. She 'had heard' that I'd been camping in 'Pumpkin' Center and was 'headin' crass country'.

'Sure must get real scary, ridin' all alone,' she said.

Maxine was all for a bit of a chin-wag. It was kind of boring work, she said, standing all day in the road with a red and green sign for company. To make ends meet, she also worked in a diner up the road where she earned $2.50 an hour for waitressing and $4 an hour if she helped out cooking. For standing all day in the sweat-soaking humid heat with her STOP/GO sign she made $6 an hour.

'Yeah, sure, it can get real tough,' she said. 'I'm hoping to start a quilt-making business but it's kinda hard to get off the ground. Folks round here just don't have the money.'

I crossed into Kansas, the Wheat State, the land of Superman, and of Dorothy from the *Wizard of Oz*. Suddenly everyone started waving to me – every motorist, every farmer, every trucker, every freight train driver. The further I was from crazy, self-obsessed California, the friendlier the people were becoming. I was entering Small Town America.

In Kansas I felt the true sense of being in the heart of a vast continent – not least when passing through Lebanon, where a small monument marked the historic geographic centre of the contiguous United States. But above all this was corn-belt country.

The cornlands of the Midwest were like an inverted golden sky – a sky so wide and so high that it seemed to swallow everything else. All day I would ride towards a horizon so infinite that I never came any closer: I felt as if I was crossing a land that would never end. Yet these views of solitary grain siloes brooding in an endless expanse of wheat and maize were somehow emblematic, moving and overwhelming. Whereas Colorado had been all mountains, Kansas was all sky.

Here in prairie-land it was impossible for the weather to creep up on me: there were no woods or edifices or high hills for it to hide behind. Instead, I watched the mighty thunderhead storm clouds growing and piling ever higher for hours. My head swivelled continually, like a periscope, scanning the skies for the tell-tale signs of a tornado – a fun-nelling demon that might whirl towards me at speeds of up to 300 mph and suck me up into its writhing and devilishly hungry vortex. Every year the tornadoes left trails of devas-tation across the Plains; towns, homes, crops, cattle, cars – all could be smashed to smithereens within seconds.

One afternoon the thick, coal-black thunderheads banking up in the east like top-heavy monsters were tinged with a menacing bilious green – a sure sign, so I had been told, that a 'twister' was a-brewing. I felt progressively jelly-like, trem-bling as I watched the sky falling to earth and realizing that I had nowhere to run.

Sheet lightning crashed and flashed in ear-shattering cracks and a wall of white hailstone clouds marched across the flat, wide plains towards me, sounding like the angry clacketing racket of an approaching train. I dived for the only shelter I could find – a waterlogged underground drain – as hailstones the size of tennis balls shot from the skies.

The next day I read in the papers that five people had been killed in that storm and farmers were not too happy about the state of their cows and crops:

'We didn't get none cut. We lost everything,' said [farmer] Jeff Boyle.

. . . Boyle said he found about 20 of his 120 herd of cattle either crippled or dead. The rest were missing.

I was turning into a nervous wreck, my life completely dominated by the torments of the unpredictable skies.

'Never had a summer like it,' I was constantly being told, or, 'It should be real fine at this time of year.' Their comments did little to boost my morale.

I was entering what the locals called 'Tornado Alley'. One night, camping in a frond-thrashing sea of maize during a severe thunderstorm, I twirled the radio knobs and tuned into the weather report. I was somewhat alarmed to learn that three tornadoes had touched down in surrounding counties and that two of them were twisting my way.

When you are lying flat on your back, quivering from head to toe, in the middle of a cornfield with nothing more sturdy than a piece of flimsy rip-stop nylon to protect you from a life-sucking horror, being warned to stay off the roads, stay indoors and shelter in a cellar tends to make you feel more than a trifle vulnerable. It also urges you into a lot of frantic praying. I lay there as helplessly as a pea in a pod waiting to be eaten.

For want of something better to do, I ran out scantily clad into the storm in a desperate attempt to batten down the hatches. But making steady the guys and placing a token rock on a peg as the whiplash rain assaulted me was little more than a futile gesture towards impregnability.

As it turned out, those raging twisters passed me by and I survived the night intact – if only just. Now my biggest fear was not so much being sucked up as washed away. By dawn I was lying in an ever-rising quagmire, and the likelihood of drowning in a field awash with cob corns was a distinct, albeit unattractive, possibility.

It is on stormy nights like these that I often notice my splayed-on-the-ground steed eyeing me bitterly with that 'how-*can*-you-leave-me-out-here-in-*this*?' look – which is as guilt-inducing as when you have kicked the cat out to face a night of force ten gales.

If you have any inkling of sensitivity or any attachment whatsoever to whatever it is that is left out in the cold and the wet, whether it be an animal or inanimate object, that nagging feeling that you have done wrong can be a touch disquieting as you lie sheltered, dry and warm. But much as I madly, truly, deeply love my bicycle, I have always felt it best not to let sentimentality wash too deep as far as preferential treatment over its owner is concerned. After all, surely my comfort is of far more importance than that of a lump of metal, albeit a distinctly useful lump of metal.

Other souls, I know, are of a different disposition. A few years ago I was zig-zagging my way up Norway's spectacularly fjorded coastline when I met Paul, a tall, typically down-to-earth Yorkshireman, who had a worrying relationship with his bicycle. He said he wanted to sleep with it. I have to say that I was a little taken aback by this unexpected salacious statement as I tried to visualize what you could possibly get up to with a couple of spoke nipples, an Allen-headed screw and a nicely lubricated bottom bracket.

But I admit that it was my mind, not Paul's, that created such fantasies. I had got the wrong end of the tube. Paul (compassionate cycle-camper that he was) only wanted to shelter his lovable steed under canvas rather than leave it to rust in the rain. I think.

Paul's problem was that his Jet Packer tent was barely large enough to accommodate his own six-foot self, let alone the company of an oily, metallic and frigid form. In his guilt towards his abandoned bicycle, he confided to me that he was actually contemplating exchanging sleeping arrangements with his mount: *it* would go in the tent to be all snug and dry, while *he* Kryptonite-locked himself to some immovable object for the night to shiver out in the rain.

Call it what you will, but I call it odd. Had Paul already been travelling for a few weeks by the time I met him, I might have felt a little more sympathetic to his dubious desires. After all, speaking from experience, cycling on one's lonesome for a while can affect the old grey matter specially if intellectual abundance is not on your side in the first place. But Paül was on a mere two-week spin, a time within which I believe it possible to remain sane.

Cold, calm Norway felt a million miles from Kansas and it was reassuring to discover that I was not the only one battling against the elements with rattled nerves. One afternoon, in a road-sweeping storm, I came across 30 Americans and 40 Belgians on a demonstration walk from New York to Nevada to protest against nuclear testing sites. Drenched, and shouting to be heard while the skies crashed and exploded around us, they admitted they had chosen a bad year for their hike. One long-haired and heavily bearded man in socks and Jesus sandals said he wished he had chosen transport. Another dishevelled character said he wished he had stayed at home.

Towards one evening, on an endless empty flatness as another storm hit me with a barrage of hailstones the size of ping-pong balls, I was saved from being pummelled to my grave by a family in a pick-up who stopped to offer me shelter. Inside were John and Vala Mosier with their chirpy daughter Jade and two small boys, Joshua and Jacob. They lived just down the road in Hoxie and said, 'Come and stay!' I didn't need much persuading.

John was a well-driller and Vala an EMT (Emergency Medical Technician) which meant that she was always on standby and constantly attached to a pager. That night she was beeped in the middle of supper and had to race out to give medical care to a local farmer who was trapped beneath his combine harvester.

'Apart from a head injury, he was fine,' she said on her return a couple of hours later. 'Round here, farmers are always turning over their tractors and combines. There are a lot who've lost their lives. It kinda gets to you when you know the guy.'

John and Vala filled me in on life in Kansas and it seemed that a lot of it revolved around cow pats. Because wood was scarce on the prairies during the last century, buffalo 'chips' were burned for cooking and heating. Today dung has other uses. There are 'Cow Pat Throwing Contests', and they also have Cow Pat Bingo – the ground inside a cow pen is marked into squares and contestants bet on which square the cow will deposit a pat.

'We're kind of weird out here, you know,' said Vala.

I said I was sure the weather was to blame.

Being keen motorcyclists (their dream was to 'ride the Rockies'), John and Vala were well informed on events such as the Kansas Motorcycle Club Poker Runs (in which a playing-card is picked from a deck at scheduled stopping points along a route) and the Biking Scavenger Hunts. In these, a rider must accumulate a number of specific objects such as a limestone rock, a picture of the Pope, a receipt for exactly $5, a Royal Crown from Burger King, a condom from a dispensing machine and, of course, a fresh cow pat.

I pedalled on. And on and on. The road never seemed to end. The flatness never seemed to end. The scenery never seemed to end or start or do or be anything other than what I had been passing for hundreds and hundreds of miles – fields the size of France overflowing with wheat and maize and soybeans and sunflowers. And because everywhere was so big and empty and wide, it was oddly wonderful.

'In the United States there is more space where nobody is than where anybody is. This is what makes America what it is,' Gertrude Stein once said.

I had never been anywhere like it. Sometimes I had the feeling that perhaps I wasn't really moving at all – I was rolling along a treadmill and I would just keep hypnotically pushing pedals through an ocean of corn until I keeled over and died. 'Gaaad! It must be so boring!' people chorused on those rare occasions when I saw anyone.

Tiring, yes, but not boring. There is always too much to be doing to get bored. Like . . . watching your feet go round. Well, maybe to some this doesn't sound particularly stimulating but you would be surprised. Feet watching, especially when the feet are your own and continuously whirring around in circles, can become extraordinarily meditative. It can send you into an agreeably painless, disembodied trance and for a while you actually forget to think about things like food, and how much you would far rather be sleeping than cycling, and how much you would far rather turn round and barrel along with a tail wind than battle at an agonizing crawl into a perpetual gale, and how much you would far rather be anywhere else other than in a solid mass of Kansas corn.

Of course, being in a hypnotic wheat-saturated state is not such a great idea when you find yourself in the path of a high-speed, groaning grain truck. But, there again, it is these sort of life-threatening events that tend to liven things up for the lone transcontinental cyclist.

Sometimes I perform mind-taxing quizzes. Where was I this time last week? (Cycling across the prairies.) Where will I be this time in a week? (Cycling across the prairies.) What might I be doing if I was at home? (Not cycling across the prairies.) After that I feel mentally exhausted and I turn my attention back to my feet for a while.

People tend to presume that, because I travel alone, I must get lonely. But I don't, and because I don't I think that maybe I should, or else why does everybody think that I do? It is one of those swings-and-roundabouts puzzles in life: alone = lonely? But sometimes travelling with somebody else can be lonely because you become cocooned in a hermetically sealed unit. It makes it harder to reach out and experience the Outside World. When you have a familiar shoulder to lean on, you lose the invigorating tension of the unpredictable opportunities and the disquieting sense of the unknown. As John Hatt says in his *Tropical Traveller*: '. . . travelling with a companion is sometimes an adventure and occasionally more enjoyable; travelling alone is sometimes less enjoyable, but it is always an adventure.'

And I am sure that raving Jonathan Raban would agree. He

says, while *Hunting Mr Heartbreak*, that 'the only way to travel is to travel alone. It opens you up to the world. It puts you in the way of luck and chance.'

Racing a storm to Junction City, I booked into a motel where a notice pinned to the back of my door declared:

ABSOLUTELY! No dogs or birds or fish in room!

My in-room entertainment cost a quarter. It was a Vibro-Bed. I slotted in the coin and then waited, clinging to the sides apprehensively, for the earth to move. Nothing happened. I gave the money-eating machine a sturdy whack with the bed-side Bible. Action! For the first minute being vibrated felt rather fun, but then I felt decidedly seasick and had to get off.

I switched on the television. The highlight of the local news was about a doddery septuagenarian in a sequinned blouse (which revealed bulging midriff fat cantilevering over her low-slung skirt) who had never eaten a Big Mac until today, her 78th birthday. The camera panned in too close, quite putting me off my banana sandwich, as her furrowed, quivering mouth closed in around her first bite of burger. After a lot of unnecessary sound effects, she was asked what she thought of it and replied, 'Geeee, you guys. Now I know why I never ate one till today!'

Flicking through an endless array of channels and finding nothing that did not make me want to slam a sledgehammer through the screen, I turned it off. Then I finished my banana sandwich and flopped out on the bed with *Time* and read about the viewing habits of children in the United States.

The average child will have watched 5,000 hours of TV by the time he enters first grade and 19,000 hours by the end of high school – more than he will spend in class. This dismaying passive experience crowds out other, more active endeavours: playing outdoors, being with friends, reading. Marie Winn, author of the 1977 book *The Plug-In Drug*, gave a memorable, if rather alarmist, description of the trance-like state TV induces: 'The child's facial expression is transformed. The jaw is relaxed and hangs open slightly; the tongue rests on the front teeth (if there are any). The eyes have a glazed, vacuous look . . .'

Recently Jeremy Campbell wrote in London's *Evening Standard*:

Violent TV shows are a factor in up to half the murders committed in America, Congress has been told. A committee heard psychiatrist Dr Rowell Houseman testify that aggressive behaviour by actors in TV movies and dramatic series can affect the outlook of children. 'More aggressive eight-year-old children grow up to be more aggressive adults and the early learning experiences that media violence provides can affect behaviour even decades later,' Dr Houseman told hearings on Capitol Hill.

In Hawaii, I had flicked through a catalogue advertising alternative energy lifestyle products. Among the solar-powered camping lanterns that never needed batteries and the 'luxurious lighted low-flow showerhead for lovers', I came across: 'One all-time favorite that most parents love . . . a bicycle-powered generator utilized to help regulate children's TV viewing. The kids have to pedal to power the TV!'

And I thought: Ingenious! But I knew that, sadly, it was an ingenuity that would never catch on.

I ventured forth through John-Boy Walton territory. Monolithic concrete grain elevators (mills) now towered up from the plains, symbolizing Kansas' wheat supremacy. They also indicated the welcome approach of a small town where I could look at something other than the approaching storms or my revolving feet.

Sometimes, excitement presented itself in the form of a gargantuan billboard that would rear up from the dizzying myriad of wavering wheat proclaiming slogans that tended to be either about abortion:

ABORTION STOPS A BEATING HEART

or God:

AT THE END OF THE ROAD YOU'LL MEET GOD

or:

IF JESUS RETURNED ON SUNDAY MORNING, WHERE WOULD YOU BE?

I estimated I should be entering Kansas City.

For once, I estimated correctly. The only thing I learnt about Kansas City was that it was a leader in soap-making as well as being home to a remorseless serial killer who ate his victims. It was also a horrible place to ride a bike and I did not linger long. I crossed the border into Missouri, dubbed the 'Show Me State'.

'Show me what?' I asked the locals, curious as to the interpretation of its nickname. Some didn't know; some who didn't think much of the place said it meant 'Show Me The Way Out State'. A school teacher gave me the more complex theory that it was named after a phrase used in 1899 by Congressman Willard D. Vandiver, during a speech in Philadelphia, who said: 'I'm from Missouri. You've got to show me.'

Just what he had to be shown is unclear. It strikes me as a rather desperate attempt to coin a motto for Missouri.

The countryside turned gloriously green and rolling, the roadsides were crowded with an enrapturing, sweet-smelling riot of vibrant wild flowers.

As I wound my way along a minuscule fraction of the

Missouri River (the country's longest at 2,466 miles) I heard
something clunking behind me. It was a bicycle and on it was
Harvey, a man of about 60, riding 'cross country' from San
Diego to New York. He had just ridden, in a little over two
weeks, what I had more or less ridden in a little under two
months. But there the similarities ended. He was hating every
minute of it, which was hardly surprising as he was riding
with his head down, seeing nothing, enjoying nothing. He
didn't stop to explore. 'I saw the sign to Monument Valley
and I thought: What the hell, and rode on.' Nor did he stop
to talk. 'Everybody in this goddam country's an airhead with
their brains up their butt.'

A trifle baffled, I asked, 'So why are you riding across
America?'

' 'Cos I've gotten myself an advanced-life crisis. My child-
hood sweetheart – my wife for 36 years – goddam got up and
walked out on me. No warning. No nothing. I always thought
we noo each other inside out. I mean, boy . . . we sure did
used to have a real swell time playing duplicate bridge
together. You wanna know the first I noo of her hate for me?'

I nodded eagerly. After all the time I had spent contemplating feet and wheat fields, this was meaty, scandalous stuff.
I urged him on.

'Well, I was reading the Sunday papers in bed three weeks
ago when in walked Thelma, cool as hell, threw me the
divorce papers and then beat it. I mean, Jeez – talk about a
crazy woman or what.'

When we stopped at a gas station to pick up a drink, I realized he was as drunk as a skunk. He announced that meeting
me was a 'God-sent blessing' and he tried to give me a very
slobbery kiss. Luckily I managed to give him the slip and
rode on through Miami Station, De Witt, Holliday, Paris,
Florida, Monroe City and New London to Hannibal, the
home of Mark Twain, who used the town as the setting for
incidents in *Huckleberry Finn* and *The Adventures of Tom Sawyer.*

Packing my panniers outside National Supermarket, I overheard a conversation between a couple of beefy youths,
sporting sleeveless T-shirts and pumped-up biceps, as they
met at the front of the store. One, looking as if he had been

pulled backwards through the blades of a combine harvester, was trussed up in slings and blood-seeped bandages.

'Jeez, Bud, what the fuck happened to you?' said the one who looked more bodily intact.

'Shit, man . . . some screwball lost his head Friday night and knived me. Guy went crazy and tried to beat the shit out of me before picking up a chainsaw. The doc said I should be dead.'

As I continued piling edible supplies into my bags, a series of passers-by stopped to say a few curious things. One, on discovering where I came from, said, 'You British sure say "bloody" a lot. Ain't that true?'

I said he was talking a load of bloody rubbish.

Another said, 'I hear your Fergie's splitting up, huh?'

A woman with blue hair and butterfly spectacles said, 'There's danger out there.'

Her friend, a wide vehicle of a woman and wearing slippers, said, 'You from England? Gee, that's just great. I know a girl from . . . ah shucks . . . some place beginning with "P" called Susie. Do yer noah?'

Randolph, who had been stationed in Torquay during the war as an ambulance driver for the Battle of the Bulge, showed me his shrapnel shrivelled arm and hand (he had only two stubs for fingers) and said, 'Ain't you real scared of being run over or raped?'

'Yes, very,' I said.

'So why naat stay home then?'

'Because it could just as easily happen there and then I wouldn't see America and meet intriguing types like you.'

Randolph, who had not left Hannibal for 50 years, thought me odd and told me so. But when I made to leave, he took hold of my hands in his wrinkled and trembling stubs and said, 'So long, hon. And good luck.'

Randolph's luck lasted me to the edge of town where the storm, which had been threatening all day, decided to strike with a vengeance.

Within the space of a few seconds the sky exploded, the clouds emptied, the streets flooded and a bolt of lightning struck a chimney above, sending the bricks tumbling down around me. I had never heard lightning strike before and the dynamic, detonating, thunder-clapping crack gave me such a shock that I skidded, aqua-planing across the street, hitting a kerb and shooting over my handlebars through the open doors of a diner.

On impact a small chunk fell off my elbow, I dented my hip and something pinged unpromisingly in my back, but apart from that all was well. Sprawled on the floor of the diner in an ungainly heap, Randolph's 'luck' returned to me in the form of an immediately likeable, dumpling-shaped cook who picked me up off the ground and sat me down to an All-You-Can-Eat feast on the house.

Over the massive Mississippi I went – America's mighty river that drains half a continent on its 2,348-mile journey from Minnesota to the Gulf of Mexico – to enter the rolling and fertile farmland of Illinois. Prosperous-looking farms adorned with handsome red wooden barns abounded, as did armies of outsized farm machinery manufactured by John Deere. At the roadside, advertising-cum-hazard signs depicting a leaping deer proclaimed:

WARNING: JOHN DEERE CROSSING!

alerting me to the very real possibility of being well and truly flattened by one of these monsters.

Round here the soil was so black and rich that early

farmers, forcing their unwilling ploughs through the thick, sticky muck, named it gumbo. Camping in it was like camping in a quicksand of muddy glue.

There were other camping hazards, in the form of a tiny creature as small as a grain of salt and as daft-looking as a crab. *Ixodes* (icks-oh-deez) *dammini* (the deer tick) shoulders the blame for the insidious Lyme disease, the second most prevalent infectious disease in the United States after AIDS.

Named for the tranquil Connecticut village on Long Island Sound where it was first reported in 1975, Lyme disease leaves its victims with a range of ills from 'flu symptoms and joint pains to heart and neurological disorders (the wife of a farmer I met had been confined to a wheelchair for life). This rampant disease had spread through 45 states, so far sparing only Alaska, Arizona, Hawaii, Montana and Nebraska.

My tent was often covered in ticks that were virtually impossible to flick off as they dug in their haunches with worrying determination. I was forever scratching and surveying my anatomy as best I could for signs of these blood-sucking blighters. After a tick bites, it holds on in there for several hours before it begins to dine off your blood; once it does, it feasts for three or four days. During that time it may deposit its infectious cargo into your system. The longer the tick remains, the greater the risks. All that makes comforting reading for the disease-prone camper.

I rode on through Springfield, the city where Abraham Lincoln had practised law, married and was buried. When I stopped to ask a workman for directions he said, referring to the numerous museums in memory of the assassinated anti-slavery president, 'You aint gonna see that Lincoln junk, are yer?'

Within minutes I passed through the two extremes of Springfield. One moment it was all clean, cobbled suburbs with fat, shiny cars wallowing in leafy streets outside tall, handsome houses. The next, I had suddenly plunged into a poverty-stricken black neighbourhood crammed with run-down peeling clapboard shacks with listless people sitting or lying idly on their porches among an assortment of tattered old armchairs and mattresses as they smoked, chatted, stared.

'Make sure you're out of that area by dark,' the workman had said, 'it's full of ghettos and gangs. I sure hope you've gotten yourself a gun.'

That night, in a seedy motel on the outskirts of town, I turned on the TV and saw Paxton Quigley (who often appears on American chat shows arguing the case for women assuming the power of the gun) talking about the classes she was running, at $150 a shot, to teach women how to shoot a man. Over the past few months she had taught 3,000 women how to shoot an attacker with one hand while lying on their backs. I thought: That's nice.

News about people killing each other was as common as BBC weathermen getting their forecasts wrong. After Paxton, the local news reported that two black teenagers had been shot dead in the neighbourhood just down the road from my motel. I had ridden through the place that afternoon.

19

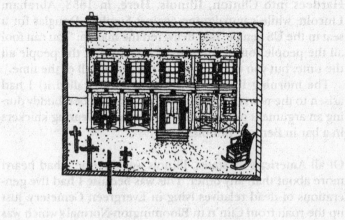

Not Normal
Behaviour

The weather yo-yoed daily between stormy and sultry. At night the humid temperature inside my tent hovered between 90° and 100°F. Sweat streamed from me as I flaked out on top of my sheet sleeping bag, unmoving, unclothed.

When it was too hot to sleep, I would lie watching the fireflies floating silently through the night, flicking their torches on and off. Fireflies (or lightning bugs) use in-built beacons, produced by bodily chemical reactions, to find mates. Each species has its own morse signal. A female perches on the ground or in the bushes, lying in wait until an alluring male throws open his raincoat (so to speak) and flashes at her. If his illuminations are impressive, she will answer him with her own show *de lumière*.

*

I rolled past the ubiquitous Dairy Queens and K-Marts and Hardees into Clinton, Illinois. Here, in 1858, Abraham Lincoln, while campaigning against Stephen Douglas for a seat in the US Senate, had delivered the maxim: 'You can fool all the people some of the time, and some of the people all the time, but you cannot fool all the people all of the time.'

The morning I left Clin'n (as the locals called it) I had arisen to the news of a man shooting dead his best buddy during an argument over whether a woman was wearing knickers in a bar in Benton, Illinois.

Of all America's 50 states, Illinois was the one I had heard more about than any other. This was because I had five generations of dead relatives lying in Evergreen Cemetery, just up the road from Clin'n in Bloomington-Normal (which was twinned with Canterbury, England, of all places).

Sometimes my parents are asked whether my love for travel runs in the family. My father says that it doesn't come from his side: for generations, the Dews have been either firemen or builders from London and stayed put. My mother's family were garage owners from New York State or shop owners from the Midwest. But she always likes to pinpoint one relative whose fidgety get-up-and-go nature I may well have inherited: my great grandfather, Hiram Myers, 'got up and went' on the Klondike Gold Rush. Fortunately he lived to tell the tale but unfortunately he returned home to Rochester, New York, a lot worse off financially. Having been away for two years, he walked up the steps on to the porch and strode right past my grandfather, Wayne Myers (aged four at the time), failing to recognize his own son.

One torpid evening in July, I met my mother off a small Ozark airline flight at Bloomington Airport. She had flown out not only to show me where she had grown up during the war, but also to sort out death duties and suchlike following my grandmother's demise, thus killing two birds with one stone, as it were.

We stayed with charming Charry Schaeffer, one of my mother's great friends from long ago, who lived with Norma from Normal in a wonderful green-and-white wooden house on East Washington, one of Bloomington's main roads. Charry's house was one of the oldest in town and had scarcely changed since the day it was built in 1857, though it was full of more modern details like a concealed chrome soap-holder, implanted in the wall above the basin, which swivelled into view only when pushed. There were other imaginative and practical fittings, the most ingenious of which was on the top floor. In the wall of the hall was a small opening like a cat-flap through which dirty washing could be deposited so that it slid down a chute to land in a laundry basket beside the washing machine situated way down below in the cool, dark cellar.

Artistic Charry was one of those genial people for whom nothing is a 'praaablem'. Despite being over twice my age, she scurried around tirelessly cleaning, cooking, gardening, shopping and a thousand other things. I felt sluggishly floppy in comparison. My excuse was that it was hot and airless and humid. Gesticulating Norma, flapping her arms like a high-speed windmill, energetically explained that these enervating temperatures were nothing compared to a normal Midwest summer. 'Usually it gets just sow haaat,' she would tell me.

It was great weather for sitting in the screened back porch, catching up on juicy home gossip and listening to the distant mournful sound of the train horns that sporadically blew over from the railroad on the 'just sow haaat' and sultry wind.

Strangely, I found that suddenly being still after having been on the move for months was far more exhausting than cycling 70 miles a day, but at one point I did finally manage to motivate myself and make Mum an enormous pumpkin pie. This, apparently, was a treat which she used to devour in abnormal quantities in the days when Normal was home.

Bloomington-Normal is a fine example of small-town America wrecked by out-of-town monster mega-malls. A small downtown store which had once been run by one of my far-off relations was now boarded up and derelict, as were the majority of those interesting, topsy-turvy buildings lining Main Street that must once have given the town such character. Instead of walking downtown to 'real quaint' family-run stores, everybody now drove a few miles down the road to shop in an enclosed expanse of sprawling, characterless concrete.

Flicking through a tourist brochure one morning at breakfast (half a melon, strawberries, blueberries, bananas and porridge), I discovered that there was a choice of three attractions for the 'What-the-hell-am-I-doing-here' visitors who found themselves stuck by mistake in Bloomington-Normal.

There were desperate lures to 'come tour one of the world's most technologically advanced automative facilities where a force of nearly 3,000 produces 63 cars an hour' (which I eventually worked out as a depressing and unbelievable 1.05 cars a minute). Or you could drop back a hundred years to 'Encounter the Prairie' in an exhibit where 'the real lives of the people of our prairie past are unfolded'. But if you were feeling a touch peckish, perhaps you could do no worse than 'tour the factory that produces the famous Bit-o'-Honeys, Laffy Taffys, Golden Crumbles and chocolate delights like Katydids and Imps. Free samples!'

Spoilt for choice, my mother and I decided that the best solution was to give all three a miss and instead get on with a more attractive option: ascertaining how many thousands of dollars worth of jewellery and family silver my grandmother had left behind in the bank's safe. Until that moment, I had been totally unaware of this appealing and potentially lucrative piece of information.

Bloomington-Normal's alluring tourist brochure was snapped shut. It is amazing how the prospect of prospecting for riches can suddenly shake off all signs of inertia, just like that. One minute I was all limp and languid; the next I was chomping at the bit and rearing to head off on our own Klondike Gold Rush.

Saddled upon our steeds (me on Zzyzx, Mum on Charry's clanking old green Raleigh), we cantered off at speed up E. Washington to Downtown Bloomington.

Our first stop was the People's Bank, where a teller called

Shirleen responded to our question of 'Where is the safe please?' by giving us an elaborate résumé of her private life, for no apparent reason. With typical British reserve, my mother and I stood patiently listening, and occasionally commiserating, until the end of her litany of sorrows. Then we haltingly repeated our enquiry but Shirleen lost herself in elaborate rhapsody again and it was a further five minutes before she answered our question. We were directed down into the bowels of the bank to Big Jesse, the safe guard, who bore a striking resemblance to Archbishop Desmond Tutu and who was on the point of leaving for his lunch. He paused to inform us that, before we could even begin to locate our potential treasure, we must first have a letter of authority from my grandmother's lawyer. We retraced our tyre tracks back down E. Washington, only to discover that the lawyer had also died recently. Fortunately Mary-Lu stepped in to help and said she would have the necessary letter ready by about 3pm.

We returned to the bank to close my grandmother's account and then back to the vaults to explain the situation to Jesse, who was just leaving for a coffee break.

As there was nothing further we could do until we had the 'letter of authority' safely in our hands, we seized the opportunity of riding up to Evergreen Cemetery to say hello to our five generations of dead relatives.

The cemetery was vast and we had no idea where our 'blood' was at rest. We visited the reception, where some old biddy (who looked like the human equivalent of a duck-billed platypus) spent 40 minutes rummaging through an antediluvian filing system to find the names of our deceased kin. It then took a further half an hour for her to locate the position of the graves on a map that resembled a kindergarten scrawl. 'X' marked the spot and off we trooped to trace the tombstones which, of course, remained elusive. Not a lot short of an hour later, we returned in irksome mood to Mrs Faff-Around Platypus who, as suspected, had sent us in completely the wrong direction.

Hoping that all our Grands and Greats were appreciating the trouble we were taking just to bid them good-day, we tried again. At last I literally stumbled upon them by tripping over their none-too-prominent 'stones. By now I wasn't in the properly reverent mood to pay my respects to those pushing up the daisies and my mother quickly put me in place when I absentmindedly propped my bike against my grandmother's gravestone. We were both feeling more giggly than sorrowful and we soon decided to abort the mission lest a Hand from above should striketh us down. We tootled off to make some sandwiches instead.

With the lawyer's 'letter of authority' safely in our hands, we hot-tyred it back down E. Washington to the People's Bank where Jesse was once again leaving just as we arrived, this time for his afternoon coffee break. Slick 'Let-me-handle-this' Stan was left to unravel our Gold Rush and looked on in faint amusement when my mother stated, 'We'd like to clear out our safe-box – one of these must be the key,' and proceeded to empty from her handbag a lifetime's assortment of keys, one of which I recognized as that of the coal shed at home.

Sifting through this clinking array, the only one we came across which provided the slightest glimmer of hope was attached to a ticket marked 402. But the glimmer quickly paled when Stan told us, 'There ain't no box with that number here.'

Then Mum went into a meditative state, referring rather incoherently to the fact that 'somewhere in my dream' she was certain there was a box her mother 'maybe had in another branch somewhere'. But she was very certain that she had left a small grey suitcase 'full of family silver' in the bank's safe after her mother's funeral. So Stan opened up the two-foot thick high-security door and in we all went, searching in bemused and boisterous mood in all the nooks and crannies for this elusive grey suitcase which (as I tried to murmur to Mum out of Stan's earshot) I was certain was in the attic at home, full of my Action Men and Corgi Rockets and Meccano.

Stan, bless his cotton gusset, was set on solving this mystery and 'phoned the other branch where in my mother's 'dream' she had another safe-box full of worldly goods.

The good news from the girl at the other branch was that they did indeed have a box numbered 402, but the bad news was when she asked if my grandmother (in whose name the box had been) was a man of Indian origin. The name of the key holder was not Katharine Myers, but Naveen Khambh.

The mystery thickened.

Detective Stan, pondering the problem, suspected that my grandmother's box had been 'drilled out' (as he put it) so that another holder could take the space. I was becoming confused. Our Klondike Gold Rush was progressively turning into the Bloomington-Normal Wild Goose Chase, which didn't quite have the same pioneering overtones to it.

Then the 'phone rang. Stan, looking a trifle baffled, said, 'Er . . . Mrs Doo, it's for you.'

Perplexed as to who could be ringing her in a bank vault, my mother took the receiver and was amazed to discover it was none other than Adeline Adams, a nigh on 100-year-old friend of my grandmother's. Adeline, on hearing that Anna 'Doo' was in town trying to sort out monetary affairs, had rung round every bank in Bloomington because she had an urgent request: would we like to come to dinner tonight?

'Why honey, it sure would make mah day,' crackled Adeline's voice, reverberating off the bomb-proof walls of the vault. 'You whaat, dear? You say you have Jawsee with you? Why, that's just great . . . laast time I saw her she was only . . .'

'Adeline,' said Mum. 'I'm sorry, but I can't really chat at the moment. We're a little bit tied up here in the safe. I'll ring you later.'

The whole thing was turning into a farce and I could tell Stan was thinking he had a couple of foreign wombats on his hands. But he was determined to get to the bottom of this and he 'phoned the other branch again. He asked to speak to somebody other than the girl he had spoken to earlier so as to get a second opinion on box #402, whereupon it was disclosed that, yes indeed, we *did* possess a box in the other bank under my grandmother's name. Hurrah! Things were hotting up.

By this time Big Jesse was ambling back from his latest

break to announce somnolently that it was closing time. Stan said that their other branch was open half an hour longer and advised us to get down there quick if we wanted to solve the mystery. After hearty handshakes all round, we raced three blocks down E. Washington as directed by Stan. There was no sign of a People's Bank and so we burned back to Bank One, which was now closed but I spotted Shirleen, the teller girl, crossing the street who, surprisingly, gave me no more life-history sob stories but told me that the bank we were looking for was not three but about 30 blocks back down E. Washington, right at the bottom, opposite St Joseph's Hospital.

So off we went again, hurtling frantically down the street to arrive sweaty and flustered but just before closing time. And then it suddenly dawned on Mum that, yes, perhaps that grey suitcase was in the attic after all (I think she saw it in a sequel to her dream) and that she was beginning to recall transferring some silver from the case to the safe-box some time ago so that she could use the case as carry-on luggage for her flight home after the funeral. We were at long last getting somewhere and, what is more, the key #402 fitted the lock.

Imagining that I would soon be setting eyes on a glinting array of heavy silver which in future years (if I played my cards right) I could well be inheriting, I was already planning what I would buy with it all; a new bicycle, a lorry-load of puncture repair kits, a new tent, a new sleeping bag, a lifetime supply of porridge . . . that sort of thing. I held my breath and gingerly turned the key.

In a nutshell, all future shopping lists and all high hopes were dealt a hasty blow. The box was almost empty. A couple of pieces of broken and gaudy jewellery and a few tarnished knives and forks – the type of thing you find in a '10p box' at a car boot sale – was all our Bloomington-not-so-Normal Silver Rush had to offer.

A momentary wave of disappointment washed over me. I knew how my great grandfather Hiram must have felt after his westward Rush. Gallantly pulling a brave face, I reaffixed my nigh-empty panniers (which I had envisaged filling to the brim with heavy duty booty) and for the umpteenth time we pedalled back up E. Washington.

We had barely gone two blocks when, in full flight, my mother's handlebars suddenly decided they would rather be pedals, and swivelled down to somewhere near her ankles, sending her shooting into the spokes. Following hot on her tail, I failed to apply my brakes in time and piled into her rear, sending us both reeling into the gutter. Despite a few dents to both bodies and bikes, we dissolved into peals of uncontrollable laughter.

It had been one of those days.

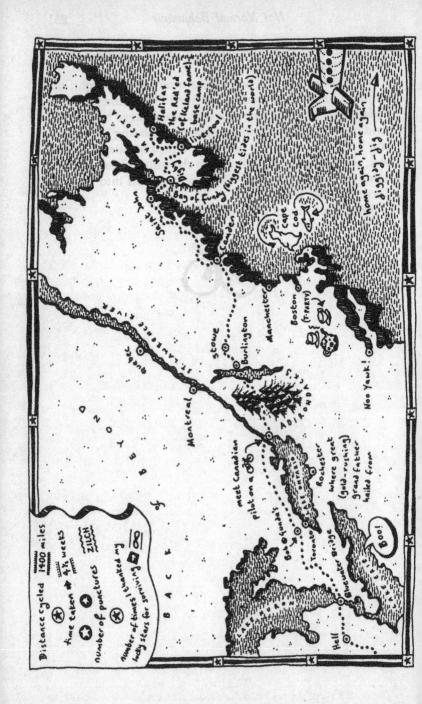

20

Hell to Halifax

All across America, I had been warned about the meaty and murderous-looking motorcycle gangs of Hells Angels who could surround you, I was told, and herd you to some lonely spot where horrific things might happen. I often came across these gangs on long, desolate roads but, despite their menacing looks, I found them far from intimidating on contact. Behind their butchery façade they were all big softies at heart.

One gang, clad in the essential tassled black leathers with skull-and-crossbones flags fluttering from the rear of their bikes, tooted and smiled and waved merrily as they passed.

Another lot bought me lunch in a gas station cafe because, they said, they were impressed with my ride. One heavy, bearded warrior with a piratical eye patch, and a sheathed machete attached to his black-leathered hip, the sort of savage who looked like he would disembowel you just for a lark, surprised me by buying me an orange juice and admitting (well out of earshot of the others) that he wouldn't be brave enough to do what I had done.

Brave? It doesn't take courage to ride a bicycle in unfamiliar lands and no one dispels this misconception better than Dervla Murphy:

> Optimists don't believe in disasters until they happen. Therefore they are not fearful and have no occasion to display courage. Nothing puts my hackles up faster than being told I'm brave. This is nonsense – albeit significant nonsense. Where is our effortless civilization at when physical exertion, enjoyed in remote places, is repeatedly mistaken for bravery?

> Genuine travellers, far from being brave, are ultra-cautious . . . before they start they suss out all foreseeable hazards and either change their route, should the hazards seem excessive and the risk silly, or prepare themselves to cope with reasonable hazards. Thus what looks to

outsiders like a daring journey is in fact a safe
toddle – unless you have bad luck, which you
could have at home.

As I cycled across the country, I discovered that people had
wary and dismissive opinions about the people in states other
than their own – states which most of them never visited. In
Kansas, for instance, I was told to be careful in Indiana:
'They're a real rough lot', 'not friendly like us guys.' In
Indiana, people would say: 'Betcha had a hard time in
Kansas – they're a kinda wild crowd.' In my opinion they
were all just as welcoming and helpful and hospitable as each
other.

In fact, during my eight months' travels in America, virtually everyone I met was friendly – often almost too friendly.
Sometimes at the supermarket checkout, feeling wearily sub-
dued and in a semi-trance state (from feet-watching), it could
be a bit of a shock to be greeted by a strident, 'Well, hi there!
How're ya doin'? Hey, that's a kinda cute accent you got
there. You travelling by bike? Wow man, you crazy or what?
Ha! Ha!'

Whenever I phoned up an organization to make an
enquiry or a reservation, I was greeted with something like:
'Hi, I'm Sunny Sandy with the over-stretched smile. Sure am
always happy to help. Your praablem's my praablem and I'd
just *lurv* to fix it.'

This treatment was a novelty at first, but after a while it
became a little overbearing and occasionally I even wished
that I could be served in that disinterested, unhelpful and
pissed-off-with-life British Rail manner.

❧

Near Morocco, Indiana, I pulled into a gas station to fill up
on 'wah-der' and was just wondering where I might lay my
weary head when I was approached simultaneously by two
separate families, each with an offer of hospitality. I ended up
having a shower and supper with Delbert and Ferol Weber
before riding up the road to camp at Randy White's farm.

Randy was all for teaching me about Midwest farming methods. He showed me how to drive his monstrous air-conditioned and computerized $125,000 articulated four-wheel-drive tractor and then, foolishly, let me take it for a 'spin', during which I narrowly missed removing half the side of his house.

Undeterred, he let me rumble forth to the edge of a green expanse of maize that stretched to the horizon. Here he gave me a lesson on how corn-on-the-cob is formed: the pollen falls from the flowering tops of the plants on to the fine strings called 'silks' and each silk forms a kernel on the cob. He told me that each of his many fields was roughly 640 acres or 1 square mile. From the yield of corn he made $450 an acre and his expenses amounted to $350 an acre which, by my estimations, worked out as a profit of $64,000 per field.

Then he pulled off four ripe cobs. Back at the house, his wife cooked them for me and I polished off all four in one sitting.

❧

More giant billboards rose up from the land with their conscience-tweaking proclamations:

DON'T BE CAUGHT *DEAD* WITHOUT JESUS

ARE YOUR TROUBLES DEEP-SEATED OR LONG STANDING? TRY KNEELING

JESUS IS EVERYWHERE BUT WHERE WILL YOU BE WHEN HE COMES?

And then I hit Amish territory, where the nineteenth and twentieth centuries co-exist. One moment I would overtake a small, rickety-rackety horse-drawn buggy driven by a sombre-suited character with a biblical beard; the next I would be sucked towards the swaying underbelly of a $200,000, 40-foot RV driven by a guy in a fluorescent shellsuit.

The Amish are said to be the most self-sufficient of all

North Americans, including the Eskimo. Grumpy Californian yuppies were finding the going rough on $80,000 a year and were thinking of punishing George Bush for their plight; while an Amish family of eight, growing and making everything for their own needs, could live comfortably (if frugally), on no more than $500 a year for the whole family. That was considerably less than a fortnight's welfare cheque for a single mother with a couple of babies in a ghetto.

But the life of the Amish was puzzling. On a bench in Nappanee I sat beside 71-year-old bonneted Fanny, who told me a little about the Amish ways. Telephones, taboo in homes, stood at the end of farm lanes; modern calculators were permissible, but not computers; their traditionally-styled clothing could not be fastened with buttons or zips but could be made from the latest synthetic materials; powerful tractors used around the barns rarely ventured into fields where modern hay balers were pulled by horses; to own and operate a motor vehicle was forbidden but they could hire cars and vans; the children could play baseball but, as competitiveness is frowned upon, they were not allowed to score.

Scooters and other small equipment (tricycles, wagons and wheelbarrows) could have rubber wheels but tractors must roll on steel. The church leaders feared that the comparative comfort of air-filled tyres on rough roads might be used to travel to town and if this was allowed the next generation might allow the use of cars, which they feared would encourage individualism, self-indulgence and the development of social status.

In stark contrast to Fanny's calm and peaceful aura, a man who looked like a pumped-up version of Arthur Scargill swaggered over to me, attached to a blaring boom-box and a bottle of beer. Stretched across his unappetising ball-of-a-belly was a T-shirt with the slogan:

I suffer from CRS – Can't Remember Shit

'Hey, I hear yer from London,' he shouted above the pumping boom. 'My great aunt's cousin's nephew's best buddy

went to England and stayed in a place beginning with "N".
Would yer know it?'

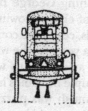

One morning I was with Cal, a doctor's wife, who was taking
me down the road to meet some of her friends. We passed a
tree festooned with roll upon roll of unravelled white toilet
paper.

'What's happened here?' I asked, somewhat baffled.

'Oh, that,' said Cal with an inscrutable smile. 'I guess one
of the kids must have been toilet-papered. We do that sort of
thing round here.'

'Pardon?' I said.

'It usually happens in High School. If a classmate's real
popular, his or her friends will sneak out to their house at
night to "toilet-paper" some tree or something in the garden. Kinda shows their appreciation. Makes their Mom and
Dad real mad, though.'

I didn't quite get the point but there again, there probably
wasn't one.

I had met Cal and her family the previous night: I was merrily riding along minding my own business when a station
wagon pulled alongside and Cal's head popped out of the
window asking if I needed some place to stay. Sizing up the
occupants, I said, 'Well, maybe.' I ended up being invited to
sleep in Cal's house, swim in her pool, wallow in her bath,
consume half the contents of her fridge, use her telephone
and washing machine, read her books and sleep in the spare
bed.

After all that, she was now taking me to meet some neighbours (millionaires) who lived on a farm. One of the many
nice things about Don and Phyllis was that they didn't *look*
like millionaires. Their white wooden farmhouse was small

and unpretentious, with a couple of rusty old Chevy pick-ups parked out front in the mud.

When Don had proposed to Phyllis nearly four decades ago, he asked her if she would be prepared to have an 'open house'. Every morning since their wedding day, Phyllis had provided bumper free-for-all breakfasts to anyone who knew about them: friends, neighbours' friends, friends of friends or just the fortunate passer-by (like me). A huge array of different fruits and cereals and breads and cakes and cookies was on offer which, for a constantly hungry cyclist, was almost too good to be true. Phyllis said she generally catered for anything up to 20 people, but this morning there were eight of us round the table.

One man, Ray, built along the lines of a Big Mac, told me how a few years back a tornado had sucked up his front and back porch (never to be seen again), leaving the rest of his house intact – apart from his dog, that is, who was chained to his kennel at the time. Ray found him the next day two miles away in a neighbour's field, dazed but alive. There was no sign of the kennel.

I crossed out of Indiana and into ovenglove-shaped Michigan (state motto: 'if you seek a pleasant peninsula, look about you.'), where I made a point of giving Detroit a very wide berth. It is the city with the highest murder rate in the country.

Instead, I went through Hell – for no other reason than to tell people that I had been there. Despite the name, it was a nice little place surrounded by a lot of water and not far from Waterloo.

The weather continued to throw nasty things at me. When it wasn't sheeting, sucking, hailing, galing, whiplashing, tornadoing or trying its utmost to incinerate me, everything from the ground to the sky was a dull, cadaverous grey. Even passing through places like Chelsea, Romeo and Rattle Run did little to lift my weather-pervaded gloom.

But passing south of Flint brought a reminiscent smirk as I thought back to the highly entertaining *Roger and Me* – an excellent budget film about how thousands of workers had lost their jobs at the Ford Motor plant in Flint, which doesn't sound very funny but it was. It also made me think of Henry Ford, who had once said that he found the design of the human body far from satisfactory because the ignition and the exhaust were located in the same area.

The day that I hit the Great Lakes, everything was wonderful. The sun showed its big, bright face and, after weeks of endless cornfields, it was invigorating and intoxicating to stand on the edge of Lake Huron and watch the boats plying the waters of this massive inland sea. I was leaving America, and entering Canada via the Blue Water Bridge – on which a Customs official told me that the shipping traffic through the St Claire River beneath was even busier than the Suez Canal. In true American fashion I said, 'Is that so?' and then sallied forth into Ontario.

I continued pedalling upways and sideways, skirting Lake Erie and Lake Ontario through gently rolling hills. Every night I was invited to sleep in someone's garden, yard, bed or barn. One night I camped among the cascading flowers of Bob and Gunda's garden, which overlooked the winking glow of distant Toronto.

After a delicious supper of salmon with Gunda's home-grown herbs, potatoes and raspberries, I lay contentedly replete with my tent door open, gazing up at a rich tapestry of stars. Then, turning on my radio, I listened disbelievingly to the story of a Toronto karaoke singer who, after performing an appalling Des O'Connor impersonation, picked up his gun and shot two men dead for laughing at him.

A short ferry ride took me across the tip of Lake Ontario, via Wolfe Island, to New York state. There I met a Canadian pilot on a bicycle and we rode across New England together. Eric had never cycled anywhere before and I think he found it a bit slow because he kept saying, 'You know, it's taking me two weeks to do what I could have done in two hours.' He invited me to go flying with him in a four-seater plane but I felt somewhat reluctant. If his flying was anything like his cycling (he had a habit of careering off the road), I didn't think my chances of landing intact looked too promising. I knew I was better off sticking to the saddle when he told me that he flew low enough to read the road signs if he became lost.

After travelling alone for months, it was fun to be with a lunatic like Eric. For two memorable weeks we had a raucous time riding over the Adirondack Mountains into the 'Live Free or Die' state of New Hampshire and through maple forests of gently trembling leaves in rusts and golds and burning reds.

But suddenly all the offers of hospitality, which had been given so generously for the past seven months, dried up. Not once did we sleep in anyone's home or back yard – it was always a campground. Although I told Eric it was all his fault for looking such a swarthy and suspect character, I knew it was because there were two of us. People tend to take one look at a couple and think that they are fine; they have someone to talk to, to have fun with, to argue and eat and sleep with. But when people set eyes on a lonesome being – especially a five-foot female – they seem to feel sorry for you, scared for you, lonely for you. In short, they want to protect you from the nasty Big Wide World.

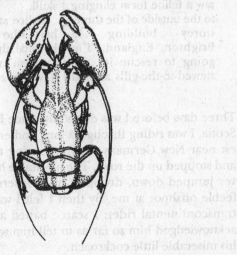

It may be fun to be with a friend but, as John Hatt says: '[It] almost invariably acts as a barrier between yourself and the country . . . most people you meet are prepared to do far more for one person than they would for a couple or group . . . Solitary travellers are altogether a more attractive proposition.'

Leaving Eric with the lobster pots on Maine's surf-battered shore, I headed north back into Canada. On the boat from St Johns, New Brunswick, to Digby, Nova Scotia, I picked up a crumpled day-old copy of the *National Enquirer* and read a story close to home:

DRUNKEN 'HERO' INJURED TRYING TO SAVE STONE CAT

A drunken man plunged 30 feet from an office building as he tried to rescue a cat – not realizing it was a stone gargoyle! Adam Pankhurst was out celebrating his 23rd birthday with pals when he saw a feline form clinging to the outside of the three-storey building in Brighton, England. 'I'm going to rescue it,' the stewed-to-the-gills animal lover announced, and he quickly began to scale the wall.

But before he could reach the life-like sculpture, Pankhurst lost his grip and fell to the pavement, fracturing his skull.

Police say the would-be hero, who is recovering in hospital, thought the stone cat wasn't moving because it was 'frozen with fear'.

Three days before I was due to fly home from Halifax, Nova Scotia, I was riding through a long and empty stretch of forest near New Germany when a logging truck overtook me and stopped up the road. The inevitable happened. The driver jumped down, dropped his trousers and waggled his feeble offshoot at me. By then I felt I was a well-hardened transcontinental rider: I scarce batted an eyelid and only acknowledged him so far as to tell him where he could put his miserable little cockroach.

Two days before I was due to fly home from Halifax, I was riding beside a wave-lashed shore near The Ovens when a car overtook me and stopped up the road. The balding driver jumped out and, expecting the worst, I was pleasantly surprised when his trousers remained firmly in place.

'Hi!' he said. 'Lady back in Riverport says you're from England. That right? I was just kinda wondering if you know Julie Morris – she's a meat inspector from a place beginning with "B". I met her briefly in Digby a coupla years back.'

I said I was sorry to disappoint him but I didn't.

'Oh,' he said, 'but I always thought England was a real small place and that you guys all kinda know each other.'

I agreed that, yes, it was a small place – Canada was 46 times larger than the UK with half the population (I had just read this truly fascinating fact that morning and was rather chuffed to find an opportunity to air it before I forgot it) – but that, no, not everybody knew each other.

Then he asked, 'Riding far?'

This was my big moment. I said what I had been longing to say smugly for a long time.

'Well, I'm only going up the road to Halifax. But I've just ridden from California.'

I waited for him to marvel.

'What the hell didcha do *that* for?' he asked, looking thoroughly unimpressed.

It was a good question and gave me pause for thought. What the hell did I do it for? Before I had a chance to answer, he said, 'You've gotta be crazy. There are easier ways to get around, you know.'

And he climbed back into his car and drove away.

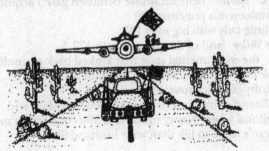

Index of People and Places

A Glossed over Glossary

Carbondale where a 16 year old girl was shot dead by a sniper
      just after I'd rolled by 223
Carl whose tropical armpits I came all too close to 45
Carmel cypress-smelling big buck town 24
Carmelita who juggled pancakes on the move with smoke
      coming out of the roof 141
Carpinteria site of the perambulating tent slasher 32
Cheap Tickets where I ate my last Hawaiian banana 159
Cindy-Lu who, thanks to Check-it-out-Linda, sold discount
      pantyhose in much the same way as a surplus of carrots 85
Claire & Jaqui hair beaders with whom I ate other peoples
      pineapples 109
Clarence see *June*
Clinton, Illinois where I learnt of a man shooting his buddy
      during an argument over whether a woman was wearing
      knickers 244
Colorado where your legs do a lot of quivering 218
Colorado River silt-carrying wonder 208
Colorado Springs Rocky-side city perched on the edge of the
      Great Plains 224
Continental Divide where I did a lot of puffing and panting
      and oohing and aahing 224

Damien, Father the 'Martyr of Molokai' 93
Dan & Bonnie who handed me an apple-banana 69; in whose
      bath I found heaven 73
Deneen, Bill top-hatted, grow-your-own, horse-and-cart-riding
      eccentric hostel owner 27
Devil's Playground where I sat watching my shadow with the
      Caterpillar driver 182–183
Diamond Head Waikiki's imposing volcano whose shadow I
      rode in 51
Digby see *Esther*
Dog Dazer shin-saving dog-zapping device 5
Dole, James D the pineapple man 79
Don see *Phyllis*
Donna love-healer horoscoper 136–137
Dorothy who announced out of the blue that she would be
      praying for me 185
Durango steam-train town near Purgatory 224

Elk Mountains which swallowed the sun 221